JAMES GREGAN

BURDENED
BUT UNRUFFLED

THE STORY OF A WORLD WAR II
SUBMARINE AND ITS CREW

JAMES GREGAN

BURDENED
BUT UNRUFFLED

THE STORY OF A WORLD WAR II
SUBMARINE AND ITS CREW

MEREO
Cirencester

Mereo Books

1A The Wool Market Dyer Street Cirencester Gloucestershire GL7 2PR
An imprint of Memoirs Publishing www.mereobooks.com

Burdened but unruffled: 978-1-86151-700-5

First published in Great Britain in 2016
by Mereo Books, an imprint of Memoirs Publishing

The address for Memoirs Publishing Group Limited can be found at
www.memoirspublishing.com

The Memoirs Publishing Group Ltd Reg. No. 7834348

The Memoirs Publishing Group supports both The Forest Stewardship Council®
(FSC®) and the PEFC® leading international forest-certification organisations. Our
books carrying both the FSC label and the PEFC® and are printed on FSC®-certified
paper. FSC® is the only forest-certification scheme supported by the leading
environmental organisations including Greenpeace. Our paper procurement policy
can be found at www.memoirspublishing.com/environment

Typeset in 10/15pt Century Schoolbook
by Wiltshire Associates Publisher Services Ltd. Printed and bound in Great Britain
by Printondemand-Worldwide, Peterborough PE2 6XD

PREFACE

ON the 4th June 1944, the Prime Minister, Winston Churchill was invited by Admiral Cunningham to visit Maidstone, to see some of the Officers and men of the Eighth Flotilla. After a stirring speech he chatted and joked with the assembled Officers oozing confidence to every single person in the wardroom as to the outcome of the campaign. When he left Maidstone tears were streaming down his face as he talked of those fine boys walking in the valley of the shadow of death.

This book is dedicated to my darling
Deborah, my wife of 40 years.

The one I love is someone
Whose face I long to see
And voice I want to hear
Who puts a love song in my heart
By simply being near.

CONTENTS

INTRODUCTION AND ACKNOWLEDGEMENTS

ALL SUBMARINES HIGHLIGHTED IN ITALICS

INTRODUCTION AND
ACKNOWLEDGEMENTS

—⊸⊶⊷⊶⊶—

IN 1999 I purchased a book detailing the exploits of HMS *Safari*, a World War 2 submarine primarily based in the Mediterranean. This single volume changed my life and I wanted to know more about the feats of submarines during this harrowing campaign. Hence, over the last 16 years I have studied the adventures of our heroic British submariners, and that of their Axis counterparts, during a difficult and deadly time in history. Boredom, daily routine one minute - gun action, torpedoing, special operations the next. No one could have written a better script.

I began investigating HMS *Unruffled* as this submarine was adopted by the townsfolk of Colchester, Essex, my home town for 23 years. The district of Colchester was charged with raising £250,000 worth of war bonds to fund the building of a submarine, resulting in a staggering £435,223 being raised by the community. I would like to thank Mr R M Webb for his help in providing me with details of the crew's visit to Colchester and Essex Archives for the program of events.

I have been a burden to Mat Knight & Alison Clarke at Royal Navy Command who have been exemplary, providing me with crew lists and cheerfully answering my never-ending questions. They must have thought 'oh no not him again', as this part of the book proved to be more difficult than one could imagine.

I must also thank Mr Barry Downer of the Barrow Submarine Museum who has also put up with all my questions, but never faltered. My thanks also go to ex-submariner Stuart Rose, who has kindly assisted me with endless technical issues and when I was at a loss, explanations as to the meaning off information detailed in the submarine logs.

All those staff at the National Archives in Kew must receive a special mention for their help and assistance during my many visits. I also thank the Imperial War Museum, London, for allowing me to explore their records.

Thanks are also owed to SM Elaine Zerafa, secretary of the Royal Navy Association (Malta) and a retired Maltese Admiral, for escorting me around the Lazaretto and old submariners' haunts.

I am indebted to the Curator, Malta Maritime museum, who kindly allowed me access to their archives.

I first met Mr George Malcolmson, archivist at Gosport Submarine Museum, during my quest to track down the Jolly Roger of HMS *Safari*. During the time it has taken me to investigate and write this book, George has been outstandingly helpful in allowing me access to the archives, and providing advice and guidance throughout my quest.

A former colleague from my Lloyd's of London Press adventure, Mr Ian Barratt, has endlessly toiled to sub-edit my original manuscript, providing help and sound advice along the long road in completing this book – thanks Ian.

I wanted to bring to the forefront this forgotten submarine, which to me was not just another piece of war machinery but a boat which helped thirty-three heroes to survive a war, when so many brave young men did not return from their fateful last voyages.

CHAPTER ONE

BARROW-IN-FURNESS

23RD AUGUST 1941 - 2ND APRIL 1942

WHEN Vickers Armstrong purchased the Barrow-in-Furness dockyards in 1897 the then-Lancastrian town was already an important centre for the smelting and exporting of steel, earning it the nickname of the 'English Chicago'. However, following the Vickers purchase, the town's industrial reputation and expertise took on a new dimension as Barrow became the leading military ship and construction facility it is today.

Several Royal Navy flagships and the vast majority of nuclear submarines, as well as numerous ocean liners and oil tankers, have been manufactured at the Cumbrian yard, and in 1901 the first Royal Navy-commissioned British submarine, a Holland-class, was built.

From that time the yard grew in stature and in 1941, Vickers Armstrong chairman Sir Charles Craven, a former submarine officer, was under constant pressure to produce ships and boats of high quality but at a record build rate. The Vickers yard was a cacophony of sound as workers struggled anxiously to launch ships of all types, as quickly as possible, from escorts to 8,000-ton cruisers and the smaller but complex submarines, ready for battle against the Axis foe.

Most of the men left in Barrow worked at the Vickers shipyard or the steelworks, or were employed in jobs that made them exempt from call-up. As overtime amongst the workers was compulsory, the only time production came to a standstill was during air raids. The Vickers shipyard and engineering works were of a particular interest to the Luftwaffe, with concentrated heavy bombing raids witnessed between 14th to the 16th April, 1941, and the 3rd to the 10th May, 1941.

Although the docks, railway and steelworks took direct hits, the main brunt of the bombing fell on the nearby local population. More than 6,000 houses were demolished and a further 1,400 severely damaged. However, this did not cause any loss of production and barely a day was lost either at the shipyard or the steelworks.

Understandably, due to the air-raids, the shipyard workers did not like the night shift so, when the warning siren was sounded, machines were stopped, tools were downed and the rush for the distant air-raid shelter began.

Dozens of blue double-decker buses lined up outside the yard at lunch time ready to take the workers to all parts of the town and to bring them back in the afternoon. In the evening the vehicles would be used again to take the workers home. Barrow must have been one of the few towns in Britain with an efficient bus service during the war. All around the dockyard, derrick cranes, heavy machine shops, battery shops, rigging lofts, mould lofts, gun-mounting shops, electric shops and the foundries combined to help fuse together the metal to mould these constructions into being. Each new crew visiting the shipyard for the first time was confronted by the sound of crashing steel, the vibrating noise of rivets being driven into place and the clatter of moving parts from the various points within this vast shipyard.

Once inside the dock area, and after picking one's way along the uneven roads, it was a case of finding the yard where your designated boat lay, surrounded by the hubbub and clatter of busy shipbuilders working feverishly on the uncompleted and complex mass of wires and steel.

This was the scene awaiting the Chief Engine Room Artificer (CERA), who was usually the first member of the permanent crew to see the submarine's construction. William Henry Ray, the CERA assigned to *P46,* later to be named HMS *Unruffled,* would have joined the boat a month before its launching. At the time of the actual launching ceremony, the craft was still just a shell and Ray might well have been the only person in attendance who was directly concerned with the future operation of the boat. The launching itself was similar to that of a surface ship, and the VIP who launched the *Unruffled*, known as the 'sponsor', would have said a few words, and then, when he/she released a silver-coloured lever mounted on a wooden lectern, wires freed the obligator bottle, which smashed against the bow. Ship workers then knocked blocks of wood from underneath the submarine, allowing it to slide stern first down the slipway and into the cold grey waters.

This action was probably witnessed by some of the directors of the Vickers board and some dockyard workers. Even though the war was at its peak, tradition did not flounder and the traditional launch ceremony still took place when a maritime vessel took to the water for the first time. Except for a Union Jack flying proudly from the bow, no visible identifications marks could be seen. Once in the water, the submarine, still without a propeller, was taken under the control of awaiting tugs and towed into the basin for completion. After the launching, the cover plates were removed and the main motors and main engines installed. The cover plates were a large part of the top of the engine room compartment. Then the main batteries were installed by passing them through the fore and engine room hatch, together with pipes and electrical and auxiliary machinery.

Vickers did not make all the component parts required for construction and had to obtain machinery from other engineering factories. For example, periscopes were made by Barm and Stroud, compasses by Sperry Gyroscope Ltd, propellers by John Thorncroft & Company and batteries by the Chloride Electrical Storage Company. There were, perhaps, a dozen or more firms employed in the supplying of machinery and parts and their responsibility was to guarantee that no material failures became fatal to the boat to ensure that the crew had full confidence in its construction and reliability.

As time progressed, Ray would have been joined by senior ratings, with the matelots joining periodically to make up the complement of crew. These ratings would have been given orders to join a new ship whilst at the Royal Navy shore-based establishment, HMS Dolphin, in Gosport, the home of submariners and the main training facility for the crews. After a long and tedious trip from London to Barrow, the ratings were understandably often exhausted by the time they reached their destination.

At Barrow they would have been met by the coxswain who, after roll-call, gave addresses and directions for where they might be able to find lodgings, with the final order to be back at the dockyard at 0900 hours the next morning. It was then that they would have congregated outside the submarine yard office to be met by the senior ratings, who had been standing by the boat as she was being built. They would also learn that the new launch was a U-class submarine with the pennant number *P46*. By the end of the first day the 'Jacks' would have got to know each other and gleaned information regarding the local hostelries in the town, the new boys benefiting from the knowledge gained by those who had been to Barrow before and knew where all the best pubs and liveliest music was to be found.

The captain, Lieutenant J.S. Stevens, joined the engineering officer in March, 1942. A few key ratings followed later, staying together to learn all the complexities of the boat. This was also the one and only opportunity for the captain to sweet-talk the shipbuilders into deviating from the original plans and make any slight adjustments to the layout of the interior. For example, if a commanding officer was of above average height, when he was standing beside the larger, high-power search periscope, a piece of machinery or pipe might obstruct his ability to achieve an all-round view. This would be the time to discuss the matter with the foreman and come to some kind of arrangement to overcome the problem. Aspects like seating and table areas might also be discussed. No two submarines were the same, and each captain or CERA would have his own agenda. Approximately six weeks before the first machinery trials the entire boat's company would have joined the submarine.

The boat was ordered on 23rd August, 1940, with the original yard number 800, and the keel laid down on 25th February, 1941. The launching was 19th December, 1941, and it was commissioned on 9th April, 1942. Though the boat had a pendant number of P46, it was later named HMS *Unruffled*, having originally been ordered as part of the batch *P31-39, P41-49, P51-59 and P61-67,* which, on Admiralty instructions, were not intended to have names. However, by late 1942, a directive from Prime Minister Winston Churchill demanded that all boats should be named by the 28th January, 1943, with the first group of names being allotted by the Ships' Names Committee.

Designed with a surface displacement of 545 net tons (658 tons gross and a submerged tonnage of 740 tons), this 196 feet 10 inches long, cigar-shaped cylindrical boat had a beam of 16 feet 1 inch and a draught of 15 feet 2 inches. It was propelled by two Colchester-based Paxman Ricardo diesel generators plus electric motors, which delivered between 615/825 bhp, and these two-shaft diesel-electric motors could produce 11.25 knots surface speed and 10 knots when submerged. With 55-ton diesel storage tanks, a range of 5500 nautical miles at 10 knots could be achieved. Test diving was set at 160 feet, with a designed diving depth of 200 feet. Four 21-inch internal bow torpedo tubes, with a complement of between eight and ten torpedoes (four permanently loaded in the tubes) and a 3-inch externally-mounted gun, completed the offensive armament.

Lessons had been learned since the original design of the Group 1 Unity class (U-class). When first designed in 1934, the U-class 1 was a cheap and easily maintained submarine intended to replace the ageing H-class and L-class boats, some of which were of First World War vintage. These elderly workhorses were used for training both submarine crews and the Air Surveillance Service (A/S). The class 2 was designed with no external torpedo tubes, and the bow lengthened and reshaped, thus allowing for improved performance and behaviour both on the surface and at periscope depth.

The class 2 had suffered delays due to engine defects. Its speed, size and limited range made this type of submarine ideal for the conditions in the Mediterranean, the most successful being *Ultor, Umbra* and *Unruffled,* with over 30,000 tons each of enemy shipping to their credit.

A submarine had just three goals: to remain undetected; to retain its ability to operate unsupported in waters under enemy control; and to deliver a torpedo and/or fire a gun within range of the enemy. It had no peacetime purpose. A British single-hull submarine with a riveted half-inch thick pressure hull sub-divided into five watertight compartments and a pressure hull and bulkheads tested to a pressure of 70 psi would withstand a depth of 160 feet. The pressure hull was pierced by four hatches: the torpedo hatch, escape hatch forward, the aft engine hatch and the conning tower hatch. Six internal main ballast tanks were fitted with hydraulically-operated vents, two end tanks forward and aft, giving free flood openings in the bottom, and four centre tanks equipped with Kingston valves. A quick diving 'Q' tank was fitted for fast diving. The 'Q' tank held 10 tons of sea water, which could be vented either in board or overboard, and was left flooded while on the surface but easily "blown" or emptied into the sea once the submarine had achieved its required depth. This enabled the U-class to get under the surface in less than 20 seconds.

Due to its restricted width, when wet the casing (deck area) became saturated and slippery, so the surface was extremely dangerous to walk on and if a rating was not tied onto the guard rail when the submarine was underway at sea, he could easily slip overboard.

The diesel engines were used when surfaced but battery power was used when submerged. While surfaced, it was usual for one diesel engine to generate forward thrust and the second engine to charge the batteries, using the engine as a dynamo. This recharge would enable the batteries to provide enough electrical power for 15 hours at an average submerged speed of between 2 and 3 knots. The rate of discharge doubled, or even trebled, if the speed was increased. In fact, a speed of 9 knots submerged would exhaust the batteries within 20-30 minutes.

Each submarine carried three batteries consisting of 112 cells each, with the total voltage of each battery being 270 volts. These batteries were joined in parallel to make one large power source. Each cell weighed half a ton and was operated in the same way as a car battery, requiring regular topping-up with distilled water. There were 331 cells in total weighing half a ton each. This meant that up to five tons of distilled water was required, especially when on a long patrol. These batteries also provided the energy source for the electric motors.

Due to a low surface speed of between 10 and 11 knots, a U-class submarine captain would find it difficult to catch up or overtake a merchant ship and had practically no chance of outmanoeuvring a warship. This clear disadvantage resulted in some heroic, imaginative, creative and strategic tactics devised by submarine masters.

When submerged, control of the submarine was achieved by the use of hydraulically-operated hydroplanes that were sited forward above the waterline and aft below the surface on either side of the rudder against the casing. The aft hydroplanes were placed so that the thrust of the propeller was directly on them. The fore-planes were used mainly for maintaining depth. They were operated by two men from the control room and they had to work in unison because efficient control could not otherwise be maintained. Once dived, balance was maintained by the shifting of weights. This was achieved by water being pumped in or out of the boat, thus establishing a stable "trimming".

The first lieutenant, under orders from the captain, maintained the submarine's depth and speed, which were adjusted accordingly from the control room. This important compartment was sited beneath the bridge and contained two periscopes. The larger of the two, known as the high power scope, was binocular and bi-focal and used for all-round vision, and included a range finder and sky search facility. It measured nine inches, tapering to five inches, and on a clear day a top range of ten miles could be achieved.

A smaller periscope, used during attacks, was known as the low-power periscope, or attack scope, and for obvious reasons was designed to leave little 'feathering' on the surface. This periscope was monocular and uni-focal, giving normal vision. The panels for the operation of the vents, Kingston valve, high and low pressure air, pumping tanks, chart table, fruit machine (a device for calculating the angle, course and speed of a torpedo run), hydro-planes control and torpedo firing order instrument were also situated here.

Going forward from the control room led to a two-foot wide corridor, where the living compartments were located. The wardroom for the officers was conveniently located next to the control room, then the galley, with the ERA's Mess next door. Next to this tiny space was sited the petty officers and leading seamen's Mess, the wash room and, on towards the final compartment, the torpedo room. The torpedo tubes, fully loaded and ready to be let loose on an unknowing foe, were in the extremity of the bow.

The toilet was located on the other side of the corridor and was split into two divided rooms, one for the officers and the other for the ratings. Each consisted of a wash basin and one toilet, the latter being difficult and complicated to operate. There were 12 different actions to be made, both before and after, and if not operated in the correct order it could lead to the contents of the bowl being blown in an upward direction. It could even result in endangering the submarine should a wrong valve be opened. Permission from the officer of the watch was required to use this facility when submerged as, due to the pressure in the boat, this was not allowed below 70 feet. Buckets were preferred by the crew and these would be emptied overboard with the 'gash' (rubbish) when recharging batteries at night.

R.A. Cunningham, in his book 'A Submarine at War', recollects that a convenience for the use of the lookouts when on duty was located on the bridge. It was similar to a voice pipe and was known by the ratings as the 'pig's ear'. The pipe led to an outlet just above the saddle tank on the port side. Cunningham comments: "It has been said that in the dark the actual voice pipe has been used by mistake, much to the disgust of the poor chap on the helm down below. He wondered why the sea was warm."

The disposing of the gash, mainly food waste and cigarette ends etc, was a nightly exercise when it was allowed by the watch officer. From the control room towards the stern could be found the W/T (wireless/telegraphy) and ASDIC (Anti-Submarine Detection Investigation Committee) office, next the engine-room, and finally the electric motor room. Sited below the entire length of the deck from the stern to the bow were the fuel and lubricating oil tanks, batteries, trim tank, magazine and stores, yet another line of batteries, auxiliary machinery (pumps), fresh water and fuel tanks, trimming and torpedo tube drain tanks and, in the extremities of the bow, the main ballast tank.

The W/T department was split into four wireless watches, each with a duration of four hours. During the watches the operator would be seated, with headphones on, reading signals from Admiralty routines and noting the address of each signal. There would be a whole batch of these prior to the individual messages being transmitted. Each submarine had its own call sign and if the call sign or DG (Delivery Group), was heard, a copy was recorded of the coded text.

These codes changed daily and it was the duty of the senior operator to change the DG for that day, a routine that was usually carried out at midnight. Radio operators were particularly attentive on the 24th-25th day of a patrol when listening for the recall to base transmission.

Because of the propagation within the Mediterranean, transmissions to the Admiralty could be somewhat of a problem. So much so, that it was easier to raise Halifax, Nova Scotia, whose Canadian operators would read the message and then re-transmit to the Admiralty in Whitehall. When dived, signals could only be received at periscope depth via the loop aerial fitted around the boat. When surfaced, there was not a problem as aerials were fixed to the jump wire stretching from the stern to bow. The jump wire was designed to protect the submarine from any obstacles that might get tangled up with the hydroplanes, the bridge – or, especially, mines. Equipped with type 129 ASDIC dome fitted beneath the hull of the submarine, the ASDIC operator, using headphones, made contact with surface ships and underwater objects by sending out sound waves (a ping that would bounce off and return whenever they hit an object). This facility also provided inter-communication with a friendly submarine. An experienced operator of the hydrophones and ASDIC apparatus could often confidently identify an enemy vessel by its propeller revolutions, shaft rotation rate and blade count. The echo from an object could be heard up to a range of two miles.

The first lieutenant was responsible to the captain for the good order and running efficiency of the boat, including discipline of the ship's company, and the engineering officer was directly responsible to the captain for the running efficiency of the main and auxiliary machinery. It was important that these two officers worked in unison in order to successfully make the submarine ready for sea. Tact and understanding were required from both sides to ensure teamwork was maintained, and as the engineering officer was usually older than the first officer, due to the experience required in engineering skills and technical issues, the term 'Sonny' was not encouraged. These two officers held responsibilities for navigation, armaments and general secretariat duties.

The wardroom that provided accommodation for the four officers on board measured 7 feet by 9 feet, with two bunks fitted opposite each other, above two settees. These folded back to form another two bunks. A narrow table on which to eat and play games was located in the centre, with lockers located beneath the settees completing the furnishings.

The petty officers were divided into two camps, with the coxswain having overall management control. The engine room ERAs were trained experts and technicians, and had their own living quarters separate from the other petty officers. The senior petty officer and the coxswain shared a Mess with a torpedo instructor, the electrician, the petty officer telegraphist and the stoker petty officer. Each member of this team had experience and technical abilities crucial to the running of the boat.

The leading ratings and petty officers were also given their own quarters, with the junior ratings having to make do with the fore-ends and the torpedo reload compartment. A two-foot corridor gave passage from the control room to the aft torpedo hatch. Loaded via the torpedo hatch, each torpedo weighed one-and-a-half tons and measured 22 feet in length and 21 inches in diameter. The torpedo was fired by a short burst of compressed air into the tube. It was first loaded into the open rear door of the tube, then the door was closed and water flooded into the tube using an internal tank. This allowed for the bow doors to be opened without any inrush of water that would have altered the trim of the boat. When the torpedo left the tube, water rushed in quickly, thus equalising the trim once again. The designated bow door would then be closed, water drained from the tube, the rear door opened and re-loading would commence.

There were three watches split into two hours on duty and four hours off. This did not include some lookouts, whose watches were one hour on and three hours off, excluding the ten minutes spent in getting accustomed to the darkness of the bridge before taking over the watch. The commanding officer, chief coxswain and chief ERA did not keep regular watches, but often maintenance work kept them busy, sometimes for as long as 24 hours or more. On top of this, the chief coxswain was expected at any hour of the day or night to play 'uckers' - a vicious adaptation of Ludo - with any officer of the watch who did not feel like sleeping. All crew slept fully clothed in anticipation of the call of 'diving stations'. In the forward torpedo room, no concessions were made in regard to the comfort of the crew. They were merely there to serve the system, fitting in between the reloading of torpedoes and stores, having to share the limited number of bunks ('hot bunking') with a shipmate from another watch and sleeping on unchanged blankets that became dirtier by the day.

This cramped space was also the storage compartment for the food, heavy tackle, blocks, wire strops, rope, tool boxes, lockers, spare gear, seat cushions, lockers and personal items. If there was enough room the seamen would sling their hammocks or lie on the floor in order to sleep in this restricted and confined compartment, but more often than not, due to the lack of space and, above all, a lack of energy, a blanket or hammock canvas was placed across the stores and either bread or soft vegetables used as a pillow.

Feet and flailing arms would often wander into someone else's face, there was snoring and grunting to put up with, and flatulence would regularly mix into the already stale atmosphere. Men were often unable to even wash their hands and face, and daily bathing and showering was impossible. On occasion it was impossible to get dry after a wet spell on watch. On war patrol, many of the crew did not shave and, due to the limited amount of fresh water, could only arrange a sponge-down a couple of times a week. After a long spell at sea, the TGM (Torpedo Gunner's Mate) might give permission to allow a salt-water shower from a cock at the rear end of one of the flooded torpedo tubes that allowed water to squirt out. Salt-water soap was substituted for ordinary soap in an attempt to get some form of lather. Lieutenant Stevens reflected: "After three weeks on patrol with the smell of diesel on your clothes you did not smell too good."

There was often a queue for the fiendishly complex toilet in the heads, but even that could not be used when submerged below 70 feet because of the exterior pressure. Thereafter the men were obliged to relieve themselves in buckets and empty bottles, the smell of which, mixed with the confined and humid odour of diesel oil and the reek of past cooking, unwashed bodies, chlorine and stale bilges, permeated every corner. When fresh provisions ran out, men were forced to eat hashes of tinned food and dehydrated vegetables and could not take proper exercise. Walking on the deck casing was not allowed in case of an emergency dive and when submerged for any length of time, crew suffered nausea and headaches; and, if the mind was allowed to dwell on the subject, incipient claustrophobia. Paradoxically, the sheer frightfulness of conditions and the sense of vulnerability and mutual responsibility engendered comradeship – irrespective of nationality – across barriers of rank, which in turn ensured a high level of morale, probably higher than in any other class of warship.

Alastair Mars, in command of *P42,* HMS *Unbroken,* said: "Routine life aboard a submarine is a dull, monotonous business. You eat, sleep, test and exercise; read, argue and write letters home; speculate and reminisce; and all the time the air becomes heavy and sour. Tempers grow short and nerves are frayed, and you curse the day you ever volunteered to serve in these sardine cans. Yet, with human perversity, you know deep down in your heart you would not be elsewhere."

So who volunteered for such an unnatural life? Before the war, sufficient numbers came forward and it was only necessary to draft a few specialist ratings, for example engineers. Some would have joined for the extra half-a-crown a day's pay, others simply had no choice, whilst the incentive to junior ranking officers was the prospect of early command compared with that of the surface fleet. Amongst the crews there was a special camaraderie and informality on board and a different kind of higher discipline, achieved by self-respect and competence. In a submarine, more than any other type of vessel, each member of the crew is vital to the team. A mistake by any one person might lead to disaster. The men were well trained and had confidence in their own skills and of those around them, and respect and comradeship bound each and every one of them together.

The main advantage the seaman in the fore-ends had over the stoker section was in regard to noise. Being forward of the engines when on the surface and with main diesel engines running meant you did not have to raise your voice to be heard. However, the vibration of the engines could be felt throughout the boat, and during a swell, the waves could be heard splashing against the hull, while the vibrating sound of the pipes and the rattle of fixtures reached a staccato pitch and ceased as quickly as it had started.

In contrast, when the boat was dived and the electric motors engaged, silence prevailed and there was no sensation of movement as the submarine glided into the depths. In the machine spaces, unlike that of the fore-ends, the engineers needed to be able to work unheeded, so no stores were kept in this area. However, the stokers had to deal with the smell of diesel and the noise of the engines, which made any conversation virtually impossible. With a crew of four officers and 29 ratings in such a small space, conditions on board were sometimes overcrowded, especially when a landing party also had to be accommodated.

I have left the subject of food until last as a category on its own because, as far as the crew was concerned, this was a vitally important subject. From the captain downwards, meal times were a significant event, and something to look forward to. Due to the monotonous daily routine of watches, sleep and games, plus occasional action stations, food and its quality and quantity were high on the list of priorities. *Unruffled* was lucky enough to have a trained baker on board. A.B. 'Wiggy' Bennett, as a willing and cheerful

Lancastrian, fitted the role to everyone's delight. Being chef was by no means an easy task and preparing and cooking food for 33 individuals in a kitchen (galley) no bigger than a closet was an undeniable challenge.

There were two cooked meals each day. Dinner was served around midnight, with breakfast being taken just before diving for the day. This was due to the fact that the galley was all-electric and it was important that battery power was conserved when the boat dived. Cold snacks and sandwiches could be made by the individual ratings when coming off watch, or if someone awoke hungry before going on watch. However, throughout the day the chef would prepare a cold meal for the entire crew, simply referred to as 'tea'.

Fresh vegetables, meat, bread and tinned food were loaded before going out on patrol. As mentioned previously, these were stored in the fore-ends. Fresh meat would last approximately two weeks, depending on how the chief coxswain managed to divide it up, but the vegetables would eventually rot, giving off an unpleasant odour. When the bread began to turn green with mould on the outside, the problem was overcome by cutting off the bad bits. Having a qualified baker on board was a big advantage because he could cook fresh bread. On many submarines, the chef was either untrained or an unwilling volunteer.

Once the fresh food had been consumed, the crew was reduced to eating tinned food such as corned beef, herring in tomato sauce, tinned ham and tinned butter. Potatoes would last longer than most food, but they would eventually begin to sprout and turn soft. On submarines, everyone was served the same food; there was no class distinction except that the officers were served their meals by the captain's steward and the petty officers, whose Mess man served their meals. The stokers and seamen usually had two ratings, who worked a 24-hour duty, bringing the food from the galley and gathering up the dirty pots and plates after each meal.

The serving of the traditional rum ration, enjoyed by all except the under-aged, was, as one might expect, the highlight of the day. The 70 per cent Barbados rum was mixed with three parts water and served by the coxswain from wicker-covered stone jars. All junior ratings were required by the King's Regulations and Admiralty instructions to draw their daily ration of one-eighth of a pint of spirit watered down. This way it would be sour unless drunk immediately. And because ratings were not allowed to smoke whilst submerged, the eating of sweets also became a prescribed ration.

CHAPTER TWO

THE CREW

‒‒‒⊱✦⊰‒‒‒

ROYAL NAVY COMMAND records held at Swadlincote, Derbyshire, reveal the crew list for P46 beginning from 1ˢᵗ March, 1942, the official date when the crew began to assemble and ratings were given their first opportunity to familiarise themselves with the boat. The crew list below gives names, dates and a short history of the Naval Personnel joining the submarine:

Lieutenant John Samuel Stevens DSO DSC RN – Commander, HMS Unruffled

Held within the Imperial War Museum archives in London is a recorded interview with John Stevens conducted on the 16ᵗʰ June, 1986 (Catalogue No. 9310). As in his book 'Never

Volunteer', published in 1971, details are sketchy and only a minimum number of the ratings' names are mentioned. His accent is, not unexpectedly, 'BBC English', as spoken by the majority of middle-class gentlemen of the day. What is surprising is that he appears genuinely to be a very shy and thoughtful person. Readers will be aware that servicemen who campaign during any war tend to keep their recollections and thoughts very much to themselves. This seems to be typical of Lieutenant Stevens, so it is difficult to accurately judge his personality or gauge what kind of man he really was.

People I have spoken to who have had the privilege of meeting him have all responded with the same comment, that "he was a nice bloke", fondly nicknamed 'Steve' by his fellow officers. Captain (S) 10th Submarine Flotilla G.W.G. Simpson, known as 'Shrimp', writing in his autobiography, gives no clue as to the real personality of the *Unruffled* captain. But when recommending him for a decoration, he states: "Lieutenant Stevens has shown a bold determination tempered with good judgment that has assured success, and I consider him most deserving for immediate award of a decoration."

Captain John Coote, who in 1950 was Officer Commanding the Rothesay Attack Teacher (OCRAT), recollects: "My favourite requalify was John Stevens, who had sunk a lot of ships in the Mediterranean in his aptly-named *Unruffled*. After listening to esoteric mathematical formulae involving rate of change of bearing and the various criteria determining the optimum spread and number of fish to be fired in a salvo of torpedoes under any given set of circumstances, to say nothing of calculating the director angle DA (or aim-off), he [Stevens] declared that a U-class only has four up the spout. So I say, if the target is worth firing at, give her the lot and, anyway, the DA is always 10 degrees (for a 7 knot merchantman that is a fair approximation). So I threw away all the graphs and most of the slide-rules and concentrated on developing basic skills within the scope of existing equipment and those in charge of it. High on my [list of] priorities were the mental aides for attacking without instruments. Over the eyepiece of the attack teacher periscope I had a brass plate fixed with the words inscribed: 'Remember, the DA is always 10 degrees'."

Dwight D Eisenhower, United States President from 1953-61 and the Supreme Commander of Allied Forces in Europe during the Second World War, described Stevens as the "maddest captain in the trade. When hitting one of Hitler's ships with a single torpedo, [he] found himself without ammunition to finish off the job".

Ralph Neville Stanbury, who sailed in *Unruffled* as Commander of a Combined Operations Beach Party group (COPP) before the Sicily landings, described Stevens as "this good-natured, jovial submarine captain. He was already, while still in this middle twenties, the possessor of a DSO and a DSC, and was one of the most famous captains in the 'trade'. The speed at which he went up and down through a conning-tower hatch was a matter of constant admiration to me, for his ample frame could allow very little, if any, gap!"

I have gone into detail with regards to Stevens' background and service record up to the point when he left *Unruffled* as I feel this information is important in gaining access to the character of a man who was not only responsible for motivating his crew but also held the boat's safety in his hands.

John Samuel Stevens was born on the 19th March, 1916, at Crouch End, North London. His father was general manager of a road transport company which delivered meat carcass from the docks to the butchers. When John was three years old the family moved to Sutton, Surrey. As far as we know, no one in his family had ever before considered a career in the Royal Navy and his interest started while at Prep school in Seaford Sussex, where one of his teachers was in the Royal Naval Volunteer Reserve service.

As a result, Stevens persuaded his parents to allow him to go to Dartford Naval College, at just 12 years of age. He went to Dartmouth in 1929 and spent three years at sea as cadet and midshipman. While on the training cruiser 'Frobisher' (1934-1936) as a cadet, he served as 'doggie' (cabin boy) to Captain Lord Tovey, master of the Rodney. He also served with Lord Mountbatten on the destroyer Wishaart in Malta and later on the Devonshire, commanded by Sir Herbert Fitzherbert, who Stevens remembers "kept a hospitable table and was a good raconteur".

He also recalls the "the ill-fated" Crown Prince Farouk of Egypt. "The Devonshire took him from Alexandria to Port Said when he was on his way to England to attend Sandhurst. This was a goodwill gesture towards the Egyptian Government during the Abyssinian war crisis in 1936. He took refreshment in the gunroom with us and he had an air of worldly experience far beyond his sixteen years," Stevens recollects.

Commissioned in 1937 as a lieutenant, he faced 18 months of shore courses before volunteering for the submarine service. Stevens, like many before him, was astutely aware that this branch of the service could provide a fast track to promotion and command compared with surface ships. He was concerned that if he did not move on he would be restricted to the role of aviation observer, and in January 1938 he was appointed third hand of a reserve group of veteran H-class submarines at Portland. In early 1939, as a junior lieutenant, he went to Barrow-in-Furness to stand by the new T-class submarine N18, *HMS Triumph,* as torpedo, armament and correspondence officer. It is relevant to add that gun action was not used in anger when he was on board.

After acceptance trials, their departure was somewhat hampered by a disciplinary problem involving the CPO Coxswain, whose responsibilities involved supervising the embarkation of the crew and their kit as well as issuing the rum ration: instead, he was found fast asleep and rather full of rum in the office in which the grog was kept. Finally leaving Barrow and after a brief visit to HMS Dolphin in Gosport, they went to Falmouth for a two-week work up period. *Triumph* operated in the Skagerrak, the strategic deep-water strait between Norway and Sweden, until mid-August 1939, when the boat was ordered to join the Second Submarine Flotilla based in Dundee reporting on board the depot ship HMS Forth.

Stevens says: "Here there was a hectic confusion as the likelihood of war approached or receded. One day we would be ordered to store for war, fit torpedo warheads and so on; the next day would see us reversing all this and getting back to a peacetime state. After this frenzied activity, it came almost as a relief to sail in earnest for our war station on the last Friday in August."

Triumph's first war patrol did not go without incident. *N18* collided with a Danish wooden fishing drifter, which subsequently sank. Stevens recalls: "I went on deck with the casing party and watched her crew hastily lower a small dinghy into the water; they threw in a handful of private possessions and then abandoned ship. Ten minutes later, we encountered another drifter and transferred them to her. Because of strict radio silence this collision was not reported until our arrival back in harbour, over two weeks later. I never heard of any official reaction to this incident."

Stevens was also the Confidential Book Officer, a responsibility which included collecting from HMS Forth, "two or three sacks" – sealed envelopes containing orders and instructions - on board the submarine before sailing. He explained: "As 3rd September drew nearer, we received a stream of signals instructing the opening of this sealed envelope or that; the orders and instructions disclosed were to bring the fleet up to war readiness. On Sunday morning we received the coded message: 'TOTAL GERMANY'; its meaning was simple – commence immediate hostilities against Germany. Later in the day, the submarine broadcast relayed the message sent to all the fleet: 'Winston is back'.

Stevens was horrified to hear of the sinking of HMS *Oxley*, the first Royal Navy wartime submarine loss. He writes that "it had been in reserve and had re-commissioned for service with the Second Flotilla. While in one of the billets on the Obrestad Line in darkness and on the surface, [the boat] was sighted unexpectedly by another British boat.

The latter challenged *Oxley* by flashing light and, failing to get a correct reply, fired two torpedoes, one of which hit and sank the boat. The captain and signalman, who had been on the bridge, were the only survivors."

A different kind of learning curve was yet to be experienced by Stevens at 2300 hours on Boxing Day when the crew was dealing with a roast and two veg. At 2306, with the moon appearing from behind a cloud, one of the four lookouts on the bridge spotted a mine floating only a few feet away. The order was given 'Hard a Starboard!' but, with the only one engine propelling the boat at low speed, the submarine was unable to answer the helm and *Triumph* struck the mine, which exploded.

"Those on the bridge heard the roar of the explosion and were temporarily blinded by the sheet of flame that erupted; it seemed to them that *Triumph* had sustained mortal damage and would go under rapidly," he writes. "My plate of roast and two veg had been flung into my face. We rushed to emergency stations and closed the watertight doors. Water could be heard spattering on to the forward side of that bulkhead (torpedo space) and the watertight doors were opened. The forward bulkhead, through which the torpedo tubes passed, were found to be split and leaking. The splits were plugged with wood and felt, which reduced the water inflow to an amount that could be controlled by continuous pumping. Able-seaman Wood was asleep in his hammock in the fore-ends, about thirty feet from the explosion, but slept on through it. He awoke only when aroused by the damage surveying party. Naturally, his messmates christened him 'Sleepy Wood'."

N18, unable to dive, 300 miles from base and still in in

enemy waters, limped home two days later. It was subsequently discovered that 15 feet of plating was missing and the force of the explosion had forced six torpedo tubes back six inches. All were loaded with live torpedoes, of which one was found to be minus its safety pin and swishing around in its damaged tube.

Stevens reflects: "On board for one operation that led to the mining was Surgeon Lieutenant Pickering RNVR, from the Firth of Forth, who was learning first-hand about the conditions under which his patients lived at sea. Over a drink in the wardroom, the captain remarked that it could have been worse for him the most, because he did not have knowledge of a submarine's capabilities. "All I know of submarines", replied the doctor, "is what I've seen in the movies where men often seem to be struggling waist deep in swirling water just before the boat goes down – we seemed to do better this time."

After being patched up in Rosyth, *Triumph* was escorted by destroyer to Chatham, Kent, for permanent repairs. Whilst at Chatham, junior lieutenant Stevens received a telephone call from Commander Mitford on Admiral Submarine staff, whose responsibility it was to nominate junior officer appointments. Stevens writes that Commander Mitford wanted (for special service) either he himself or Sandy Nott, a fellow junior officer and good friend on *Triumph,* who had taken the same Submarine Officers' course. Nott was due back from leave the next day when Stevens was due leave himself. "All right," said Commander Mitford, "you take your leave, but warn Nott he'll be going elsewhere in a day or two."

Nott was transferred as liaison officer on the Polish

submarine O.R.P. *Orzel,* which was sadly lost in the Skagerrak, with the loss of all those on board, in May 1940. Explained Stevens: "Sandy and I tossed a coin to settle which of us should go on leave first; had the coin fallen the other way it would have been my fate to join *Orzel".* Stevens was to receive another hammer blow when in November 1941 *Triumph,* having been transferred to the Mediterranean, was sunk with all hands. Some of the original key ratings who had joined the boat at Barrow-in-Furness three years earlier perished with her.

Stevens left *Triumph* on the 14th April, 1940, after being ordered to report to 'Cyclops', an elderly depot ship based at Harwich under the command of Captain P. Ruck-Keene. Here he was allotted 'Special service' and consequently joined the French submarine *Circe* as liaison officer. This task was to assist with coding and cyphering radio messages. He recollects: "Each day, all four officers and myself squeezed into the tiny wardroom for lunch. This was an excellent four-course meal, with copious [sic] wine rounded off with coffee and a liqueur. The crew was allowed wine, pumped up from a bulk wine tank. Later in the war, with normal wine resources cut off, the supply people had quite a headache getting adequate amounts of this vital commodity through to free French forces."

Once again Stevens was involved in a collision, this time with another French submarine, which caused a holed after-main ballast tank. As German forces began to overrun France, the French flotilla was called back home and liaison parties recalled. Having received orders to report on board *H50,* a First World War relic based at Harwich, he was greeted by the-then Captain (S) G.W.G. Simpson. Having been promoted to first lieutenant *H50*, Stevens spent the next couple of months carrying out patrols off the Dutch coast as part of an anti-invasion force, after which he again received new orders. This time it was to stand by a boat at Cammell Laird shipyard, Birkenhead. Upon his arrival, and much to his surprise, he found himself standing by *Thetis,* which had sunk during trials in June 1939 and had been salvaged and repaired. He found the engineer officer, Jack Northwood, and six key senior ratings standing by the boat, which was to be renamed *Thunderbolt.* Three days after his arrival, he was presented to the King and Queen, who had come to inspect the boat. Whilst the King was escorted below, "I was privileged to tell the Queen of some of our purposes. I have never forgotten her genuine interest, her charm and capacity for putting us at ease," he says.

There was no fuss made at the renaming ceremony, as the Admiralty wanted to keep the subject as low-key as possible due to the circumstances behind the *Thetis* incident. Upon completion in late October, 1940, *Thunderbolt* left Mersey under the command of Lieutenant Commander C.B. Crouch. There was plenty of tension in the air, for everyone was aware of the past history of the boat as it headed for trials at the Scottish WWII naval base sea loch of Gairloch, where, much to the relief of the Admiralty and the crew, trials and work-up were completed without problem.

On the 3rd December, 1940, *Thunderbolt* left the British coastline on her way to her first war patrol – destination mouth of the River Gironde, in the Bay of Biscay. Whilst submerged on station, it encountered an enemy submarine, thought at the time to be a U-boat, being escorted by two steam trawlers. Lieutenant Commander Crouch ordered diving stations and prepared the torpedoes for an attack.

Stevens enthusiastically continues the story. "Quite soon, *Thunderbolt* gave a slight shudder as the first torpedo – the first fired in anger in this commission - went on its way. For most of us, and certainly for me, it was the first such torpedo in this war – an exciting moment." They had, in fact, hit the Italian submarine *Tarantini*, which sank rapidly, leaving five or six crew in the icy waters. One officer and three ratings survived the ordeal. This success exorcised the demon of the *Thetis* and resulted in a superb morale-booster not only for the crew but the Admiralty. It was not long before the boat was transferred to Halifax, Nova Scotia, on convoy escort duties. The port of Halifax was extremely busy, with Bedford Basin, a large natural anchorage, ideally suited for use as an assembly area and meeting point for all the merchant ships readying to cross the Atlantic.

Liquor laws were disliked by both the Royal Navy ratings and merchant seaman, as there were no bars and only an overcrowded Fleet Club, which was heavily supervised. For five months *Thunderbolt* carried out her duties, escorting merchant ships halfway across the Atlantic before returning to her mothership HMS Forth back in Nova Scotia, to await another convoy. In company with HMS Forth they sailed for St John, New Brunswick, where they were both entered into dry dock for three days of underwater cleaning and painting. They then sailed for St John's, Newfoundland, where shortly after arrival Stevens received orders to return to the UK to participate in the Submarine Commanding Officer Course, fondly known amongst submariners as the Perishers. He travelled on board the Frigate Leith, a convoy escort vessel, arriving in Liverpool, and in August reported back at HMS Dolphin in Gosport, where he spent three weeks, occupied by lectures and simulating dummy attacks on the mechanical training teacher.

Two further weeks were spent on sea attacks in the submarine *Oberon,* based at Rothesay, on the Isle of Bute, where he qualified as a submarine commander. Six weeks later he left Dundee with orders to take command of the Londonderry-based *H44,* which was employed on training exercises with the Western Approaches Escort Forces. The official joining date is recorded as the 6th November, 1941. Four weeks after joining, *H46* was ordered for a refit at Sheerness, Kent. On the trip to the Isle of Sheppey, the starboard propeller became fouled and temporary repairs had to be made in Portsmouth. On completion, the submarine joined a Sheerness-bound convoy off Spithead, but almost immediately after arrival he received a signal directing him to join *H32* to replace the captain, who had gone sick whilst it was finishing off a refit. Stevens joined the boat on the 6th December 1941, a command that was to last until 26th February, 1942.

Conditions on board this veteran submarine were somewhat primitive, with the three officers having to live behind a curtained area in the confines of the torpedo room, which had to be dismantled when the torpedoes were being overhauled. It was not long after he joined, and the boat had returned to Portsmouth, that *H32* was ordered on a patrol area five miles to the seaward of Cherbourg as part of the 'Iron Ring'. The German Battleships Scharnhorst and

Gneisenau had been rumoured to be preparing to sail from Brest. It was not until New Year's Day 1942 that all submarines involved in the operation were stood down. Unfortunately, *H34,* the sister of *H32*, failed to return to port. *H32* was then ordered to report to the Londonderry Exercise Training areas, where Stevens was relieved on the 4th March and told to travel to Barrow-in-Furness to stand by a new boat – *P46* - which he resumed command of on the 6th March 1942.

Lieutenant John Samuel Stevens died on the 12th November, 1991 after a long and distinguished naval career.

1st Lieutenant Gordon Maurice Noll

Noll joined HMS Dolphin submarine course on the 4th March, 1940. Upon completion on the 20th April, he was appointed to the 6th Submarine Flotilla, HMS Elfin at Blyth, on the Northumberland coast, and was transferred to the 7th Submarine Flotilla on the 10th July, 1940 to report on board HMS Cyclops at Rothesay. On 15th September 1940, he received orders to report to Vickers Armstrong in Barrow-in-Furness, to stand by in readiness for the completion of the submarine *N65* (HMS *Usk*) as 3rd hand. *Usk* was commissioned on the 11th October, 1940, and sailed for trials and training on the Clyde. Seventeen days later it returned to Barrow where it remained for five days. One can only presume that a fault had been reported and the boat returned to Barrow for repairs. While on passage to Portsmouth, *N65* was ordered on its first war patrol, some 20 miles off Ushant, France, when it was reported that the German pocket battleship Admiral Scheer was making for port. *Usk* was to be lost with all hands some time after 25th April, 1941, while on patrol off Cape Bon, Tunisia.

Shortly after arriving at Portsmouth on the 11th November, 1940, Noll was told to report to HMS Dolphin, where he remained until 1st February, 1941, when he reported to HMS Cyclops for duty on board *H50* as first lieutenant. On the 5th July, Noll was on the move again, this time reporting on board HMS Forth, based at St John, Nova Scotia, to report on board HMS *Tribune* as first lieutenant. This commission was again short-lived and by 4th November he had joined *P511,* a former US Navy Submarine (*R-3*), which had been transferred to the Royal Navy.

After passage to Plymouth, Noll was stood by HMS *Unruffled* on the 6th March, 1942, as first lieutenant departing the boat on the 17th October, 1942, to HMS Dolphin, where he successfully completed the perisher's course. On 10th November, 1942, Noll became the commander of *H34.* He was moved on again on 1st February, 1943, to take command of a new boat, HMS *Untamed,* being built at Vickers Armstrong. Unfortunately, 36 men were lost when *Untamed* failed to surface while completing trials off Campbeltown, on the 30th May 1943. The Admiralty decided to salvage the stricken boat and it was retrieved from the depths and taken to Barrow. During close inspection it was found that a valve had been incorrectly fitted, which gave a false reading to the crew. When the flooding compartment was evacuated the watertight door failed to seal. After spending four hours attempting to resurface, the crew evacuated into the engine-room in order to escape, and began flooding the compartment and using the internal pressure to force open the outer hatch. Unfortunately, another faulty valve, which showed it was open when in fact it was closed, prevented the flooding and it was not until some time later that another valve was opened to attempt to flood. However, incoming water also entered the bilges, which meant it took even longer to flood the engine-room. It should at this point be noted that carbon dioxide built up rapidly, preventing clear thinking by the crew. They are laid to rest at nearby Dunoon cemetery. *Untamed* was re-named HMS *Vitality* and joined the 7th Submarine Flotilla as a training boat.

2nd Lieutenant Oliver Lascelles DSC MBE

Born on the 5th March, 1921, and a descendant of William the Conqueror, Lascelles joined the Royal Navy in 1939 just before his 18th birthday and retired in 1965. He reported on board HMS Forester and later HMS Malaya, a 33,020 deadweight tons Queen Elizabeth class battleship.

Oliver recalls that at one stage, while on route to the USA, they had loaded a "million tons of gold" as part payment for military equipment. Having visited Alexandria, Malta and Gibraltar, one unfortunate incident typically illustrated the discipline and protocol exercised in the Royal Navy at that time. Lascelles, 20, whilst coxing a picket boat, failed to see an Admiral in his barge nearly half-a-mile away, so he neglected to slow down and salute as procedure demanded. The unnamed Admiral reported the regrettable misdemeanour by signal to HMS Malaya, which resulted in Lascelles later receiving six cuts with a cane; this, at a time when servicemen were being killed fighting for their king and country.

Undertaking the submariners' course on the 18th November, 1941, and passing out, Oliver was sent to the 5th Submarine Flotilla at Blyth on 15th January, 1942. On the 1st March, 1942, Oliver was appointed to stand by a new boat at Barrow-in-Furness, HMS *Unruffled (P46)* as gunnery officer, joining on board on the 10th. He was promoted whilst on war patrol on the 16th April, 1943, to first lieutenant and awarded the DSC on the 7th September of the same year.

When *P46* was designated her official name, Lascelles was not too impressed. In fact, he believed *Unruffled* to be an awful name. Described as having a wicked sense of humour and "a good man to have with you when you wanted a run ashore", Oliver also had, as the ladies described, a "twinkle in his eye". He later went on to take command of *Unruffled, U-249, Trusty, Umbra, Unbending, Seneschal, Meteorite, Turpin, Telemachus, Explorer* and *Anchorite*. Lascelles was later promoted to commander and was involved in experimental work involving submarine engines. He died at the age of 78 on the 10th October, 1999.

Sub-Lieutenant Ronald Max Seaburne-May DSC

Born in Kenya, Seaburne-May survived the sinking of the battleship 'Royal Oak'. He served in submarines from 30th June, 1941, having completed his submariners' course, after which he was appointed to the submarine depot ship HMS Cyclops at Rothesay. On the 5th August, he was appointed third lieutenant on board the submarine *H33*.

After receiving orders on the 12th March, 1942 to stand by *P46,* he travelled to Vickers Armstrong as the appointed third officer, which included the role of navigating officer. He was to be appointed first officer on the 20th October, 1942 and awarded the DSC on the 4th May, 1943. G.W.G. Simpson, captain (S) Tenth Submarine Flotilla base in Malta, recommended an Award of Decoration, stating "for skill and leadership as first lieutenant and second in command of the submarine. His constant devotion to duty and fine example in action has contributed greatly to the success of the submarine".

Seaburne-May went on to take command of HMS *Urtica* and HMS *Vigorous* at the age of 22. At the time of his promotion to lieutenant-commander, he was the youngest officer of that rank in the Navy. He died, aged 30, in Hong Kong, after being struck down with polio on the 13th June, 1955, whilst serving on HMS Tamar in the Far East, and was buried at sea from HMS Cockade.

Acting Chief Engine Room Artificer William Henry Ray DSM DSC MiD– (D/M38397)

Ray, whose home was at Bentley, Hampshire, began his submarine Royal Navy career as engine-room artificer second class on board HMS *Pandora,* following his appointed on the 6th May, 1941. Ordered to stand by *P46* on 31st August, 1942, where he was to be CERA, he was awarded the DSM on the 4th May, 1943, to go with his Long Service Medal, Good Conduct Medal, two Mentions in Despatches (1941/1944) and a DSC (5th June 1945).

G.W.G. Simpson, in his recommendation for decoration dated the 18th January, 1943, wrote: "For skill and leadership in charge of the engine-room department, by keeping the submarine free from defects, he has made a direct and most valuable contribution to the success of this submarine."

Ray transferred from *Unruffled* on the 1st March, 1943, having been appointed warrant engineer in *Storm* on the 7th June, 1943. He was promoted to lieutenant engineer in *Tradewind, Acheron* and *Totem*.

Able-seaman Arthur Addison MiD – (D/JX 238056)

Addison was drafted to *Unruffled* as an ordinary seaman on the 16th March, 1942. He was awarded a Mention in Despatches on the 7th September, 1943. After leaving *Unruffled* in January 1944, he rejoined his old boat in June 1944.

A.B. Geoffrey 'Wiggy' Bennett – (P/JX 237495)

Bennett joined *Unruffled* on the 16th March, 1942, as an acting able-seaman and is one of only a few crew mentioned in J.S. Stevens' autobiography in which he is described as "a willing and cheerful Lancastrian".

Before his call-up, he had been a baker, which gave him enough cooking experience to be designated chef. He had to feed 33 hungry seamen in a cramped working area and had few ingredients with which to work. Being a baker he would have been able to make fresh bread when supplies ran out and no doubt was envied by other submarine crews.

The brunt of much joking, moaning and respected praise, he needed to be a cheerful character. He remained on board throughout *Unruffled*'s commission.

Petty Officer William S. Carter – (P/JX 132187)

Carter joined *P46* on 16th March, 1942, and served until 12th June, 1942, when he was lent to HMS Forth.

Ordinary Seaman
William B. Cunningham – (D/SSX 20981)

Cunningham joined *P46* on 16th March, 1942, and stayed with the boat until June 1944. He was promoted through the ranks and became temporary acting leading seaman on the 1st January, 1943.

Ordinary Seaman William G. Dale – (P/JX 235929)

Dale was from Levenshulme, Manchester, and served on *P46* from the 3rd April, 1942 until 1945. He was promoted to able-seaman in January, 1943, whilst serving on board *P46*.

Ordinary Seaman Albert L. Davies – (C/JX 290207)

Davies joined *P46* on 17th March, 1942. He was promoted to able-seaman on 1st January, 1943.

Stoker Petty Officer William Dinsmor – (D/KX 81058)

Dinsmor served on board *P46* from the 1st February, 1942, until 9th March, 1942.

Temporary Acting Leading Stoker Geoffrey Ronald Brill-Edwards MiD – (P/KX 89910)

Brill-Edwards joined the Royal Navy as an adult on 13th October, 1936, and later volunteered for service in submarines, joining a training course at HMS Dolphin on

1st April, 1940. Subsequently he joined the submarine HMS *L23* on 7th May, 1940, returning to HMS Dolphin on 26th September, 1941. He was to join HMS *Unruffled* on the 24th February, 1942. He was the recipient of the Palestine Medal and was recommended by G.W.G. Simpson on the 18th January, 1943, for a Mention in Despatches for his "skill in working the periscopes during attacks and for efficiency in carrying out his routine duties as Outside ERA's mate". On leaving *P46,* he joined HMS Medway as spare crew on 1st May, 1944, returning to HMS Dolphin as spare crew on 18th September, 1944.

On promotion to petty officer, he was transferred to general service on 15th November, 1944. He was awarded a Mention in Dispatches *London Gazette* 4th May, 1943, in a series of awards made to HMS *Unruffled* for Eastern Mediterranean war patrols from August to November 1942. Two supply ships and other vessels were sunk. He died at Barrow-in-Furness on 20th November, 2014, aged 96.

Petty Officer Charles Edward Farr DSM – (P/JX 126235)

Farr joined *Unruffled* on the 4th February, 1942. On 18th January, 1943, Simpson recommended a decoration, writing: "For skill and ability in carrying out his duties as torpedo gunner's mate, which enabled [the submarine] to fire seven salvos and two single torpedoes with no tube failures and no torpedo failures due to causes under his control." Farr continued to serve on *Unruffled* until 1945.

Able-seaman Cyril Green – (D/SSX 29769)

Green served on *P46* from 16th March, 1942,
until 2nd April, 1942.

Engine Room Artificer 2nd class
Arthur Lumley Griffiths DSM - (D/MX 51586)

Designated to HMS *Unruffled* as third class ERA on the 24th
February, 1942, Griffiths was promoted and recommended
for decoration by G.W.G. Simpson on the 18th January, 1943,
for "skill and ability in his duties as outside ERA, both in
action and while on maintenance work: the efficiency with
which he has carried out his important work and excellent
example he has set have done much towards the general
standard of efficiency".

Other than leaving the boat for a short period at the
beginning of 1943 – rejoining on the 1st April, 1943 –
Griffiths served throughout *Unruffled*'s war patrol.

Leading Telegraphist William
Stanley Haines – (D/SSX 31914)

Born 6th April 1918, Haines served in submarines from May
1940 until September 1946 in submarines *L26*, *H44*, *H28*
and *Unruffled,* which he joined as telegraphist on the 16th
March, 1942, until January 1944. He died in March, 2011,
aged 92.

Acting Leading Signalman
Ronald 'Ginger' Hiles DSM – (P/JX 156018)

Hiles, from Retford, Nottinghamshire, was drafted to

Unruffled on the 24th March, 1942, as signalman. He would have had a lot of input into the making of the Jolly Roger. He was awarded the DSM on 7th September, 1943, and left *Unruffled* early 1944. He died in 1983, aged 61.

Temporary Acting Leading Stoker Alfred Hedley Hines, MiD – (D/KX 85976)

Hines joined *P46* 24th February, 1942, as temporary acting leading stoker, and departing *Unruffled* on the 12th June, 1942. He was later promoted to acting stoker petty officer in *Seraph* on the 9th September, 1943.

Telegraphist Frederick L. Horner – (D/SSX 31914)

Horner served on *P46* 16th March, 1942, until 1945.

Acting Leading Stoker Cecil Brinley Howells DSM – (C/SKX 114)

From Cheltenham, Gloucestershire, Howells was drafted to HMS *Unruffled* as stoker 1st class on the 16th March, 1942. He was awarded the DSM on the 7th September, 1943. Departed *Unruffled* June 1944.

Stoker 1stClass Ceiriog Jones MiD – (D/KX 115308)

Jones was drafted to submarines and joined *P46* as stoker 1st class at Barrow-in-Furness on the 16th March, 1942. He was mentioned in despatches and G.W.G. Simpson recommended him on the 18th January, 1943, reporting: "For quiet efficiency in his work as a stoker and for skill in operating the hydroplanes in watch diving stations. His coolness and cheerfulness have been a perpetual source of inspiration to all about him." Ceiriog departed *Unruffled* early in 1944.

Petty Officer Telegraphist Joseph Norman Victor Lewis DSM – (C/JX 134555)

From Peckham, South London, Lewis served as a telegraphist from 1936 to 1946 in submarines *H44*, *L69*, H32, *Seawolf*, *Sealion*, *O10*, *O14*, *Wilk* and *Unruffled*. Drafted to *P46* as temporary acting petty officer on the 24th February, 1942, he was to be later awarded the DSM on 7th September, 1943. He died on the 24th July, 1993. Joseph was also a poet and three of his three poems survive today. The first, titled 'Underneath the Surface', is a parody of the Flanagan and Allen song 'Underneath the Arches':

Big ships we never cared for
And cruisers you can keep
There's only one place that we know
And that is where we sleep
Underneath the surface, we'd dream our dreams away
Underneath the surface on battery boards we'd lay
Every night you'd find us, tired out and worn
Happy 'til they shake us, or wake us, with those klaxon horns
Then everyone gets busy, the Tiffies and the Swains
Working vents and blows and hydroplanes
When the panic's over we'll crash down again
Underneath the surface, we'd dream our dream away

His second poem is sung to the tune of another Flanagan and Allen song, 'They're building flats where the arches used to be', from a film released in 1936:

Underneath the surface is where we used to stay
But they shifted us one day and sent us on our way
We packed our bags and hammocks and wandered back to Gens
What's become of our homeland midst the submarine men?
They've built a fairground where Blockhouse used to be
They've got giant dippers where we used to load kippers
They're playing games where we once lived heart free
And there's no captain (S) to say
Start another long patrol today
Side by side we look with pride, at our old HQ
And we wonder what Gens is like now the war is through?
We're walking round now as sad as can be
They've built a fairground where Blockhouse used to be

This third poem is yet another Flanagan and Allen tune 'Leave us alone let us wander':

Leave us alone let us wander, back to good old civvy street
We're tired of war and sailing in these boats
We're fed up with Malta, the heat, the stink, the goats
Gone is our craving for the sunshine
Give us instead snow and sleet
The seas are too wavy, so you can have the Navy
Take us back to good old civvy street.

Acting Engine Room Artificer 4th class Malcolm McNeil – (D/MX 73392)

McNeil joined *P46* on the 16th March, 1942, and was promoted to 3rd class ERA whilst serving on *Unruffled*. Later joined HMS *Ultimatum*.

Stoker 2nd class Jack Padgett – (P/KX 126801)

Padgett joined *P46* on 16th March, 1942, and departed on 25th April, 1942.

Able-seaman Stanley Harry Baden Powell DSM – (C/JX 155976)

From Ipswich, Suffolk, Powell, was drafted to *Unruffled* on the 28th March, 1942, at the age of 21. John Stevens described him as "the gun layer. Powell was a dedicated man – he lived for that gun. In harbour he spent long hours polishing and oiling metal-work with loving care". G.W.G Simpson, in recommending Powell for an Award of Decoration, said: "For skill as gun layer, which resulted in the destruction of an enemy minesweeper, and damage to a railway train, and for never failing keenness and fighting spirit." Stanley departed *Unruffled* in June 1944.

Able-seaman Henry Victor Preece – (C/JX 155976)

Born 1st January, 1922, and from Liverpool, Preece served on submarines until 1953, rising through the ranks to reach chief petty officer coxswain. He served on the submarines *H33*, *Unruffled*, *P614*, *Vitality*, *Vagabond*, *Auriga, Sentinel*, *Statesman*, *Teredo*, *Turpin* and *Totem*. During his time as a crew member on board *Unruffled*, he took up the roll of gun

trainer from the 16th March, 1942. Departed *P46* June 1944.
Died on the 4th May, 2011, aged 91.

Leading Seaman William J. Reed – (C/JX 140015)

Reed, 25, a torpedoman from London, was welcomed on board
P46 on the 16th March, 1942. Left *Unruffled* June 1944.

Temporary Acting Stoker Petty Officer
George S. Reed – (D/KX 82615)

Reed was on board *P46* from 24th February 1942.

Able-seaman John Rice – (D/SSX 24013)

Rice was on *P46* from 16th March, 1942,
until 23rd March, 1942.

Acting Leading Seaman Edward Richardson
D.S.M. – (P/JX 141872)

Richardson served on *H32* and *H43*. He joined *P46* on the
24th February, 1942, gaining promotion to temporary acting
petty officer on the 1st January, 1943. Ended his career in
the Royal Navy in March 1949. He was promoted through
the ranks to petty officer electrician. Also serving on *Unison*,
P614, *Springer* and *Aeneas*.

Temporary Leading Telegraphist
Robert J. Rook – (D/JX 142920)

Rook joined *P46* on the 16th March, 1942. Having departed
Unruffled early in 1943 to participate in courses to further
his career, he rejoined *P46* on the 1st April, 1943, departing

in January 1944, having reached the rank of temporary acting petty officer telegraphist.

Leading Stoker John Robert Sherwin MiD – (P/KX 12810)

Sherwin, from Bristol, was drafted to submarines, joining *P46* on the 16th March, 1942, as stoker second class. Awarded a Mention in Despatches whilst serving on *Unruffled*.

Able-seaman Donald Joseph Stephens DSM MiD – (P/JX 217674)

From Abergavenny, Monmouthshire, Stephens was drafted to submarines, being designated to *P46* on the 6th March, 1942. Mentioned in Despatches as recommended by G.W.G. Simpson on the 18th January, 1943, "for keenness and skill in maintenance and operation of the ASDIC apparatus. This rating is less experienced than most senior A/S ratings of submarines but by his coolness and ability he has been of great assistance in evading counter attacks". Donald was awarded the DSM dated 7th September, 1943. Whilst serving on *Unruffled*, he was also promoted to Temporary Acting Leading Seaman and awarded a Mentioned in Despatches.

Able-seaman Henry Taylor – (C/J104741)

Taylor joined *P46* 19th March, 1942, until 23rd April, 1942.

Acting Chief Petty officer Gerald Desmond Walls
DSM MiD – (D/JX 136741)

Walls joined *HMS Regent* on 1st August, 1941, as petty officer and was transferred to *P46* on 24th March, 1942, to assume the role of coxswain. He was mentioned in despatches for eight Mediterranean war patrols. G.W.G Simpson, in his recommendation for the award of a DSM on the 18th January, 1943, wrote: "For skill when working the hydroplanes in action and for unfailing keenness and good example as lookout, and also for efficiency and cheerfulness in carrying out his duties as coxswain. By his conduct he has greatly assisted in keeping the morale of the ship's company at a high level."

Able-seaman Joseph E. Weston – (P/JX 156397)

Weston joined *P46* 16th March, 1942, until 31st March 1942.

OTHER OFFICERS AND RATINGS KNOWN TO
HAVE SERVED IN *UNRUFFLED*

Lieutenant John Munro Crosland Fenton DSC

Fenton was from Greenock in Scotland and joined *Unruffled* as 3rd officer (navigating officer,) replacing Gordon Noll when he left to take the perisher's course on the 17th October, 1942. He was awarded the DSC for successful patrols in *Unruffled* and *Unbroken,* which he joined as first lieutenant. Also second in command of *United* and promoted to commanding officer in *Unsparing*, *U-825*, *Seraph*, *Tantalus* and *Artful.* The recommendation for decoration dated 13th August, 1943, described Fenton's actions as follows: "During the period which this officer served in *Unruffled*, she inflicted the following losses on the enemy: sunk 9 merchant vessels, 3 schooners. Damaged: 1 cruiser, 1 tug. Enemy escorts have carried out a number of depth charge attacks on her. *Unruffled* has been noticeable for the efficiency of her attack instrument workers of whom this officer was in charge."

The recommendation continues: "This officer has served 10 months in *Unruffled,* during which time the ship has carried out 14 war patrols in the Mediterranean. His skill in working attack instruments, his correct actions and alert lookout as officer-of-the-watch, has greatly contributed to successful attacks. Prior to joining *Unruffled,* he served for two war patrols in *Unbroken* (*P42*). While on the second patrol, two Italian cruisers were hit by torpedoes in one attack, and over 200 depth charges were fired at the submarine in counter-attack".

Lieutenant Alan Harold McCoy DSC

On the 3rd August, 1941, McCoy was appointed to *Sunfish* as torpedo officer. He joined *Pandora* as navigating officer on the 25th October, 1941. On 1st December, 1942, he was appointed to the 10th Flotilla at Malta and was ordered to report to *Umbra* as first lieutenant where he was awarded the DSC on the 5th May, 1943. The next day he was told to report to *Porpoise* as first lieutenant. Having returned to the UK, on the 8th July, 1943, he reported to HMS Forth *in* Holy Loch, having been appointed to *Tantalus* again as first lieutenant. On 15th December, 1943, he was appointed to

HMS Dolphin to undertake the perisher's course, which he successfully completed. He resumed command of *Unruffled* on the 5th December, 1944.

Lieutenant Robert Francis Park

On 22nd March, 1941, Park was serving on HMS Forth in Halifax, Nova Scotia. He was transferred to HMS St Angelo (arsenal) in Malta with the 1st Flotilla until 5th September and then joined HMS Medway at Alexandria before moving to the submarine *Osiris* as third hand. On arriving back in the UK, he was sent to the USA to stand by *Severn,* which was re-fitting. On the 24th April, 1943, he returned to Holy Loch but returned to *HMS* Dolphin on the 21st May, reporting for the perisher's course. Upon completion, he joined *H33* as commanding officer before joining *Unruffled* on the 17th June, 1944. After a year in command he was told to report to HMS Cyclops at Rothesay to command *Sceptre,* which was refitting. On the 21st August, 1945, he reported on board HMS Forth for submarine duties. On 10th March, 1946, he was sent to Australia to join HMS Adamant 4th Flotilla based in Sydney. He took command of *Talent,* returning to the UK at Christmas 1946. *Talent* was refitted and he remained on board until 25th February, 1948, he later commanded *Trump* and *Tiptoe* in June 1954.

Sub Lieutenant Arthur James Anderson

Anderson was appointed to HMS Seaborn in Halifax, Nova Scotia and joined *Unruffled,* which was undertaking ASW training, as navigating officer on the 29th January, 1945. This was followed by a move on the 18th March, 1945, to

Upright, which was also in Halifax for ASW training. On his return to the UK he reported to HMS Cyclops on the 15th October, 1945, as spare submarine officer. He then stood by *Alaric,* which was being completed at Cammell Laird, Birkenhead.

Temporary Sub Lieutenant Robert Anthony Cobb

Cobb reported to the depot ship HMS Cyclops on 14th February, 1944, only to be told to report to HMS Dolphin the next day. He was appointed to *Unruffled* as temporary sub-lieutenant on the 15th February. Ordered to HMS Forth at Holy Loch on the 15th May, 1945.

Sub Lieutenant Michael John Norman Dean

Dean reported on board *Unruffled* on the 29th January, 1945, as third lieutenant for ASW training in Halifax, Nova Scotia. Joined *Upright* on the 18th March, 1945, and returned to the UK at HMS Dolphin standing by *Sirdar* during a refit on the 21st December, 1945. On the 26th September, 1947 he reported on board HMS Montclare at Rothesay.

Sub-Lieutenant David Wright Lupton

Lupton served in submarines as a sub-lieutenant to lieutenant commander from 29th January, 1945, when he joined *Unruffled*. Also served in *Sceptre, Truncheon* and *Teredo.* He then completed the Submarine Commanding Officers course and took command of *Trespasser* from February, 1946. He went on to command *Springer* and *Tapir.*

Temporary Sub-Lieutenant John Rayner

Rayner was appointed to HMS Forth, 3rd Submarine Flotilla at Holy Loch, on the 2nd February, 1943, and then onto HMS Talbot, 10th Flotilla in Malta by 15th March, when he joined submarine HMS *Unruffled* as third hand, joining 16th April, 1943. On 16th September, 1943, he was appointed liaison officer *P714* ex-Italian submarine *Bronzo*. He returned to HMS Forth on the 1st December and headed for home, returning to Dundee where he joined the submarine depot ship HMS *Ambrose* on the 8th. On 29th October, 1945, he was appointed to HMS Cyclops to the 7th Flotilla.

Sub Lieutenant Brian
Gordon Richard MBE, BEM, MiD RNVR

Richard was appointed to the submarine base HMS *Talbot* 10th Flotilla in Malta on the 12th December, 1942 as navigating officer in HMS *Unbroken* and in *Unruffled* from the 24th July, 1943 in the same role. He was awarded MiD on the 28th September, 1943. After *Unruffled's* victorious return home, he was sent to Vickers Armstrong in Barrow-in-Furness to stand by *P81*, HMS *Varne* as first lieutenant.

Sub Lieutenant Arthur Richardson

Richardson was appointed 3rd hand on *HMS Viking* on 24th April 1944, after which he was transferred to *Unruffled* on the 15th April, 1945, as first lieutenant at Halifax, Nova Scotia, for ASW training. He reported for duty on the 25th February, 1946, on board the depot ship HMS Adamant *to* the 4th Submarine Flotilla in Sydney. Joined *Talent* as first lieutenant in Hong Kong on the 8th September, 1946, being transferred to HMS Adamant, which was then based in Hong Kong, on the 26th February 1947, for submarine duties.

Temporary Sub Lieutenant
Arthur Farnsworth Savage

Savage joined *H33* as navigating officer on the 16th February, 1944, at Rothesay. He joined *Unruffled* on the 23rd April, 1944, again as navigating officer. He was ordered to report to *Trespasser* whilst refitting on the 30th April, 1945, as navigator. On the 20th December, 1945, he was appointed to HMS Dolphin for submarine duties.

Acting Sub Lieutenant W. S. Sherwood

Sherwood was appointed to *Unruffled* on the 26th January, 1945, as navigating officer at Halifax for ASW training. On returning to the UK, he joined *Seraph* on the 11th October, 1945, as navigating officer. On 25th September, 1947, arrived on board HMS Montclare at Rothesay for submarine duties.

Temporary Sub Lieutenant Peter Stanley Worth

Worth reported to HMS Talbot, 10th Flotilla Malta on the 3rd May, 1943. He joined *Unseen* as navigating officer on the 5th July, 1943, departing on 2nd January, 1944. On his return to the UK, he reported to HMS Dolphin and joined *Unruffled* on the 16th June, 1944, as first lieutenant, an appointment that was to take him to Canada for ASW training.

On the 9th June, 1945, he was appointed to *Storm,* which was refitting as first lieutenant. He reported for submarine duties at HMS Dolphin on the 4th December, 1945. In October 1946, he was serving at HMS Pembroke at Chatham and was promoted to lieutenant commander on the 22nd September 1953. In April 1956, he was serving at HMS Gamecock, the Royal Naval air station at Bramcote, Warwickshire. In April 1958, he served on board HMS Kenya and in 1960 in HMS Excellent.

Chief Engine Room Artificer John Eric Horton DSM

Horton was born on 8th July, 1915 and served in submarines as an ERA, being promoted to CERA from 1937 to 1950. He served in the submarines *Clyde*, *P39*, *Trump*, *Umbra*, *Unbending*, *United*, *Unruffled* and *Alaric* and was awarded the DSM while on Far East patrols. He died on 4th November, 2009, aged 94.

Acting Chief Petty Officer Ernest Alfred Thomas DSM & Bar – (C/J99723)

Thomas was born on 27th October, 1904, in Plumstead South London, and was drafted into submarines to serve on board HMS *Utmost* where he was awarded the DSM on the 21st November, 1941, and also a Bar on the 5th May, 1942. 1st April, 1943, Thomas, 39, joined *Unruffled* as acting chief petty officer (coxswain). He departed *P46* June 1944. He lived in Eltham, South-East London.

Stoker 1st Class Samuel Adams – (P/KX121201)

Adams joined *Unruffled* on the 1st January, 1943.

Temporary Leading Telegraphist
Donald P Arthur – (SSX24214)

Arthur joined *Unruffled* January 1944, until June 1944.

Acting petty officer Joseph Bell DSM – (C/JX141130)

Bell was born on the 20th October, 1917, and was known to his shipmates as 'Joe'. He hailed from Sacriston, Devon. He served on board HMS *Oberon* and *Taku* before joining *Unruffled*. He was awarded the DSM on 7th September, 1943. After reaching the rank of chief petty officer he went on to serve on board *United*, *Seraph* and *Tapir*. He died, aged 90, on the 5th December, 1997.

Reginald Bennett

Bennett was born on the 26th August, 1925, and he joined *Viking*, *Volatile*, *Unruly*, *Unruffled* and *Sceptre*. He was a member of *Unruffled*'s crew until 1945.

Temporary Acting Petty Officer
Daniel Blythe – (CD/X2482)

Blythe joined *Unruffled* June 1944.

Leading Telegraphist Albert Cain

Cain served in the submarine *Untiring*, *Unruffled* and *L23*. He passed away on the 25th January, 1996.

Stoker 1st Class James Cleland – (KX140411)

Cleland joined *Unruffled* June 1944.

Able-seaman Robert Godfrey – (JX369637)

Godfrey joined *Unruffled* in June 1944.

Ordinary Seaman Robert W Goundry – (JX554585)

Goundry was born on the 18th May, 1925, and served as torpedoman from June 1944 until 1945 on board *Unruffled*. He passed away on the 10th May, 2008, aged 83.

Telegraphist William S. Hames – (SSX31418)

Hames joined *Unruffled* January 1944.

Temporary Leading Telegraphist Basil E. Hatch – (JX149399)

Joined *Unruffled* January 1944 until June 1944. Died in 2011, aged 92.

Acting Engine Room Artificer 4th Class Andrew Henderson – (KX156315/MX583226)

Henderson joined *Unruffled* January 1944, until June 1944.

Temporary Acting Leading Seaman Arthur Hill MiD – (JX208461)

Hill, from Swansea, was drafted to *Unruffled*. He was mentioned in despatches in the London Gazette dated 7th September, 1943.

Able-seaman Robert Hill – (SSX35984)

Hill joined *Unruffled* June 1944.

Telegraphist Peter J. Hodgkinson – (P/JX225393)

Hodgkinson joined *Unruffled* on the
1st January, 1943, until 28th February, 1943.

Telegraphist Robert G. Houlder – (P/JX216078)

Houlder joined *Unruffled* on the 1st April, 1943.

2nd Class Stoker Brian Joyce – (KX610229)

Joyce joined *Unruffled* June 1944.

Petty Officer Shafto Kerr – (JX138596)

Kerr joined *Unruffled* June 1944.

Stoker 1st Class Robert E. King – (KX117743)

King joined *Unruffled* January 1944, until June 1944.

Acting Stoker 1st Class Joseph Lamb – (KX156217)

Lamb joined *Unruffled* June 1944.

Able-seaman David T. Lougher – (JX208613)

Lougher joined *Unruffled* June 1944.

Stoker 1st Class Albert Megson – (KX135315)

Megson joined *Unruffled* January 1944, until June 1944.

Temporary Leading Seaman
Reginald J. Moller – (J72183)

Aged 42, from Liston, Essex, Moller was drafted to *Unruffled* on 1st January, 1944, until it had arrived back in the UK in 1945.

Stoker Petty Officer John T.H. Moxham –
(D/KX83174)

Moxham joined *Unruffled* on the 1st January, 1944.

Engine Room Artificer 4th Class Gilbert Nelson –
(MX73517)

Nelson joined *Unruffled* January 1944.

Engine Room Artificer 5th Class James H.
Nicholson – (MX509180)

Nicholson joined *Unruffled* January 1944, until June 1944.

Stoker 1st Class Henry Parry – (KX165926)

Parry joined *Unruffled* June 1944.

Temporary Acting Leading
Stoker Melville Percival – (KX92973)

Born on the 4th December, 1910, Percival served as Stoker first class, promoted to leading stoker mechanic during his 1941 to 1950 career. Having served in the submarines *Trident, Tigris, Seawolf, Unruffled, Alcide* and *Ambush*. He joined *P46* in June 1944. He died in October, 2005, aged 94.

Engine Room Artificer
4th Class John Pye – (MX75515)

Pye joined *Unruffled* June 1944.

Temporary Acting Leading Stoker James H.
Reynolds – (KX85028)

Reynolds joined January 1944, until June 1944.

Stoker 1st Class Phillip N W Robson – (KX102014)

Robson, 24, a gun loader from Gateshead,
was drafted onto *Unruffled*.

Able-seaman John Simpson – (JX155808)

Simpson joined *Unruffled* June 1944.

Stoker 1st Class Gerard Smith – (KX93369)

Smith G joined *Unruffled* January 1944, until June 1944.

Leading Signalman Leslie Smith DSM – (JX134370)

Smith L joined *Unruffled* January 1944, until 1945.

Able-seaman Thomas Smith – (JX542849)

Smith T was born on the 17th December, 1925, and served
as a torpedoman 1943-1946 on *Oberon* and *Unruffled,* which
he joined in June 1944. He died on the 6th October, 2010,
aged 86.

Able-seaman Horace A.G. Waldron – (P/JX136741)

Waldron joined *Unruffled* on the 1st January, 1943.

Leading Cook (S) Ernest Wallace – (MX56850)

Wallace joined *Unruffled* in January 1944 until June 1944.

Temporary Leading Stoker
Harry Whitehouse – (KX86154)

Whitehouse joined *Unruffled* June 1944.

Temporary Acting Leading
Telegraphist Josiah Wilde – (JX178361)

Wilde joined *Unruffled* June 1944.

Ordinary Seaman Alexander Yoxall – (JX54370)

Yoxall joined *Unruffled* June 1944.

CHAPTER THREE

Commissioning Day

3rd April 1942 – 12th May 1942

———∞———

1000 hours 3ʳᵈ April, 1942:
This was the time and day when *Unruffled* was commissioned. The boat, having been inspected and pronounced fit for trials by the captain, was then handed over to the new crew, with the ratings being given instructions by the coxswain at midday. Lieutenant Stevens addressed his newly-formed crew in direction, his vision for the forthcoming patrols and his expectations of crew behaviour, performance and discipline.

This would have been the first time he had spoken to the crew in its entirety and it was imperative for the success of future patrols that the team talk was an inspiring one. The following week was considered a good time for the ratings to get to know the boat intimately, having already been shown all the nooks and crannies by the heads of departments. They learned the whereabouts of their diving stations and the requirements expected of them. This period also presented a good opportunity for the captain and his fellow officers time to get to know one another, as well as the rest of the crew. It was a time when, according to Stevens, "sailors know what officers are thinking about".

It was also explained to the crew at this juncture that trials would take place on their route to Scotland. As the boat was still in the hands of the contractors, it was expected that any faults would be rectified by them, plus any snags that might crop up during the run. At 1300 hours dinner was attended to and at 1430 hours the process of loading stores on board began. As all hands were still billeted ashore, by 1700 hours the boat was secured and the crew made their way to their lodgings and then for a night out on the town.

4th April:
The loading of stores in preparation for their impending voyage continued throughout the day. One crew member reported sick.

5th April:
The loading of ammunition and stores was the order of the day and by 1300 hours cleaning of the boat began. The crew again went ashore at 1700 hours.

0745 hours 6th April:

P46 slipped her moorings and proceeded to Buccleuch Dock, Barrow-in-Furness, arriving at 0825 hours. The crew then continued loading provisions and commenced cleaning the boat from 1300 to 1600 hours.

0900 hours 7th April:

All hands were once again employed cleaning the boat until 1330 hours when *P46* proceeded to Ramsden Dock, also part of the Port of Barrow, at an engine speed of 440 rpm in a F4 south-westerly wind. By 1702 she secured alongside HrMs Jan Van Gelder, a Royal Netherlands Navy minesweeper, which served as an escort ship with the British submarine flotilla. That evening all the crew remained on board and settled in for their forthcoming adventure.

1701 hours 8th April:

P46, having embarked dockyard personnel, Admiralty officials, observers and a mandatory pilot, who had disembarked 41 minutes later, exited the lock and proceeded into the open sea, escorted by the Jan Van Gelder. Their destination was Holy Loch. The short journey would act as the boat's 'trials' and, depending on the outcome, it would then be accepted into the Royal Navy fleet. It would be the first time the new submarine and crew would be tested as preparations were made for their first submerging.

For Lieutenant Stevens, this was not the first time he had experienced standing by a boat awaiting completion. Early in 1939, as a junior lieutenant, he was at Barrow-in-Furness standing by HMS *Triumph*, a new class of ocean-going 'T' class submarine capable of a torpedo salvo of 10 torpedoes, almost double the size of *Unruffled*. *Triumph* was lost in the Mediterranean in December 1941. At this time, with the war only weeks away, new boats and crew experienced only a two-week work-up period at Falmouth, and this did not provide any time for practice on target ships, torpedo practice or experience for the four-inch gun crews, who had to make do with static soap-box targets.

0600 hours 9th April:
P46 continued throughout the night on a northerly course, reaching the outer buoy and, after passing the Gairloch boom at 1153 hours, the boat embarked a pilot at 1202 hours to see it safely into the loch. At 1332 hours the klaxon sounded bringing *Unruffled*'s ship's company to diving stations and the boat, filled to the brim with dockyard personnel, Admiralty officials and observers, prepared to dive. All hatches, with the exception of the conning tower hatch, were closed and the captain must have looked a lonely figure as the sole occupant on the bridge. It was a proud moment for Lieutenant Stevens, who would have felt a mixture of excitement and exhilaration as he gave the order down the voice pipe: "Slow ahead group down, open one and six main vents."

As the vents opened, the air in the ballast tanks was replaced by an inrush of water and John Stevens gave his final order, "Periscope depth", before going down the hatch and pushing home the clips that held it in place. As this was to be a slow, deliberate dive, all actions were not rushed. Down below, the crew must have been apprehensive and nervous, especially as for some of the crew this was their first time in a submerged submarine. In the control room, the nerve-centre of the boat, Gordon Noll, the first lieutenant responsible for the trim, stood behind the hydroplanes operators, coxswain George Walls and stoker Ceiriog Jones, the second dicky. Noll issued instructions to outside ERA Arthur Griffiths, who stood alongside assistant leading stoker Geoffrey Brill-Edwards, who operated the tank control levers and periscope levers ready to obey Lieutenant Stevens' command.

These orders allowed water to be taken out or let it in to any auxiliary tanks either forward or aft, thus maintaining maximum trim. Also in the control room were Lieutenant Lascelles, the gunnery officer, and Ronald Hiles, whose job it was to maintain the gyro bearing angle of an enemy target. Behind them stood the navigating officer, Sub-Lieutenant Seaburne-May, at his table. In the engine-room, the chief ERA, William Ray, stood alongside the SPO (stoker petty officer) Edward Richardson and Malcolm McNeil, who operated the large switches that controlled the main propulsion motors used to drive the submarine when it dived. Right back aft in the after-pump space, stoker Jack Padgett stood by the main propeller shafts and the after-pump, as well as the hydraulic accumulator, looking for leaks. In the fore-ends by the torpedo tubes, the Torpedo Gunners Mate (TGM), Petty Officer Charles Farr and his torpedomen, were ready watching closely for any leaks that might occur when dived. In the wireless office sat Petty Officer Ronald 'Ginger' Hiles and William Haines. On the ASDICS apparatus set was Donald Stephens.

At the same time as the tanks were flooded and the boat sank beneath the waves, the order was given by Noll to open all main vents. The coxswain, on the hydroplanes, applied a hard-a-dive movement by turning the control wheels in a downward direction. This, in conjunction with the motors, took the submarine in a gradual slow, regulated dive until she reached the required depth of 27 feet. When the order to level off came, the trim was adjusted with the use of the auxiliary tanks forward and aft. When levelled off, Stevens gave the order "Up periscope" and, with a look around the loch, no reported leakages and, satisfied that they had got over the first hurdle, the captain decided it was time to go deeper so he ordered "Down periscope, group up on the main motors" to give a bit more push to the downward thrust. He turned to the No 1 and said: "Take her down to 60 feet and level off." Noll gave the necessary order to the outside ERA, who opened the vents to take the boat down.

Once again the coxswain on the planes went hard down, and as they did they watched the movement of the depth gauges and the bubble in the spirit level. At 60 feet they levelled off. Now came the crucial moment in the exercise. If there were going to be any leaks, then this would be the moment when they would show up. Commencing from aft, the Vickers engineers checked the stern glands of the propeller shaft, then worked their way forward through the boat until they came to the fore-ends.

Stevens must have been intrigued to notice the degree of stability inside the control room once the boat had dived. The only sign that the boat was submerged was a slight motion of the bow going down and, later, a gentle levelling off. No notion of panic or claustrophobia was experienced by the crew as they were too intent on going about their routines or checking for leaks and any other defects that might have developed. When satisfied with the outcome, surface instructions were given at 1551 hours and the boat gently rose to the surface where the conning tower was unclipped and opened once again. Having exited Gairloch and turned for their new temporary home at Holy Loch, the trials party disembarked at 1645* and *P46* secured alongside HMS Forth for the first time. The 'Jacks' (sailors) were then employed on servicing and preparing the torpedoes in readiness for the next day's exercises.

*(*Author's note: I am unable to answer two intriguing questions. It was usual for the captain to order the submarine to dive to its design depth of 160 feet whilst on trials. This would enable the Vickers engineers to test for leaks at depth. Secondly, there is no reference to when Stevens signed the papers transferring ownership from Vickers to the Royal Navy. Under normal circumstances, once docked, this was carried out on board HMS Forth. However, there are references to some submarines having been signed over within the boat at the completion of the trials.)*

At this time, Holy Loch was the main training facility for new boats and recently refitted submarines, providing the opportunity to fine-tune the crew and boat into a fighting unit. There was a floating dock and the accommodation ship HMS Forth, built in 1939 by John Brown & Co. of Clydebank. Equipped with eight 4.5 inch guns, pompoms and smaller arms, the Forth was credited with shooting down the first German aircraft on British mainland soil. She provided facilities such as a floating workshop, rest area for the submarine crews and a supply vessel. She also transferred fuel, ammunition and torpedoes. It would have been possible to purchase cigarettes on board, get a haircut, have a bath and wash laundry. Old destroyers and armed yachts provided targets for torpedo practice. Captain (S) at the time was Hugh Meynell Cyril Ionides CBE, an ex-submariner commanding *H32* and *L52*.

1315 hours 10th April:

P46 slipped her moorings and proceeded to Loch Long in the Tay Valley, Argyll, for independent exercises. This location was the torpedo range for Royal Navy submarines between 1912 and 1986, diving at 1411 hours resurfacing at 1655 hours. By 1810, the first day's exercise was complete, with the boat secured alongside HMS Forth, and two-thirds of the crew was given shore leave.

11th April:

The boat proceeded to Arrochar, near the head of Loch Long, and anchored. On board a torpedo party was busily employed working on the torpedoes in preparation for the next day's torpedo range exercise, while the remainder of the crew cleaning ship. Leave was granted for two-thirds of the crew between 1800-2300 hours.

0911 hours 12th April:

The boat slipped its moorings and, while still on the surface, fired one practice torpedo at 0942 hours. Having anchored at 1014, the boat then proceeded on its way at 1125 hours and at 1210 hours fired another torpedo. It anchored at 1251 and proceeded back to the range at 1400 hours, having fired a further torpedo at 1435. At 1445 the boat anchored and repeated the exercise, firing a torpedo at 1637. At 1658 hours the boat anchored two cables distance from Arrochar pier and, while two-thirds of the crew was granted leave and headed to the nearest bar, a torpedo party and duty watch were employed to embark torpedoes.

13th April:

P46 was once again summoned to the torpedo range, diving at 1123 hours and firing a salvo of four practice torpedoes. By 1155 hours the boat was once again on the surface. This exercise was repeated at 1623 hours when two practice torpedoes were fired from the surface. *P46* then returned to Arrochar and anchored.

14th April:

The crew was employed cleaning the boat before heading back to Holy Loch at 1330 hours. On the way back, Lieutenant Stevens ordered diving practice at 1425 hours, only to resurface at 1511 and repeat the exercise at 1523 hours. Leave was again granted for some crew, except for the duty watch. The liberty boat would have landed those ratings and officers lucky enough to have received shore leave at a small pier at Sandbank, from where they could either catch a bus to convey them to Dunoon, a 20-minute journey away, or visit the Ardenaden public house located on the other side of the Sandbank jetty. Here the beer was cheaper than in Dunoon but it was a lot quieter in respect of entertainment. Dancing was held every Friday and Saturday in the local social hall, providing the men with the opportunity to meet the fairer sex.

0830 hours 15th April:

P46 secured alongside *N89*, HMS *Upright* to embark

torpedoes. Those not involved in this duty would be detailed to clean the boat. Leave was granted from 1730 until 0730 hours. The ratings would have washed and changed on board the Forth, returning in the early hours for some much-needed sleep.

0900 hours 16th April:

The attack team to exercise (practise) with the rest of the crew busy cleaning. Dinner was served at 1200 hours, after which the lookouts went to the 'attack teacher', an ingenious device using a model of a target ship which could be made to alter course and speed, while the operator at the periscope gave his orders as if he was carrying out an actual attack. Leave was granted to all but the duty watch and two crew members who had reported sick. Over the next two days, still with two ratings on the sick list, various exercises took place, including dummy attacks and gunnery practice aimed at the Holy Loch 'fleet'.

Diving, resurfacing, action stations and control at dive depth were refined, developing team work and routine. The torpedo crews repeatedly practised their drill for firing several torpedoes in rapid succession, much to the annoyance of those in the fore-ends whose mess was being overrun, but it was essential that the torpedo crews all knew every valve and switch in the tube space so that mistakes would be avoided when firing took place.

It was also a time for the development of personal contact between the ratings and officers. The bonding together of everyone in such a small and confined space was vital, and it was important that nothing remained secretive among the crew, and that everyone by this time were aware of each other's good and bad personal habits, life history, character, idiosyncrasies and personal hygiene. Every individual, from the captain downwards, practised diligently their individual roles in making the submarine a widow-maker.

0800 hours 22nd April:

The day began with *P46* practice diving and carrying out dummy attacks on the flotilla 'fleet'. Once surfaced, gunnery practice took place. This exercise was repeated throughout the day. There were a number of personnel changes, with Stoker second class Jack Padgett and able-seaman Henry Taylor being replaced by Stoker first class Albert Megson and acting able-seaman Arthur Hill.

1st May:

P46, having embarked a pilot and a naval 'trials' party comprising Admiralty officials, proceeded to Gairloch, where the submariners were put through their paces during final 'acceptance trials' in preparation for war patrol. Having completed the necessary routines, by 1645 hours, the 'trials party' disembarked and *P46* secured alongside HMS Forth back at Holy Loch by 1727 hours. No leave was granted, with a torpedo party instructed to work on the torpedoes and duty watch called. The crew of *P46* were no doubt aware that their first war patrol was close at hand.

0800 hours 2nd May:

P46 slipped its moorings and made way, destination Campbeltown. The boat dived at 1124 hours to exercise in dummy attacks. It surfaced again at 1244 hours and dived again at 1300 hours in a repeat exercise. It then surfaced at 1513 hours and once the practice run had been completed, continued to Campbeltown, arriving at 1851 hours and securing alongside 'New Buoy'.

0800 hours 3rd May:
The boat left its securing and prepared for more exercises. A delay of 40 minutes occurred due to the late arrival of pre-arranged surface craft, but then it began an underwater attack exercise until 1232, before resurfacing. This was repeated, with diving commencing at 1248 hours and resurfacing at 1555 hours, and there was another dive at 1611 hours involving a submerged attack on HMS St Modusen. This exercise lasted 16 minutes. On resurfacing, *P46* returned to Campbeltown at 1732 hours, with leave being granted to all but duty watch at 1800 hours until 0700 hours.

Campbeltown, being a pleasant small fishing port, was popular with the submariners. It had as many public houses as there were streets. Able-seaman Cyril Green bade farewell to his companions, having departed the boat.

0800 hours 4th May:
Today was the start of a 24-hour exercise starting at 0915 hours and continuing until 0835 the next day when *P46* secured alongside HMS Forth at Holy Loch. After making dummy attacks and screen attacks and doing diving exercises and gunnery practice, which started at 2345 hours, the exercise finished at 0500 hours.

0500 hours 5ᵗʰ May:

The exercise completed, *P46* returned to Holy Loch. At 0900 hours all hands were employed cleaning the boat, with a break at 1200 hours for dinner. At 1400 *P46* shifted berth to secure along the port side of SS Al Rawdah, which was built in 1911 and requisitioned as a military base/prison ship for Irish Republican internees and prisoners. Able-seaman Green departed the boat and was replaced by Temporary Acting Leading Seaman Joseph Bell.

0830 hours 6ᵗʰ May:

The submarine departed for the outward journey to Clyde DG (degaussing) range where a magnetic field was passed over it to reduce the chances of it attracting a magnetic mine. This action took 26 minutes and by 1039 hours *Unruffled* was back at Holy Loch and secured alongside HMS Forth. A dinner of roast beef and roast potatoes was served at midday, after which crew members were deployed cleaning the boat. After tea, leave was granted at 1600 hours.

0815 hours 7ᵗʰ May:

The boat departed from Holy Loch on a short voyage to Kames Bay, Argyll, where *P46* entered Admiralty Floating Dock No 7 (AFD VII) and was chocked down ready to have her propeller changed, an operation that also gave the crew the opportunity to paint the boat. The work finished at 1600 hours when two-thirds of the crew were granted leave. The boat undocked the next day and returned to Holy Loch alongside HMS Forth. Leave was granted after the boat was cleaned.

(*Author's note: The Unity class submarine had an ongoing problem, not only due to engine vibration but also with propeller noise, known as 'singing propellers' which, if not rectified, allowed for easier detection by the enemy when on patrol. Propeller noise was an inherent problem from the first design of the U-class submarine. In order to rectify the problem, the design of the class II incorporated a modification of the stern. This included lengthening the overall size of the boat and reshaping the stern. Modification and replacement of the propeller at regular intervals was required throughout the life of the Unity class, but the problem was never solved. The usual procedure for a boat on - or finishing - trials was for it to return to the builder's dockyard, but this was not done and leads me to the conclusion that the remedy chosen may have been ordered by Captain (S) Hugh Ionides because of the urgent need of P46 being required in the Mediterranean.)*

1030 hours 9th May:

The boat slipped its mooring and proceeded to swing compasses. Owing to the structure of the boat, metal objects or electrical equipment can change the position of the magnetic field. The adjustment would have involved taking a compass bearing from the bridge and adjusting any deviation by way of adding magnets around the gyrocompass. This was completed by 1130 hours, when P46 secured alongside SS Al Rawdah. All hands were employed in make-and-mend, departing the submarine at 1630 hours to find a Mess on board HMS Forth.

1030 hours 10th May:

All hands to Divine Service, which meant the crew had to be dressed in their finest naval uniforms, after which the ship's company was granted leave.

0830 hours 11th May:

All hands were employed storing the boat for sea. This was a time when rumours and arguments started between crew members as to where they would be sent on their first patrol. Betting odds were laid as to their destination, with money and tots of rum placed on the various locations scattered around battle scared Europe, Mediterranean or even the Far East.

0830 hours 12th May:

Hands employed cleaning the boat, with leave granted from 1330 hours until 0700 hours.

CHAPTER FOUR

FIRST WAR PATROL

13TH MAY 1942 - 25TH JUNE 1942

—⊃∞⊂—

0830 hours 13th May:

Once again all hands were employed cleaning the boat and
embarking the fresh provisions required for their first war
patrol. At 1730, *P46* left Holy Loch accompanied by the
Dutch minesweeper Jan Van Gelder, HNLM submarine *0-
10* and *P614*. *0-10* was to patrol in the Atlantic Ocean to
protect Russian convoy PQ16, on an outward-bound voyage
from Iceland to North Russia, against German Surface
forces.

P614 and her sister ship *P615*, having been originally
ordered by the Turkish Navy, appeared in the 1943 film 'We
Dive at Dawn', starring John Mills and Eric Portman. *P211,*
HMS *Safari*, before heading off to War Patrols in Malta, also

appears in the same clips. As normal procedure dictated, the area for this patrol was classed as a warm-up exercise and so a 'safe' area was chosen to allow the crew work-up time, and a chance to refine their techniques, before being sent to the more active battle line.

0045 hours 15th May:

P46 sighted HMS Renown and four destroyers. Renown, a 36,800 gross tons battlecruiser, completed in 1916 with six 15-inch guns, had been transferred to the Home Fleet in November 1941 to provide cover for inbound and outbound convoys to the Soviet Union. 'Renown' became the flag ship of Force W, which was formed to escort carriers carrying fighter aircraft to besieged Malta in April 1942. She rejoined the Home Fleet in May until October, 1942 when she was stationed in the Mediterranean. At 0130 hours Stevens sighted a southbound convoy and began zigzagging every seven minutes on a 20-degree angle. This tactic of continually altering course was used by surface ships in an attempt to avoid attack from enemy U-Boats and E-Boats. *P46* entered Lerwick South Harbour at 0001 hours.

0130 hours 16th May:

The submarine secured alongside an oiling barge at Lerwick North Harbour, to embark diesel and lubricants for the forthcoming voyage. Having loaded the necessary fuel by 0315, at 0604 hours *P46* slipped her moorings and proceeded on her first war patrol. Because the boat was now considerably heavier, she dived at 0627 hours for a test trim, surfacing ten minutes later. Then, due to the sighting of an unidentified aircraft, she dived again at 0837 and resurfaced

13 minutes later to continue her way to the designated patrol area. At 2200 hours they encountering their first equipment failure, when the boat's log, a device for measuring the boats speed through the water, had to be repaired. Lieutenant Stevens remarked: "At this time of the year in the northern latitudes there was no real darkness, so a direct surface passage to a position 200 miles off the Norwegian coast was feasible." Inside the submarine, illuminated by a dull glow of dim red lighting, the crew settled down to a leisurely smoke and a game of cards, chess or uckers, and a tot of rum.

0304 hours 17th May:

Continuing to zigzag, *P46* received a message to investigate a crashed Catalina aircraft. At 0605 they passed a floating mine. At 0645 hours the boat found itself in position 63 deg 10 min N 00 deg 47 min W, where it was able to exchange identities with another Catalina that was searching for the downed plane, and remained in contact until 1100 hours when the aircraft returned to base. No sighting of the crashed aircraft was seen or ever recovered. Another floating mine was sited at 0912 hours. Having set course for the original patrol area, at 1430 hours another message was received to alter course and take up a position, replacing the French submarine *Q185*, FS *Minerve*. The crew of *P46* continued to proceed to their patrol area, sighting aircraft at 1430, 1700 and 2015 hours.

0400 hours 18th May:

Submerged. Land sighted at 0530 hours. Routine patrol was maintained throughout the day. Aircraft sightings at 1200,

1500, 2000 and 2130 hours. At 1400 hours they passed a lifebuoy but were unable to identify the ship it had come from. Throughout the day they twice had equipment failure, and again had to repair the log. Stevens outlined the aim of the patrol, which "was to discourage sorties by the heavy German ships from the Norwegian ports against the PQ convoys. The routine was to stay dived constantly except for five hours daily spent surfaced charging the batteries".

0107 hours 19th May:
Surfaced to recharge the batteries. The main meal of the day probably consisted of lentil soup, beef steak pudding, boiled potatoes, tinned carrots with tinned fruit and custard for a sweet. At 0115 hours they began zigzagging 20 degrees to either side. *P46* proceeded to its designated patrol area, Zone K33. Forced to dive due to the sighting of a Fokker Wolf Condor, at a height of 300 feet, at 2122 hours. The boat resurfaced at 2150 to continue recharge the batteries. The next few days passed without incident.

0146 hours 24th May:
Sighted aircraft. Repeated at 0644 and again at 1042 hours. *P46* surfaced at 1056 hours, zigzagging 30 degrees either side in an attempt to confuse enemy U-Boats. At 1251 hours *P46* had an unexpected encounter with the Norwegian submarine *Uredd,* which surfaced within 2,500 yards off *P46*'s starboard beam, an incident which startled the crew for no-one on board had heard *Uredd* A/S challenge. Lieutenant Stevens takes up the event. "I heard a shout down the voice pipe from the bridge, 'Submarine in sight... captain on the bridge'. I rushed there in double-quick time

to find the Officer of the Watch working the signal lamp. 'She's just surfaced and made the challenge,' he said, 'I'm just giving her the correct reply'. A quick look through the binoculars confirmed that she was of British design, a sister U-Class boat. Then identities were exchanged by signal lamp – she was the *Uredd*, commanded by Lieutenant R. Roren R.Nor.N. Her signal lamp started flashing again 'Good morning, I am happy now not to have torpedoed you'. 'Me too,' was the fervent reply that our signalman flashed back. Later, we found out that *Uredd* had been stalking us from the time that we had surfaced not far away from her until just before Roren was going to fire his first torpedo. One of our zigzag alterations, of course, enabled him to recognise us as being on his side."

Stevens continues: "Since leaving Lerwick, skies had been overcast and no navigation sun or star sights had been possible. We had been navigating by dead-reckoning, but the ocean currents had been playing tricks with estimations, which had led to this unexpected rendezvous."

In fact, *P46* was some 90 miles from her patrol line position and the taking of a sun sight at 1300 hours and again at 1715 hours confirmed that *Uredd*'s position was correct and Stevens immediately ordered a change of course for Zone K33, her designated patrol area, arriving in the vicinity at 0030 hours on May 25th. Almost a year to the day later *Uredd* was struck by a mine and lost with all hands.

0001 hours 25th May:
Wind direction NE blowing F4, decreasing to F2 as the day wore on. The boat surfaced at 0158 hours to recharge and dived at 1514 due to the sighting of a Fokker Wolfe Condor

at 1000 feet. It resurfaced again at 1808 hours to take star sights for navigational purposes, diving just five minutes later. At 2320 hours, distant underwater explosions could be heard throughout the boat. For many of the crew, this was the first time that they had experienced such a noise under war conditions. Many looked up to the sky and kept their own thoughts firmly tucked away, while others joked and tried to maintain a level joviality of the situation.

0115 26th May:
Aircraft sighted and repeated throughout the morning at 0325, 0530, 0738 and 0800 hours. At 0400 and 0440 hours, underwater explosions some distance off could be heard throughout the boat and by 0800 hours, at a speed of 3 knots, *P46* changed course, and surfaced at 1012 hours for a navigational sighting. Three minutes later the boat dived and resurfaced at 1054 in order to recharge batteries. At 1320, with the submarine travelling at 4 knots, William Haines reported very fast and loud hydrophone contact on a bearing of red 150 at approximately 350 revs. Within two minutes *P46* had dived and altered course to red 90, with the hydrophone contact now making 200 revs.

P46, later to be known as *Unruffled,* transmitted the submerged identity letter several times with no response, leaving Lieutenant Stevens and first lieutenant Gordon Noll believing that an unidentified submarine was close by. By 1330 hours, and on red 130, contact bearing grew aft and then faded. At 1500 hours, and much to the annoyance of the crew, a pronounced whistling could be heard on the port shaft between 150 and 200 rpm. That darn propeller again! More distant charges could be heard at 1812 hours. At 1930 hours a moderately close underwater explosion was felt throughout the boat and diving patrol commenced at 2000 hours. At 2252 hours an unidentified aircraft was sited at 800 feet.

0032 hours 27th May:

Today began with an unidentified aircraft sighting and distant underwater explosions being heard between the hours of 0130 until 0400. Aircraft sightings continued throughout the day, though *P46* remained surfaced between 0944 until 1558 hours to recharge batteries using a 30-degree zigzag pattern. Otherwise the day was one of daily routine.

0308 hours 28th – 30th May:

A Fokker Wolfe Condor, in position 72 deg 22 min N 15 deg 48 min E was sighted by the bridge watch, so *P46* dived to a depth of 70 feet, rising back up to periscope depth at 0325. Aircraft were once again seen at 0330, 0932 and 1330 hours. *P46* surfaced at 0557 in accordance with instructions received to proceed to Lerwick. The crew were in happy mood in the knowledge that the journey home from their first patrol had at last begun.

Talk amongst the ratings centred on how long leave would last, which pub to go to first and which girl was to be met. However, just 12 minutes later a Fokker Wolfe Condor was again spotted and at 0618 hours *P46* was forced to dive. The boat surfaced at 0630 and commenced zigzagging 20 degrees either side. At 0931 the klaxon sounded and diving stations was called as another Fokker Condor was sighted. The submarine surfaced at 0944 and continued to zigzag back to Lerwick.

Nothing of note happened for the next three days, which allowed the crew time to clean the boat and get ready for the inspection by Captain (S) 3rd Submarine Flotilla upon arrival in Holy Loch. This task included polishing the brass fittings, cleaning the boat throughout, sweeping the deck, cleaning the gun and, in general, preparing the boat for the arrival home.

1840 hours 31st May:

Their make-and-mend was interrupted and *P46* dived following the sighting of an unidentified monoplane. However, Lerwick was not too far in the distance.

1730 hours 1st-4th June:

The crew of *P46* arrived back on British soil after completing their first war patrol. The following day *P46* left Lerwick accompanied by HMS White Bear, a submarine tender commanded by Commander Charles Flemming, and headed for their final destination - Holy Loch.

0030 hours 5th June:

After awaiting the passage of an outward-bound convoy, *P46* arrived alongside HMS Forth. Lieutenant Stevens reported directly to Captain (S) Third Submarine Flotilla, Hugh Meynell Cyril Ionides, who, as an ex-submariner himself and having commanded both *H32* and *L52*, was fully aware of the needs of submarine commanders and the importance of getting the best from each of them. Together they would go through the patrol, no doubt over a well-deserved gin, and discussed the conditions, sightings and notable activities of any Axis contact. Any information in respect of the patrol areas was useful to Captain Ionides, as this would be helpful to all future patrols leaving the depot ship HMS Forth. Stevens informed Ionides that he had experienced moderate weather with low cloud and occasional mist. The aircraft sighted were, in the view of Stevens, on passage and in the patrol areas.

At 0830 hours the fore-end ratings were employed working on the torpedoes. This continued throughout the day, half the crew being granted three days' leave. Shore leave was also granted to a further quarter of the crew, leaving the other quarter remaining on board.

(*Author's note: Within the port log, Lieutenant Stevens did not report any defects to Captain (S), though the propeller noise had caused some concern whilst on patrol).

0830 hours 11th June, 1942:

P46 sailed for the degaussing range and returned back alongside HMS Forth at 1030 hours. At 1315 hours all hands were undertaking the task of storing provisions. By 1600 those who had been granted a three-day pass had returned to the boat, bringing *P46* back up to her full complement. Two-thirds of the crew was granted leave from 1800 hours until 0700 hours, allowing the 'Jacks' time to wash, change, write letters home and partake in a few beers. Temporary Acting Leading Stoker Alfred Hines and Petty Officer William Carter left the boat, to be replaced by Temporary Acting Leading Stoker James Reynolds.

0830 hours 12th June:

The crew prepared for sea and at 1000 hours, *Unruffled* slipped her mooring and made for the fairway to 'swing compasses' before returning alongside HMS Forth 63 minutes later, after which time the crew continued to replenish the boat with stores. This continued until 1500 hours when the boat was secured. At 1745 hours the crew of *P46* waved goodbye to HMS Forth on her outward voyage to Gibraltar, test diving at 1848 for trim purposes, and at 2000 hours rendezvoused with 'Jan Van Gelder', which was to act as escort. Lieutenant Stevens officially tells the crew their destination, resulting in jubilation for some and commiserations for others.

(*Author's note: According to the Port Log P46 was also accompanied by P222 but there is no mention of this in the Submarine Log. P222 was commissioned on the 4th May, 1942 under the command of Lieutenant Alexander James Mackenzie. It completed trials at Holy Loch and was also destined for Gibraltar to operate in the Mediterranean. On the 30th November, P222, yet to be named, sailed from Gibraltar with a complement of 48 officers and crew. It was sent to patrol off Naples and her last communication was heard on the 7th December. The Italians claimed to have sunk a submarine on the 12th December by depth charges from the Italian torpedo boat Fortunale).

0205 hours 13th – 15th June:
The crew was kept busy due to aircraft sightings and exercises. At 1330 hours *P46* hove-to and transferred stores from Jan Van Gelder before diving for exercises involving coastal command aircraft. Once surfaced, the boat continued to follow astern of her escort until 2240 hours, when Jan Van Gelder parted company. *Unruffled* began a zigzagging procedure. The next couple of days involved the crew going

through exercises at the captain's discretion, including diving, surfacing and gunnery practice. A reference is made in the submarine log that a sick member on board Jan van Gelder was transferred to a tender for hospitalisation.

0011 hours 16th June:

P46 surfaced and began evasive manoeuvres 20 degrees either side. At 0403 hours lights from a possible fishing vessels were sighted in the distance. The submarine kept its distance and dived at 0423 hours. At 0935 hours The Officer of the Watch sighted two fishing trawlers through the periscope and at 1155 hours a Sunderland aircraft passed overhead. It surfaced to take navigational sights at 1500 hours and a minute later another trawler was observed, forcing the submarine back under the surface. Once again it surfaced for navigational purposes, this time at 1829 hours, and three minutes later they dived. Trawler lights were again encountered at 2300 and 2320 hours.

0035 17th June:

P46 surfaced and immediately spotted 20 trawlers with lights showing to their starboard beam, together with a single aircraft crossing the horizon. At 0142 three fishing trawler lights were observed, again off to starboard, followed by aircraft circling around the vessels. At 0217 two lights were spotted on the port bow, indicating approaching boats. A white flare was dropped by the aircraft at 0230 hours, approximately two miles on the port beam. *P46* chose to remain on the surface and did not dive until just before sunrise at 0442. Surfacing at 1015 hours and began a zigzag course 20 degrees either side. *P46* was forced to dive once more at 1210 hours, having spotted an unidentified object, and resurfaced seven minutes later.

The sighting of a Hudson aircraft at 1704 hours resulted in the klaxon sounding with the call to dive and at 2130 until 2145 distant explosions could be heard, which was thought by Lieutenant Stevens to be an attack on the Wild Swan.

(*Author's note: The Royal Navy destroyer HMS Wild Swan (D62), commissioned in 1919 and at the time commanded by Captain Claude Edward Lutley Sclater DSO, was returning to Plymouth to refit. She was steaming through a Spanish fishing fleet after being detached from a convoy when she came under heavy attack from a squadron of German Junkers JU88 bombers. The German squadron, having been despatched to attack the convoy, mistook the Spanish trawlers as the convoy and started to attack, sinking three boats in the process. HMS Wild Swan also lost steerage after a near miss and collided with one trawler, sinking her almost immediately. After picking up 11 survivors, HMS Wild Swan was also hit and sank, leaving survivors in the water. After a period of time these were picked up by HMS Vansittart, which retrieved ten officers and 123 ratings, five of whom were seriously injured, and 11 men from the Spanish trawler. Thirty-one British seamen lost their lives. She was sunk in latitude 49 deg 52 min north, 10 deg 44 min west. P46 was in the position 49 deg 20 min north 13 deg 28 min west at 2054 hours).

18th-23rd June:

Breakfast on the 19th of June probably consisted of grapefruit, bacon and liver, with a lunch course of tinned soup, corned beef, pickles, baked beans, and cheese and biscuits. For supper a menu of pea soup, roast chicken, tinned cauliflower and a desert of boiled jam roll. The boat zigzagged on a continuous course, but no sightings or contact were observed. Daily routines were carried out by the crew. In the forenoons those off watch tried to sleep or read after the nightly din of the engines, some in a bunk with curtain drawn, giving privacy and solitude from the rest of the boat. Others stretched across the tops of locker stools, slung hammocks or simply lay on the deck. Small noises, particular sounds which everyone had come to know well, cut the general silence in the semi-darkness: the wheezing snuffle as the periscope lifted up on well-greased pulleys, and the sharp crack as it came to the end of its run; the gentle sound of the Officer of the Watch, as he worked his way round the periscope well; the Vickers telemotor pump and the hydroplane wheels grounding softly over their bearings; the navigator passing his parallel rulers over the chart, checking a bearing of a landmark. Then the noise of the telemotor again as the periscope reached the bottom of its run – silence prevailing, until, after only a few minutes, the repeated action would begin all over again.

1434 hours 24th June:
P46 exchanged identities with a lone Hudson aircraft and the rest of the day was spent at routines.

0440 25th June:
P46 sighted Cape Trafalgar, followed by Cape Spartel, and finally met up with its escort HMT Harlem, which escorted them into Gibraltar Harbour at 1015, docking alongside HMS Maidstone at exactly 1032 hours.

Lieutenant Stevens boarded HMS Maidstone to report to Captain(S) G.A.W. Voelcker and provided a detailed report of the voyage from the UK. Officers and crew boarded the depot ship at 1200 hours for dinner, reassembling back on board the submarine at 1315 hours to begin disembarking stores. These included spare parts, which were in short supply on board Maidstone. Leave was granted to two-thirds of the crew from 1600 to 2200 hours.

(*Author's note: Though written in the port log as 'HMT Harlem', I believe this to be HMT Haarlem (FY 306), an armed anti-submarine trawler. She was commissioned in July 1940 and, though owned by a Dutch Company, was requisitioned by the Royal Navy and commanded by Captain Leslie Bertram Merrick RNR).

CHAPTER FIVE

GIBRALTAR

———◦◦◦———

THE Eighth Submarine Flotilla in Gibraltar was served by the depot ship HMS Maidstone, which was launched at Clydebank and completed on 5th May 1938. This modern floating submarine base arrived on station in March 1942, and in doing so provided to all visiting and assigned submarines valuable workshops, electrical and torpedo repair shops, spare parts, stores, plumbers, carpenters, spare batteries, diving and salvage equipment and foundry and leisure facilities.

Capable of supplying over 100 torpedoes and mines, HMS Maidstone was designed to care for nine operational boats. Her facilities included steam laundries, baths, showers, a cinema, a hospital with fully equipped operating theatre and dental surgery, a chapel, two canteens, bakery, mail office and a barber's shop.

She was commanded by Captain (S) G.A.W. Voelcker, an ex-submariner and depot ship captain. He took command on the 30th March, 1941, but was replaced in July 1942 when he took command of HMS Charybdis, a new 5,600-ton cruiser. She was sunk in action after being torpedoed off the French coast by the German torpedo boat T23 on 23rd October, 1943 whilst heading a destroyer squadron, which had been detailed to intercept enemy shipping. Tragically, 460 lives were lost, including Captain Voelcker's, with 107 men rescued.

The Rock itself was well fortified as the Axis alliance was in command of the entire seaboard, except Gibraltar, Egypt and the Palestinian coasts, with the three main operational ports being Malta, Alexandria and Gibraltar. As a vital British port, Gibraltar commanded the entrance to and exit from the Mediterranean. In fact, it was doubly important because the only other route into the Mediterranean was via the Suez Canal, which, apart from exposing the British forces to greater danger, was further in nautical miles.

Gibraltar was home to 20,000 British, Commonwealth and Allied personnel and, in addition to searchlights and fighter planes, was strongly fortified by anti-aircraft defences totalling 365 gun emplacements, which were well hidden from view. G.W.G. Simpson summarised the strategic value of Gibraltar when he said: "Of the 62 German U-Boats which entered the Mediterranean in 1941-1945 no less than 48 were sunk."

Gibraltar was not a popular place, for two reasons: beer

was expensive and there was a dearth of female company. Spanish workers (Spain was a neutral country) crossed the border gate at 0800 hours and departed at 1700 hours, and many of those workers were women. There were six nurses at the hospital and the youngest, at 45, had a diary full of dates with fleeting admirers. The local brew, Cerveja, was lukewarm and cost twice the price of a British pint. The usual port of call was the Trocadero bar, in Main Street, where the biggest attraction, apart from the beer, was a brash and noisy all-female band, who invariably drowned out the noise of the drunken sailors, many of whom were often unceremoniously thrown out against their will. The naval patrol would put the offenders into a waiting truck before taking them back to headquarters until the following day, when they would appear before their respective commanders to hear their punishment. This was either a fine or a leave penalty - sometimes both. Some ratings could even be taken off submarines altogether, reporting for duty on surface ships, though to merit this action the offence had to be extremely serious.

If the Trocadero was full, there was a similar establishment, known as the Universal, further along Main Street where a pianist called Bobby was renowned for his affection for sailors. In fact, if he took a fancy to a certain matelot then he would play any tune they wanted - all night long. This led to much embarrassment and banter amongst the crew.

R.A. Cunningham, who served on HMS *Taurus,* portrays life on board a submarine in 1942-44 as seen through the eyes of one of the crew in his illuminating book 'A Submarine at War', vividly recollecting that Bobby would shout out "Anything you like, darling?" in a rather effeminate voice. "Most of the old hands who had seen Gibraltar before knew the stories concerning the Alameda [Botanic] Gardens situated on the outskirts of the town. The sailors had to pass the area on the way back to their ships but none would venture into the gardens because of rumours that circulated around the fleet concerning the goings-on there after dark. For that reason it was taboo for the young matelots to enter the gardens, except during daylight hours."

In Arthur Dickison's book 'Crash Dive: In Action with HMS *Safari*, 1942-43', published in 2003, the author, a leading telegraphist, describes Gibraltar leisure time comprising a "few runs to the free cinema on board the depot ship. The only problem was that one had to queue up for about an hour before it started to get a seat". Officers could visit La Linea and Algeciras, two towns immediately adjacent to Gibraltar, but ratings were confined to the limits of the British territory. Dickison writes: "Some of our leisure time was spent with an occasional liberty run ashore. The shops were well stocked, with quite a number of things that could not be purchased in the UK – soaps and little luxuries like boxes and bars of chocolate, face powder and hair grips." Silk commodities such as pyjamas, underwear and stockings were freely available for purchase and though they were not allowed to send these back to the UK, the matelots could take them home when they returned.

For the younger members of the crew who were under the legal minimum age to consume alcohol, and those who perhaps might not want a beer, there would be an invitation, perhaps, from the naval chaplain to go climbing on the Rock with the opportunity to feed the famous Barbary apes. R.A. Cunningham recollects: "There was a quick tour of the gun emplacements and then it was down to the canteen for tea and buns, but no beer." There was also a rest camp, which was open to ratings on three days' leave after a patrol. This military establishment, called Governor's Cottage Camp, was a palatial residence situated between Europa Point and Governor's Beach. Matelots enjoyed swimming at nearby Catalan Bay. There was also the opportunity of a luxury food hamper. ENSA (Entertainments National Service Association) occasionally provided shows for the servicemen, which made a pleasant change from the usual leisure time pursuits of swimming, sunbathing and fishing, making the wearing of shorts, which had been stowed away with thick white submarine sweaters, almost obligatory.

Ronald Max Seaburne-May, in his position as sub-lieutenant, would unofficially have quietly given the nod to, say, signalman Richard Hills that it might be a good idea if he stocked up with essentials such as toothpaste, soap, tobacco and packed shorts, singlets, towels and sandals, as a lot of sweating was in prospect. This was the closest hint the sub-lieutenant could give as to the crew's future movements. The rest of the crew members were, via the grapevine, also soon given an inkling of what might lie ahead and, by the time it came to sailing, not one single small space was left vacant to provide some of life's small luxuries that could also be used as an opportunity for useful future bartering currency. Mail was received and distributed back at HMS Maidstone, providing a highlight for the crew. For example, the Scottish newspaper the 'Daily

Record' sent a box of 'comforts' to all Scots serving on broad. These parcels, known fondly as 'Jock's Box', contained bars of chocolate, toothpaste, books and magazines, as well as much sought-after cotton shorts and tops. And, of course, a copy of the 'Daily Record'.

Officers enjoyed more freedom, having access to excursions to Algeciras and La Linea. Rear-Admiral Ben Bryant, arguably the most successful submarine commander to survive the war, writes in his memoirs 'One Man Band. The Memoirs of a Submarine C.O.' published in 1958: "The Italian Consul in Algeciras had a room at the Reina Christina hotel, the windows of which looked out across the Strait of Gibraltar and enabled him to report all shipping movements by day into Gibraltar or beyond. I remember a run over to Algeciras with two other COs. We did ourselves really well with food and drink, and later amused ourselves by staring up at the lookout window of the Italian Consul, doubtless he was too used to such demonstrations to be embarrassed." Lieutenant Stevens also reported: "The war had not stopped visits into Spain: passes allowing the holder to go as far as Algeciras could be obtained and there was less fuss at the frontier post than there had been since 1965."

Lieutenant Stevens informs us that "a handsome cat joined our company by walking on board from the dockyard one day. He was christened Timoshenko after the Russian general Semyon Timoshenko, who was making headlines at the time." Timmo was a cat of extraordinary character and, as he had a habit of disappearing ashore after a spell at sea, and it was regarded as unlucky to sail without him, considerable and sometimes frantic, efforts would be made to get him back on board before leaving port.

Vic Preece, who served on various submarines until 1953 and was, until he died in 2011, the last surviving crew member of *Unruffled*, also provides us with a detailed account of the ship's cat. "The P.O.Tel (Joseph Lewis) was walking through the dockyard when he was accosted by a WREN, who produced a tiny bundle of fluff (a kitten) and requested a home for it. Being a kind-hearted sparker, Lewis took the kitten back on board and the crew accepted it immediately as a good-luck charm. They firmly believed that Timoshenko had been an 'outside wrecker' in a previous life as he made his diving station and attack team station under the control panel. He always used his litter box in the Petty Officers' mess, part of his part three (boat training)." Timoshenko did 20 war patrols with the boat from Malta. The crew was convinced that he was a lucky mascot to such a degree that on one occasion when he went missing, departure for a patrol was delayed 24 hours on the orders of the Captain (S).

Preece adds: "Timmo must have fathered many a cat in Malta as, just like any other red-bloodied submariner, his needs were great on his return from patrol. On the trip back to the UK for refit, he got off at his home port of Gibraltar, never to return to the boat. He probably found it nice that the lady cats spoke his native language and decided to settle down, after living through all those times when his world went bang and oxygen got short – or it could have been that the boat sailed at 1300 hours, the time he was usually ashore."

Able-seaman William Dale, from Manchester, also remembers Timoshenko with affection. Quoted during an interview with a local newspaper, he commented that before the crew went into action "Timmo always walked up and down the deck mewing. It was an unfailing warning and we never took our clothes off when he started to behave in that manner. Timmo's uncanny sense made him into a sort of living hydrophone".

Petty Officer Telegraphist Joe Lewis also gives us an account of 'Timmo' the cat, describing his behaviour when at diving stations. "He would yawn and mew when a fish left the tube. He was quickly house-trained and used to do his 'georges', as the captain quaintly called them, in a box. Should he forget himself at any time, there was always a willing hand to use the heads and blow the indiscretion over the side. Timmo was awarded a collar with a silver plate bearing his name. Gzira front owed their existence to Timmo's eye for a pretty cat. One sure thing was that on arriving from patrol, Timmo would disappear for two or three days, returning with what one can only describe as a satisfied smirk on his face.

"Timmo gave us a scare when he fell ill and we discovered it was cat flu. We prepared for the worst. A vet looked him over, diagnosed a chill, and gave him some Friars' Balsam. Timoshenko was soon his old self again. Will anybody who saw the fight ever forget the routing of the Alsatian dog in the Lazaretto? I certainly won't. I thought our brave lad was a goner until, yelping with pain, the dog bolted, leaving the field to Timmo. Our spell over, we headed west and Timmo found himself back in the land of his birth. He developed a daily routine during our stay in Gibraltar. After breakfast he would go ashore and not be seen again until about 1700 hours when he would settle down for the night. Our final departure was timed for 1300, so it was plain that if we couldn't keep him on the boat we would lose him. The first lieutenant (Lascelles) suggested that we secure him to the gun and this was done. A miserable creature of a kellick L.T.O. (leading torpedo operator) said that was no way to treat a cat and set him loose. Goodbye, Timoshenko, I think I can paraphrase the poet and say:

Hail to thee, Blithe Spirit,
Cat thou never were!

"He was succeeded by Timoshenko II and III but neither of these approached the master and I'm sure all old *Unruffled*s will agree with me when I say NO cat ever will."

Due to the fact that *Unruffled* was destined to join the Tenth Flotilla, based in Malta, and the impending Operation Pedestal, the famous British attempt to get desperately-needed supplies to Malta in August 1942, July was to prove a quiet time for the officers and crew. A five-day run-up patrol was organised off the nearby Alboran Island, with the sole intention of providing the crew with training and acclimatisation to the weather and sea conditions experienced in the Mediterranean. Even Lieutenant Stevens succumbed to the heat when he "found that being bearded in the July heat was prickly and uncomfortable; the red 'set', which I had besported for nearly three years, came off. I have not been bearded since".

One important piece of information to be found within the submarine log for *N19*, HMS *Utmost* dated 15th July, 1942 indicates that "at least two attempts were made daily to call *P46* on A/S but without success" and seemingly had not been noted by the captain (S) on board HMS Maidstone or actioned by any of his staff. This proved to be an ongoing problem for *Unruffled* during her war patrol to Malta.

Destination Malta: Commenting on the mission of submarines during Operation Pedestal, Stevens remarked: "This was a covering role for submarines in support of Operation Pedestal. With major fleet support, a 15-ship convoy of fine freighters and tankers fought its way against expected heavy enemy action at Malta."

31st July, 1942:
Unruffled was fully provisioned with fuel, lubricants, fresh food, water and torpedoes. Also loaded on board was ammunition, spare parts and special cargo items for the beleaguered Maltese Island.

1700 hours 1St August – 3rd August 1942:
With the captain on the bridge, Noll reported: "All hands and Timoshenko on board, sir. Ready for sea," and *P46* slipped her moorings alongside HMS Maidstone and proceeded out of harbour into the gathering dusk on route W.M.P.17 as per her routing orders and instructions for Operation Pedestal, which were intended to resupply Malta with oil, grain, ammunition, aircraft and food. It comprised a convoy of four aircraft carriers, two battleships, seven light cruisers, 32 destroyers, 14 merchant ships, three heavy cruisers, three light cruisers, 15 torpedo boats and 11 submarines. Waiting for them to enter the Mediterranean were the Italian and German air-forces, based in Sardinia and Sicily, and U-boats. On August 10th the flotilla passed Gibraltar and within 24 hours it was attacked. On reaching Malta, only three merchant vessels limped into port, including the American tanker SS Ohio, which was heavily damaged and tied between two destroyers due to loss of

steering. Eventually she had to be scuttled in the harbour.

Allied losses were heavy, totalling one aircraft carrier, two light cruisers, one destroyer, nine merchant vessels and two submarines sunk and one aircraft carrier, two light cruisers, one heavy cruiser, one light cruiser and one submarine damaged. Approximately 400 sailors were lost. On the Axis side, 42 aircraft were lost, two submarines sunk and two cruisers damaged. Unable to protect the convoy against aircraft, the submarines were used as decoys, remaining on the surface as much as possible to attract attention to themselves rather than the distant ships.

Over the next three days no sightings and no action took place. The crew remained in routine patrol mode, settling in and undertaking their routine task and shifts. Tension was running high, with the crew at optimum efficiency due to the task in hand, and conversation turned to their possible next port of call.

0915 hours 4th August:

A merchant vessel was sighted hull down on a 360-degree course. 'Wiggy' Bennett, having already served a breakfast of cornflakes, bacon and eggs, settled down for a quick nap.

0355 hours 5th August:

Lights from a merchant ship on course 340 degrees were sighted. Having prepared and served lunch of tinned soup and tinned lobster with mayonnaise and potato salad, Geoffrey Bennett handed out oranges and mugs of cocoa. Timoshenko feasted on the lobster, visiting each compartment as he toured the boat.

2230 hours 7ᵗʰ August:

The submarine adjusted course and speed to comply with orders received. A defect with the ASDIC set was reported by PO Tel Lewis to Lieutenant Stevens, who informed his captain that repairs could not be made at sea. Lieutenant Stevens commented on this matter by remarking that "it was particularly unfortunate, since the successful positioning of submarines for Operation Pedestal depended upon ASDIC efficiency".

1835 hours 10ᵗʰ August:

Made a landfall sighting off Marettimo in position 38 deg 03 min N 11 deg 52 min E and, whilst maintaining a holding position, the Officer of the Watch summoned the Captain to the bridge after sighting a 3,000-ton enemy supply merchant ship bearing 80 degrees. She was on a 270-degree course and was being escorted by a flying boat. *P46* went to diving stations, the crew not taking long to reach them and First Lieutenant Noll taking a shorter time to adjust an attack trim. Matelots who had been asleep just moments before rolled out of their bunks and, still half asleep, attended their action stations. The passageway that had been clear was suddenly crowded and filled with men, some going forward and others heading for a position astern of the control room. Once the ratings had settled and the clash of Kingston valves opening and closing and the rapid orders followed by counter replies had finished, silence reigned as the boat manoeuvred to the attack. Stevens relayed his orders to the attack team. Glued to the periscope, sweeping a full circle and at the same time making observations on the target, he took a general look around the horizon and

sky for other ships or aircraft. The periscope was up for only
seconds. Brill-Edwards on the operating lever kept busy as
Stevens ordered the periscope up and down in short
snatches.

The Captain changed to the attack periscope in
readiness for the attack but, as Stevens recorded, "shortly
before the first torpedo should have been sent away, I
glimpsed the Cant flying boat escort flying straight at the
periscope. I ordered a rapid depth change to 120 feet, as
there was a doctrine that submarines should treat aircraft
with respect in the clear Mediterranean waters. Minutes
later (1909 hours) we returned to periscope depth, and fired
three torpedoes from longish range. They missed, which was
a disappointing first effort against the enemy. We consoled
ourselves with the thought that there would be plenty more
opportunities later".

Unbeknown to the crew, this merchantman had been
attacked 14 minutes earlier by *Utmost* with one torpedo
hitting home. Stevens allowed for a speed of eight knots
when calculating the firing pattern. However, *Utmost* had
allowed for a speed of 14 knots when their torpedo struck.
P46 was two-and-a-half miles from *Utmost* at the time of the
attack. At 2200 hours, the submarine surfaced and
proceeded by route through QBB.255, passing through the
position at 2259.

1043 hours 11th August:
In position 38 deg 20 min N 12 deg 51 min E, the boat
sighted an unidentified bomber at a height of 200 feet. The
crew was put on alert as they passed through the Sicilian
minefields, the order 'diving stations' was given and the

crew listened out intently for any sounds indicating a close encounter with a mine. No sound was heard. ASDIC also remained silent.

1430 hours 12th August:
The boat was in position for Operation Pedestal. As per orders, *P46* was in a position between *P34* HMS *Ultimatum,* commanded by Lieutenant Peter Harrison DSC, and *N19,* HMS *Utmost,* whose captain was Lieutenant Anthony Langridge, which created a five-submarine patrol line spaced out south of Pantelleria. With the ASDIC out of operation and thus being unable to communicate with the two other submarines, Stevens endeavoured to conform to the line of operation, reluctantly adjusting his position northward of the line and changing course once they were able to surface. At 1843 hours a Junkers 88 was sighted flying at 100 feet and at 1905 William Haines heard HMS *Ultimatum* and HMS *Utmost* in communication with one another. A British Blenheim was sighted at 2000 hours. At 2345 hours the submarine set a new course as per orders.

0530 hours 13th August:
Having reached its designated position, HMS *Utmost* was in communication bearing 120 degrees and at 0745 she was at a bearing of 160 degrees. At 0800 *P46* surfaced and changed course when *Utmost* was sighted four miles away on a bearing of 165 degrees. The speed was altered to five knots. At 0907 *Unruffled* dived and altered course to comply with orders received. At 0955 a British Sunderland aircraft was sighted through the periscope on a 360 degree course. At 1015 heavy distant depth charges were heard by the

crew. A solitary Junkers 88 was spotted at 1100 and at 1540 a Wellington bomber was spotted flying at 200 feet. At 1630 a Blenheim aircraft was also recognised as it passed in the distance. At 2107 the boat proceeded on the surface on a course North East of a line between Gozo and Pantelleria.

1915 hours 14th August:

P46 proceeded on an ordered course of 324 degrees. Because of the extension to Operation Pedestal due to the damage to the tanker Ohio, HMS *Utmost* remained at sea, whilst *Unruffled,* because of the defective ASDIC set, was ordered to Malta. An expectant crew enjoyed their tot of rum and discussed their leave plans when reaching Malta.

0225 hours 15th August:

The boat set course for Malta and with trepidation entered the minefield that had been laid by the Axis powers on the approaches to the port of Valletta and just outside the harbour entrance. Several boats had already succumbed to this menace whilst trying to re-supply the Island from Alexandria. Lieutenant Stevens called for diving stations and ordered "slow ahead group down on one motor only", ready to stop immediately if required. Their depth was adjusted to pass below the mines, with strict instructions passed throughout the boat for silence.

Able-seaman Donald Stephens on ASDIC was concentrating hard to detect any sounds around them. The silence seemed to last forever, with only the swishing of the propellers audible throughout the boat. Any cough, sneeze or flatulence was greeted with a look that could kill from the captain or other members of the crew. Even Timoshenko was sleeping and was not disturbed.

For just over an hour not a whisper could be heard, even though confidence throughout the crew began to grow that the minefield had been crossed. Then, out of the blue came the sound they all dreaded: a scraping noise coming from the bows, the sound of metal upon metal. Then silence. Moments later the sound was repeated, but this time it was much louder and further aft. Heartbeats quickened and silent prayers were offered as the thought occurred to the crew that they were in the middle of a minefield. As the noise drifted aft towards the propellers the question was raised: Would the wire become wrapped around the spinning blades? There was a huge sigh of relief when the final sound of the wire detaching itself from the submarine was evident.

Suddenly there was an awful bang, causing everyone to either jump or duck – another mine close by with its mooring wire dragging along the hull. Would it drag clear, would it clear the conning tower? This was a tense time, felt by all. Men held their breath as the mine passed along the saddle tanks without incident. The minutes ticked by in silence and the crew began to relax, whispering to their mates and discussing the close encounter just experienced.

Once clear of the minefield, *P46* surfaced, with nothing more being heard on the ASDIC until 0410, when the sound and sighting of a bow wave crossing the stern from starboard to port forced *P46* to dive. Fifteen minutes later the submarine surfaced and proceeded on her way to Malta and was finally escorted by a minesweeper into Marsamxett Harbour.

On the bridge, signalman Ronald Hills had a grandstand view of their approach into Lazaretto Creek and witnessed the terrible destruction caused by bombing. Encountering small boats rowed by a standing oarsman, Lieutenant Stevens explained that these were water taxis called *dghaisas* which could be hired to ferry members of the crew across the creek to the town of Valletta.

Ahead of them was a small jetty, with pontoons strung out from along the shore. Waiting for them to arrive was Captain (S) G.W.G Simpson and a few other officers and once the gangway had been put in place, Stevens left the boat. He then made his report, which included the aircraft sightings, the reason for firing three precious torpedoes, and explained that W/T reception had been good throughout the journey. An officer from the flotilla immediately came on board *P46* and spoke to Lieutenant Noll, explaining that two sentries should be posted, one on the jetty side of the submarine and the other on the boat side, and emphasised that no one should be allowed on board, especially the local Maltese workmen, because, due to the food shortages, stealing was a big concern. It was also advised to have a casing sentry to stop any dghaisas which came alongside. The officer explained that he would try to organise a good dghaisa and that the submarine would have to pay him a monthly salary and, preferably, draw up a contract. Coxswain Gerald Walls was sent ashore to the spare crew office to obtain further information. The officer's last words to Gordon Noll as he left *P46:* "Oh, and by the way, welcome to Malta."

CHAPTER SIX

MALTA

16TH AUGUST 1942 - 16TH OCTOBER 1943

DURING 1941 and 1942 Axis forces had only one objective as far as Malta was concerned, and that was to starve the people, to break the will of the inhabitants and bomb frequently and heavily the structures and infrastructure of the island. In order to achieve victory in North Africa, Malta had to be restrained and over a period of just six weeks 6,700 tons of bombs fell around Grand Harbour alone. Twenty-one Royal Navy warships were sunk within the harbour walls, or in its approaches, and 13 others were damaged. A total of 275 air-raids were recorded in March 1942 alone and a further 283 in May, and over a course of three months there were only 11 nights free of air raids. The island had to endure 3,340 air raids or air-raid alerts in a two-year period, during which time 35,000 homes were destroyed or damaged.

During air-raids, submarines submerged in Marsamxett Harbour close to the submarine base at HMS Fort Talbot on Manoel Island. This was a disused ex-quarantine building once inhabited by Lord Byron and now operating as the land base for British and Polish submarines. Bombing became so intense that the 10th Submarine Flotilla was forced to withdraw from Malta in May, 1942 relocating to Alexandria, Egypt, and only returned on the 31st July at 1230 hours when HMS *Unbroken*, commanded by Alastair Mars, once again entered harbour to take up station.

The long-suffering citizens of the island lived in subterranean shelters and endured unimaginative hardship, with rationing and shortages of all material items. Life could only be described as a living hell, but the Maltese population continued their everyday lives as best they could, even going to work each day in the bombed-out city of Valletta and dock area, repairing ships of all types, unloading any vessel that had managed to limp into port and generally carrying on with their normal jobs and daily activities, as well as helping in the defence of the island.

The second half of 1942 looked grim for the island. Morale was at a low, food stocks and fuel became critically short, with no rice, sugar, oil, soap, meat, tea or butter. And when coal ran out there was no electricity, either. The staple diet was chiefly bread and soup. Thanks to the large mine-laying submarines, HMS *Porpoise* and HMS *Clyde*, precious 100-ton cargoes, unloaded during darkness, offered some relief, though the main cargo consisted mainly of precious fuel, ammunitions and spare parts.

Due to the initiative and skill of the Flotilla chief engineering officer, Commander E. 'Sam' Macgregor, new facilities had been built into the rock using Maltese labour, providing sleeping quarters, a sick bay, a dental surgery, offices, a chapel and an operations room. A full-size cinema, showing the latest American films delivered by submarine and courtesy of Royal Navy Cinema Service in Gibraltar, provided entertainment for crew. For exercise, swimming at Sliema and hockey on Manoel Island was available. G.W.G. Simpson, Captain (S) of the Tenth Flotilla, explains: "Fresh water for all purposes at Lazaretto was never rationed. Hot baths for the crews in from patrol were essential, and were guaranteed by Macgregor, a large domestic boiler having been acquired. Commander Macgregor would watch with close attention the progress of his under-rock workshop, a beautiful arched-roofed vault, measuring 120 feet by 60 feet by 20 feet high. The amount of rock removed weekly varied directly with the calories in the workmen's ration, which fell in 1942 to 900 a day from the 3,500 which is normal.

"Radio receivers were privately owned by many people, but there was also the local Malta broadcast. In Lazaretto, we were all fans of Lord Haw-Haw [the wartime traitor William Joyce] and the wardroom loudspeaker was always tuned in to receive 'Jairmany calling! Jairmany calling!' which was considered good entertainment." Simpson, or Shrimp, as he was fondly called, was without doubt, loved, respected and admired by all those under his command. A man of strong character, a go-getter and superb strategist, he was a man of action, who went on to become Commodore Destroyers of the Western Approaches and a Rear Admiral CB, CBE. Lieutenant Stevens described Simpson as "disdaining red tape, most likeable and approachable, he suffered some hard knocks when casualties occurred among the submarine crews for whom he cared so much."

Outside the confines of the naval establishment, entertainment for the crew was limited due to the lack of alcohol, so the main form of leisure activity, when air-raids permitted, were simply swimming and sunbathing. Those who ventured ashore found only three bars, serving local beer and distilled local spirits. The shops stocked only essential items and even then were expensive. A reel of cotton cost 15 shillings and sixpence and a small potato was about one shilling. It was impossible to purchase lipstick, which could only be obtained through bartering. The bar bill and black market purchases were paid for in notes rather than coins, as bronze and silver were practically non-existent in Malta, and even the smallest coin was hoarded. All of this add to making the jack a dull boy.

One favourite meeting place on the island was the Dun Cow, now a pizza emporium, on Sliema sea front. Sydney Hart, from the submarine HMS *Taurus,* gives us an insight into the scene awaiting the men after arriving back from patrol. "As we entered the Dun Cow, after crossing the little bridge from the Lazzaretto to Sliema front, Anne, the bar owner, greeted us with her usual welcoming smile and, in her quaint English, exclaimed, 'Ah, truants back. Drinks on me first, boys!' The bar was always spotlessly clean, offering a cordial welcome with its gaudy drapes hanging at the windows. As we sat around the little table, Anne brought over the drinks and chatted with us until she was called elsewhere.

"She was a great favourite amongst the submarine

crews, especially if one's finances were low. 'Pay me any time', was Anne's useful motto, and if any of us wanted the loan of a few pounds she would always come to the rescue. Many a time I have known her lend money to her 'pets' [favourites] just before they sailed on patrol. Anne really did have a heart of 24 carat gold."

Tony's was another bar frequented by the matelots, and to this day it is still open and serving drinks. It had a small area with a bar at the far end with a sea frontage and served a local brew known as Ambite. Quite often the ratings would be violently sick after just a couple of pints. Despite the lack of spirits there was plenty of gin, so the matelots passed away the time happily enough.

Arthur Dickison says that Tony, the owner, helped the matelots in his own special way. "Some submariners had a novel way of having refreshments when they returned from sea by saving up their tots [rum] in a bottle. They would bring it ashore to Tony, who would stick a label with their name on it and then put it in a locked glass case behind the bar. When they returned from patrol they came by the bar, collected their bottles and sat down for the evening with a few rums mixed with ginger or lemonade supplemented by Ambite". Then there was the 'Cairo' bar, which served mainly gin and orange. It had a piano and was very popular, especially with the locals.

Dickison adds: "We toured around Valletta and what a state it was in! What devastation after dreadful bombardments! The smell was terrible and from time to time it was necessary to hold a hankie to one's mouth. Wherever we went people asked for things such as packets of cigarettes, soap and toothpaste. It was quite a state of affairs."

Sand-flies were a real irritation, especially with living conditions being so far from ideal. They came in swarms, and Dickison recalls: "Their bite was worse than a mosquito. They were at you all night and your arms, face and legs came up in large bumps. If you broke the skin with constant scratching, you ended up with a nasty sore, which took time to heal". Due to the lack of fats in the Maltese diet, scabies was rife, with most of the island suffering.

Petty Officer Walls returned on board and assembled the crew in the fore-ends, where he informed the matelots that due to the continuous air raids they had to mess 80 feet underground in an area not dissimilar to an air-raid shelter which did not smell too pleasant. Once inside their new quarters the men were advised by members of the spare crew (ratings awaiting allocation to a submarine) to leave as much of their own personal property on board as possible, because petty theft on the island was rife. On this score, ratings were just as bad as the locals. The two-thirds crew using the shelter were advised that it was best to return to sleep on board the submarine whenever possible because conditions were not as good on shore and, in any case, the light in the sleeping area of the shelter was constantly turned on so it would always have been difficult to sleep anyway.

These ratings would not have been required in the event of an air-raid; the duty of diving the boat when the siren sounded would have been the responsibility of the other one-third crew left on board the boat, which would then sit on the seabed until the all-clear. Food was also served in the confines of the shelter with the Maltese workmen constantly around looking for scraps. As there were no facilities for a rest camp and the beaches were wire-fenced, it was considered a time to 'loaf' around when leave was given.

Second Patrol

0800 hours 23rd August, 1942:
Loaded torpedoes, fuel, lubricants, fresh water and stores ready for patrol. The water had a distinctly unpleasant taste which some crew members described as "horrible". Most of the matelots added lemon or orange in an effort to disguise it. Though food was rationed throughout the island, submariners fared extremely well due to their dietary requirements in such a confined space. Though fresh eggs and tins of ham were not available, the men had plenty of tinned food, such as Spam, dried potatoes, spinach, peas and beans. Fresh provisions included Maltese potatoes, which were not a particular favourite amongst the ratings, lettuce, tomatoes and goat veal. With the exception of olives, no fresh fruit was available, but tinned prunes were plentiful. Bread was rationed to one slice per man per meal and, as a sandwich was always eagerly sought when on patrol; the chef was encouraged to bake rolls on a daily basis.

There was a daily submariners' newspaper published by the 'Daily Mirror' named 'Good Morning', which the coxswain handed out while on patrol. It consisted of snippets and photographs of relatives, wives and girlfriends of serving submariners, with exciting accounts of everyday heroism of successful submarines. There was even one particular cartoon featuring a ship's cat, with the caption 'I said tinned fish. Not tin fish', referring to the torpedoes. Due to the impending sailing of the boat no leave was granted and the crew remained at the Lazaretto.

1600 hours 24th August, 1943:

Lieutenant Stevens is informed by 'Shrimp' Simpson that his patrol line will be an area off Misurata, Libya. Simpson had deliberately chosen this area knowing that it was a good work-up position to enable the crew to acclimatise and sample the conditions associated with the western half of the Mediterranean. *P46* slipped its mooring and proceeded out of harbour at 1715 hours, practising the firing of the deck gun at 2045 before proceeding on her way for Area M at 2050. The crew resumed routine patrol, talk and chatter in the various compartments confined to the expectation of the forthcoming days.

1400 25th August:

While in a position 34 deg 33 min N 15 deg 00 min E, fast hydrophone contact could be heard on a bearing of 050 degrees, but nothing was sighted through the periscope. This contact was repeated and again nothing sighted. At 1530-1555 similar H.E. was heard and faded on a course of 300 degrees. *P46* continued on the surface during the night to recharge batteries, diving at dawn for routine patrol. Able-seaman Bennett was already in his confined kitchen making rolls for the Scotch broth he would later serve. Uckers was in play amongst the crew, with a chess match also underway.

26th-29th August:

During the three days in an area patrolling four to ten miles off the coast between a line from Marsa Dsima and Ras Khara, nothing was sighted by night and only small open fishing boats by day. On the 27th *P46* passed a drifting floating buoy at 1410 and observed the flashing white light every five seconds from the Ras Zorugl lighthouse from 2200 hours until 0015. The next day an Italian floating mine was observed. Due to the sighting of a convoy in the area, and having received instructions from Malta, the boat altered course to Appollonia at 2152 hours on the 29th. PO Lewis reported to Lieutenant Noll that communications were being hindered as a loud crackling noise in the headphones prevented most signals from being read when dived. No defect could be found, but the problem continued throughout the rest of the patrol. Donald Stephens, on ASDIC, reported a loud crackling that prevented its use for listening from the 28th August, a problem that continued throughout the rest of the patrol. No link could be found between the crackling and the noise heard by the telegraphist over the W/T. Oxtail soup, veal, boiled potatoes and tinned runner beans, followed by a sweet consisting of pineapple and custard, was the main meal of the day/night.

0511 hours 31st August:
The boat dived in position 33 deg 07 min N 21 deg 33 min E and proceeded submerged to its patrol position. Aircraft were sighted throughout the day. Breakfast included grapefruit and fried fish. The submerged lunch was tinned soup, with tomato and lettuce salad. The occasional letter was written, to be sent back to the UK when the boat returned to Malta.

0103 hours 1st September:
The lookouts heard aircraft every half-hour until diving at 0508 hours. The boat continued to spot aircraft throughout

the day on a regular basis. Timoshenko became agitated, pacing up and down the boat from one compartment to the other, mewing as he progressed. At 1155 hours smoke was sighted through the periscope and at 1205 the mast and funnels of two ships bearing 050 degrees were sighted westbound through the periscope lens. The ships appeared to be one merchant vessel and one trawler. An escorting Cant aircraft, flying at 300 feet, was observed searching the area to the bow of the two ships. *P46* endeavoured to close the two vessels but could not make up the distance. At 2050 hours the submarine surfaced and set a zigzag course 20 degrees either side at a speed of four-and-a-half knots. The boat continued to hear aircraft in the distance. Total submerged time: 15 hours 42 minutes.

0505 2nd September:
Dived. *P46* sighted the funnel of a large hospital ship eastbound bearing 360 degrees. At 2128 hours a message was received from Malta ordering *P46* to a new patrol position as a small tanker had been sighted at 33 deg 37 min N 22 deg 25 min E. The boat surfaced at 2002 hours to recharge the batteries. Those on the deck could smell oil and see it on the surface of the water. The submarine changed course to a new bearing after flares were sighted by a lookout at 2320 hours. Total submerged time: 14 hours 57 minutes.

0048 hours 3rd September:
P46 resumed course onto her original heading as the flares were considered to be over seven barges that had been reported by an earlier aircraft signal. To the delight of a

disappointed crew, the return to Malta signal was received. Talk amongst the crew focussed on their forthcoming liberty. At 0240 hours the course was set for Valletta. At 0505 hours the boat dived and the only further contact on the return journey was at 2016 hours, when, after surfacing, an illuminated hospital ship was observed, eastbound on a bearing of 080 degrees. Total submerged time: 15 hours 8 minutes.

0512 hours 4th September:
Dived. The crew began to clean the boat ready for their entrance into Valletta Harbour, including bright-work cleaning (cleaning the brass work). Surfaced at 1235 for navigational purposes and dived five minutes later. Surfaced again at 1643 for the same reason, diving five minutes later. Aircraft sighted at 1732. Gyro was checked and corrected by using the sunset. At 2020 the submarine surfaced and began recharging the batteries, zigzagging 20 degrees to either side. Total submerged time: 15 hours 5 minutes.

0515 hours 5th September:
With the sound of the boat's klaxon bringing the crew to diving stations, *P46* gently slipped below the surface to begin another periscope patrol. The boat's compass was checked at 0830 hours. It surfaced at 1405, zigzagging 30 degrees to either side. Aircraft were spotted by the lookouts at 1700 hours. Total submerged time: 8 hours 50 minutes. Breakfast began with grapefruit, buttered eggs and cornflakes, with lunch comprising tinned soup, corned beef and baked beans. Midnight dinner/supper was pea soup,

roast veal, roast potatoes, tinned cabbage. Tinned apricots finished off the meal.

0029 hours 6th September:
Revs set at 400 rpm. Aircraft sighted at 0335 hours. The minesweeper escort that the lookouts were searching for finally came into view at 0505 and *P46* dived at 0534 after the minesweeper hosted a red flag indicating that the submarine should dive. Surfaced at 1412 to proceed up channel astern of minesweeper. No Jolly Roger would be flown as they entered the entrance to the harbour at 1600 hours and secured alongside HMS Talbot at 1630. *P46* tied up beside the Lazaretto to be greeted by Simpson. Stevens reported the communication and ASDIC problem to Simpson but added that the echo sounder "gave excellent results from 310 fathoms upwards and was a useful navigational aide off Misurata". At 1700 hours two-thirds of the crew was granted leave and immediately headed for the tunnel for a hot bath and something to eat.

0815 hours 7th September:
All hands fell in and were employed cleaning and unloading the boat. Dinner was partaken at 1200 hours ashore and make-and-mend called at 1330. Leave was granted to half the crew from 1330-0730 hours.

0815 hours 8th September:
All hands fell in and were employed cleaning the boat throughout the day. Three days' patrol leave was granted to half the boat's company. Trot sentries watches on the casing of the submarine were ordered, with a loaded revolver at the

ready to repel all boarders. This routine continued, while the remaining matelots left on board were employed cleaning, scraping paintwork and repainting, a task that involved painting approximately 10,000 pipes, each one with a different coloured identification, and painting the boat externally. Leave was granted to a lucky few from 1330-0730 each day.

Lieutenant Stevens' memoirs recounts the start of the next patrol by relating to the circumstances behind a fast sailing. "One afternoon towards the end of our rest period, the staff officer (operations) at Talbot found me drying off in the sun after a swim," says Stevens. "'Captain (S) wants to see you in half an hour, meanwhile get your boat ready for sea', he said. I made the arrangements, dressed and reported to 'Shrimp'. Normally a short written Operation Order, containing the aim, intelligence and other details, was issued before a patrol. This time was, perhaps, characteristically different. 'No time for formal paper, old chap,' said Shrimp, handing me a small piece of paper with only a latitude and longitude position on it. 'Just get to this position as fast as you can, fighter cover arranged till dark. I'll send you a signal when I know more'".

Within Simpson's patrol report he explains that *P46* had orders to make his best speed towards Kuriat in an endeavour to intercept a ten-knot large tanker which air reconnaissance showed south-west-bound from Naples. With this objective, the RAF provided fighter protection throughout daylight hours so that *P46* could proceed on the surface.

Third Patrol

0815 hours 18th September:

Hands employed cleaning the boat, dinner taken at 1200 hours in the confinements of the Fort Talbot tunnel. At 1400 hours, the boat slipped its moorings, escorted by the minesweeper HMS Hythe. At 1600, the escort left to return to harbour. *P46* surfaced and set course for Ras Mahedia. Gun practice took place at 1645 hours and was completed at 1659 when a 20 degree zigzag each side was set on a course of 264 degrees at 460 rpm - best speed.

(*Author's note: There does not appear to be any information regarding the storage of P46 for this patrol and one can only assume this took place sometime during the preceding days.)

HMS Hythe (J194) was built by Ailsa Shipbuilding Company and launched at the Scottish west coast port of Troon on 5th March, 1942. Ordered under the launch name of 'Banff', she displaced 656 tons and was 174 feet in length, with a beam 28.5 feet and a draught of 8.25 feet. She was part of the 14th/17th Minesweeper Flotilla based in Malta and had a complement of 60 crew. She was torpedoed and sunk by U-371 whilst off Bougie, Algeria, on the 11th October, 1943, with the loss of 50 lives.

0547 hours 19th September:

Dived. Several unidentified aircraft were sighted throughout most of the day at heights of between 500-1500 feet. At 1310 *P46* received instruction from Malta to maintain position, as early reconnaissance showed the tanker to be in Palermo Harbour. At 1430, with the coast eight miles distant, *P46* altered course to the north to patrol an area between Ras Mahedia and Kuriat Island. At 1718 hours smoke was sighted bearing 205 degrees. H/E (Hydrophones) contact was made at 1932 hours and the submarine changed course to investigate. The mast and funnels of a convoy of three small vessels were sighted close inshore. Stevens, not willing to compromise *P46*'s position in anticipation of the tanker leaving Palermo for North Africa, left them to continue their journey unmolested. Surfacing at 2005 hours when H/E contact had disappeared, *P46* continued through the night on the surface, identifying aircraft activity at 2012, 2027, 2035 and 2053 hours.

0545 hours 20th September:
After having successfully fully charged the batteries, the boat dived. Aircraft were spotted throughout the night. At 1325 hours *P46* set course for a position 090 degrees off Kuriat Light to intercept a 6,000-ton tanker which had been reported by air reconnaissance to be southbound off Kelibia. At 1750 the submarine was in position and awaiting arrival of the tanker. Expectations were high when H/E contact was made at 1757 with increased air activity overhead. At 2033 hours *P46* surfaced, receiving reports from Malta at 2120 that the convoy would pass Kuriat Light at an estimated time of 2130. Stevens was in a patrol position eight miles from the advised position. At 2245 a darkened vessel was sighted proceeding southbound, on a bearing of 240 degrees, and *P46* pressed ahead to investigate.

0017 hours 21st September:
The vessel was identified as a large three-masted auxiliary

schooner – later to be acknowledged as the Italian-registered N10/Aquila – and not the expected 6,000-ton ship. There was one small motor craft in station astern. It was a calm moonlit night when Stevens made the decision to order "Stand by gun action" in anticipation of attacking the schooner with gunfire. Down below decks the gun crew waited below the conning tower, contemplating the chance of action. Second Lieutenant Lascelles would be ordering the range and trajectory, with able-seaman Stanley Powell firing the 3-inch gun. Once the order "Gun crew to station" was given, they would rush up the ladder onto the bridge and over the rails and prepare the weapon, with fellow crew members forming a chain and standing by to bring up the ammunition.

The small craft was difficult to identify and Stevens could not decide whether or not it was an escort. On three occasions when closing the schooner to open fire, her small consort altered course towards *P46,* which withdrew. At 0105 in position 33 deg 33.5 min N 11 deg 08 min E the small craft had dropped astern to about five cables. *P46* opened fire on the schooner at approximately 1,000 yards and closing. Twelve rounds were fired, of which eight hits were observed. The crew abandoned ship after the first round was fired. A delay in shooting between rounds was caused by the extractors failing to eject the first two rounds, which had to be withdrawn by hand. Down below the crew cheered as the result of each hit was relayed back to them. The attack was made upmoon from the quarter, which gave good light conditions. The schooner was set on fire and the glare could still be seen four hours later. The small boat is presumed to have altered course away when *P46* opened fire, as she disappeared in the dark area away from the moon. Stevens withdrew to the north-east on the surface and it was thought later that the small craft could be seen in the glare of the flames picking up survivors. The schooner was towing a skiff astern, but this was not seen after the shoot. Stevens later described his justification in the sinking by proclaiming that it had been "a large motor schooner, undoubtedly taking cargo to an African harbour that would comfort Rommel".

At 0130 hours a lookout reported a possible target, with the resulting action being that Stevens immediately gave the order to proceed and investigate the lights of a vessel bearing 330 degrees on a southerly course. At 0200 the vessel was seen to have French colours with the name 'Liberia' illuminated on the side. The shore station from the vicinity of Ras Mahedia was seen to be using a signalling projector. Liberia answered with an all-round lamp above the bridge. The flashing could not be understood. Stevens recalls: "I was astounded when the officer of the watch pointed out the navigation lights of a ship to the north. Tunisia was under the Vichy regime and neutral, but we were well offshore, so investigation was called for. At full speed we closed this mystery ship."

Lieutenant Stevens comments: "The status of such a ship was uncertain, so I went below to make a quick study of C-in-C Mediterranean's orders on the subject. These stated clearly that Vichy shipping was to be sunk on sight if underway after dark or outside the three-mile limit of territorial waters. She fulfilled both these conditions." The attack took place in accordance with operational B.S. article S.B. (d) which ruled that all ships in Tunisian waters south of 35 deg 46 min N were to be considered hostile at night.

Stevens ordered "Slow together! Starboard ten!" The engines slowed and the submarine came on to her firing course. "Steady as she goes! Stand-by tubes" ordered the Captain. At 0213 the order to "Fire one" was given, resulting in *P46* launching two torpedoes for the first time in anger, with depth settings set at 10 and 12 feet and 20 seconds apart, from a range of 1,000 yards. The first torpedo circled to starboard with a gyro failure and narrowly missed the submarine that had fired it. The second torpedo hit the target vessel, after running for 45 seconds, just abaft the mainmast. At 0228 the ship was seen to sink within sight of the schooner that had previously been attacked and was still burning furiously. G.W.G. Simpson described the torpedo failure as belonging to "*P46*'s outfit supplied by Maidstone and the gyro had not been prepared by the Tenth Flotilla torpedo repair party".

Diving at 0541 hours, *P46* continued on its way. After an eventful night it was back to routine, with only aircraft being sighted for the rest of the day until resurfacing to charge the batteries at 2025 hours. At 2330 hours expectations grew throughout the boat when *P46* changed course to investigate a darkened shape. Fifteen minutes later that shape was identified as land.

No further information is available regarding the N10/Aquila, except she was known to be of 306 tons. *SS* Liberia *was* built in 1905 by Russell & Co Ltd, of Greenock. Owned and operated by the Vichy French Government, she was 3,890 gross tons, with a length of 112.7 metres, a beam of 14.9 metres and a draft of 8.4 metres.

0241 hours 22nd September:

While on the surface Lascelles, who was officer of the watch, observed smoke bearing 045 degrees and summoned the captain to the bridge. At 0300 hours the object was identified as a small unescorted merchant ship southbound. Stevens passed the necessary orders to the control room to close the vessel and alter course for an attack. Having sounded the klaxon to bring the crew to diving stations, at 0325 in position 35 deg 53 min N 11 deg 09 min E, *P46* fired two torpedoes, leaving phosphorescent tracks that were clearly visible on the calm surface. Both missed, probably due to an over-estimation of the enemy's speed and under-estimation of the track angle. Five minutes later gun action was called and four rounds were fired at a range of 1,000 yards, resulting in two hits, but the enemy retaliated with unpleasantly close machine-gun fire, so *P46* dived.

The boat surfaced ten minutes later at 0350 and Stevens made the decision to shadow the vessel until moonset, keeping to just within range of sight, with the option when the opportunity arose to attack with torpedoes. Enemy speed, previously estimated as eight knots, was found to be six knots. The ship was heard to be transmitting by W/T the word 'LISA' repeatedly. At 0448 hours and having gained position on the port bow, Stevens fired three torpedoes at an estimated range of 2,000 yards. The torpedoes were set for a depth of eight feet, with a firing interval of 18 and 21 seconds. Stevens was aiming for just ahead of the vessel, the funnel and the stern, with the outcome, after a run of 1 minute and 49 seconds, being one hit registered amidships. This resulted in the entire vessel bursting into flames, which led to the conclusion that, as this was not a tanker, she must have been carrying petrol in drums. It is believed that a second torpedo also hit the target.

Later she was discovered to have been an Italian cargo vessel, SS Leonardo Palomba, built in 1899 by Strand slipway Co. Ltd, of Monkwearmouth, Scotland, with a gross tonnage of 1,097 tons. At 0510 hours Stevens reached the conclusion that having only one torpedo left, of which the gyro was suspect, it was time to lay a course back to Malta.

At 0602 hours *P46* dived. The boat was unable to send a signal back to base notifying its estimated time of arrival until 2030 hours that evening. At 1115 the watch officer reported an unidentified object to the captain, who attended the control room within seconds. On investigation this was found to be a lighthouse. Aircraft continued to be sighted five times until dark prevailed and *P46* surfaced at 2000 hours.

Now, with the hatch open, permission was given to smoke, enabling crew members to assemble below the hatch for some much-needed fresh air, which was blown through the boat due to the engines sucking in air. Signalman Ginger Hiles went straight to work on the making of the Jolly Roger ready for their arrival into the Lazaretto base. The skull and cross bones symbol was flown from the wireless mast by each submarine when returning to harbour after a patrol. On the flag were sewn white bars for torpedoing a merchantman or a red bar for a naval vessel. Similarly, a red or white star denoted a sinking by gun action. There were also special symbols for cloak-and-dagger operation, train destruction and for laying mines. *P46*'s flag would proudly contain two white bars and a star.

1259 hours 23rd September:

The boat dived to negotiate a minefield, surfacing when it was safe to do so at 1545 hours. At 1815 *P46* exchanged signals with its escort, Hythe, and headed for Marsamxett Harbour. At 2054 hours, flying the Jolly Roger, the proud submarine arrived at HMS Talbot, securing alongside berth U4 to be greeted by Simpson and his fellow staff officers.

Back down the tunnel in the Lazaretto over a glass of gin, Lieutenant Stevens briefed his commanding officer on the gun actions, torpedo firings, weather, air activity, communications, ASDIC and navigational information during the patrol. Simpson remarked: "Lieutenant Stevens decided to return to Malta, since only one torpedo remained and the gyro was suspect. This decision was quite correct. In a brief five days from leaving port, *P46* destroyed two enemy vessels and one Vichien all-by-night attack, and this well-earned early success has been most valuable to the whole ship's company. Lieutenant Stevens' actions and decisions throughout were bold and offensive, and attended by the success they deserved. The correct assessment that the motor boat following the schooner was not an M.A.S. (Motoscafo Armato Silurante or Torpedo Armed Motorboat) enabled [the] attack to be carried out and I have nothing but praise for the action taken, but would stress the danger of a night attack on enemy shipping escorted by motor boats. Having been given five Electrical Artificers from Captain (S) Eight in July 1942, and these men not having been replaced to date, it seems unfair, though necessary, to remark that out of five torpedoes fired by *P46* and supplied by the Eighth Flotilla, two had circling gyro failures."

0815 hours 24th – 28th September:

All hands were employed cleaning the ship, with patrol leave being granted at 1320 hours, which enabled half the crew to enjoy a rest period, with a further quarter of the ratings granted leave until 0730 hours the following morning. As *P46*'s last home-coming, the same routine was imposed with trot sentries posted to protect the boat and the remaining crew cleaning and painting the boat.

0800 hours 29th September:

With all hands reporting back on board, the submarine, including two new shipmates, Temporary Acting Leading Seaman Joseph Bell and Stoker First Class Albert Megson, the boat slipped her mooring to embark seven torpedoes from the storage depot located further upstream. After completion, all hands returned to cleaning the boat before it moved to pontoon U3. There was speculation amongst the crew as to when the next impending patrol would be. Leave was granted from 1630 until 0730 hours. The routine of cleaning and painting continued.

0815 hours 30th September:

Cleaning the boat continued and after dinner the crew was ordered to embark the loading of stores, a sure indication that a patrol was imminent. This continued until 1600 hours, when leave was granted until 0730 hours the next morning.

Fourth Patrol

1355 hours 1ˢᵗ October:

P46 slipped her moorings and left the channel astern of her escort Hythe. At 1600 it dived for a dummy attack on Hythe, resurfacing at 1642 and diving once more at 1648 for another dummy attack. At 1655, the boat surfaced and at 1845 fired four rounds during gunnery practice. Total submerged time: 51 minutes.

0607 hours 2ⁿᵈ October:

P46 dived and proceeded submerged at a depth of 80 feet through the minefield. After continued sweeps of H/E, able-seaman Donald Stevens reported no contact or other underwater noise heard through his headphones. Meanwhile, telegraphist Frederick Horner tried unsuccessfully to make contact with HMS *Parthian*. At 2300 *P46* surfaced and zigzagged 30 degrees to either side, 15 minutes later reducing this to 20 degrees.

Seaburne-May, finding nothing in sight, was unable to take a navigation fix from Marettimo lighthouse because it was not burning and he had to rely on dead-reckoning for navigational purposes. Stevens made the decision to remain on the surface to recharge batteries. Total submerged time: 16 hours and 53 minutes.

HMS *Parthian (N75)*, commissioned 13ᵗʰ January, 1931, made numerous successful patrols transporting much-needed aviation fuel and ammunition to Malta. She was sunk early in August 1943, thought to have hit a mine.

0006 hours 3rd October:

Three heavy underwater explosions shook the boat, with no indication as to the origin. Between 0500-0600 hours Max Seaburne-May was able to take navigational fixings from Maraone, Levanzo and St Vito Light. At 0600, with the dawn light improving, Stevens sounded the klaxon and *P46* dived to periscope depth. After a quiet day, it returned to the surface at 2000 hours. A searchlight sweeping the sea from the direction of Cape St Vito was encountered at 2250 hours. Total submerged time: 14 hours.

0100 hours 4th October:

P46 commenced a patrol line off Cape Gallo some ten miles off. Hearing aircraft in the distance on five different occasions during the night, the submarine dived at 0549 hours, having completed recharging the batteries. After having breakfast, those members of the crew not on watch settled down for forty winks, only to be woken at 0915 hours by the sudden cry of "H.E. ahead, sir", which reverberated throughout the boat. Contact was made with a small 800-ton motor vessel through the haze of the periscope and Stevens identified a mast and called for the bearing to be taken. "Down periscope, port 25, Group up – up periscope." Stevens relayed the orders thick and fast until finally he had manoeuvred the submarine into the best available firing position.

Having fed all the relevant information into the 'fruit machine', at 0947 hours two torpedoes were fired from a range of 700 yards. The laden ship, which was described as having a large Samson post as well as a mast and derricks forward, altered course to starboard after sighting the run

of the torpedoes after they crossed the ship's wake – a miss.
The rest of the day was quiet and one of routine for the
disappointed crew. The boat surfaced at 2000 hours to
recharge the batteries and begin surface patrol. Total
submerged time: 14 hours 11 minutes.

0530 hours 5th October:
P46 dived. Unidentified distant explosions were heard at
1117, 1143 and 1205 hours. Having resurfaced at 1958, the
only sightings encountered by the bridge watch were
aircraft throughout the night. Total submerged time: 14
hours 8 minutes.

0212 hours 6th October:
Engines stopped in order to listen for any contact, but the
only sound to be heard was that of aircraft passing in the
distance. Dived at 0540. *P46* encountered an inquisitive
Italian Cant aircraft, which passed overhead flying at a
height of 700 feet at 0815 and returned an hour and a
quarter later at a height of just 300 feet. At 1020 hours,
distant explosions were heard throughout the boat and at
1515 the mast and two funnels of a large hospital ship were
sighted to the west. Surfacing at 2000 hours, the crew
settled in for the night. Total submerged time: 14 hours 19
minutes.

0001 hours 7th October:
Simpson's dummy wooden periscopes are jettisoned
overboard. These are perfect copies of a periscope, weighted
so as to float vertically showing three feet above the water
line. The thought behind these decoys was that the Italians

would waste time and fuel in attacking them. A rude remark was painted on each one by the crew, expressing their thoughts towards Mussolini.

Dived at 0547 hours and at 0915 ASDIC contact was made with two schooners, but as the contact could not be identified through the periscope the watch officer continued to monitor the developing situation. Finally, after clear physical contact with a convoy at 0945, Lieutenant Stevens was awakened by the officer of the watch, who had sighted through the periscope two merchant ships and three schooners in the distance, as well as increased aircraft activity. After careful assessment of the situation, Stevens came to the conclusion that the convoy was too far ahead and could not be caught up. Once again at 1515 the captain was called to the control room after a lighted vessel, with a mast and funnel was sighted. It was finally identified at 1530 as a Virgilio class hospital ship. Having spent a total of 14 hours and 15 minutes below the waves, Stevens surfaced the submarine at 2002 hours, setting a course for Cape Suvero, to begin another night on the surface.

0542 hours 8th October:
P46 dived. At 0655 a convoy of three 3,000 tons merchant vessels, in ballast (unloaded) and one Partenope class destroyer were sighted through the periscope, heading northbound, three miles offshore. Stevens concluded that as the vessels were travelling in ballast, they did not qualify as legitimate targets and he would save his precious torpedoes for a more suitable victim. At 0710 the leading ship was identified as being camouflaged blue and grey, with the remaining two painted grey. *P46* was by now off

the Calabrian coast, where the mountains run down close to the sea, and the railway connecting Rome to the toe of Italy and Sicily runs along the water's edge. Lieutenant Stevens decided that as Operational Orders pointed out the possibilities of gun action against southbound trains, *P46* would try her luck against such a target. Having sighted a 200-ton schooner to the north of their position at 0720, the submarine commenced reconnoitring the coast for the possibility of night gun action against a train.

During the morning Stevens, with Noll and Lascelles, examined the charts of the area on the wardroom table, formulating a plan and identifying the best location for an attack, considering the coastal defences and 'what if' scenarios. After much debate, Stevens eventually announced that the operation was "on" and a plan of action was formulated. The news went round boat and enthusiasm quickly spread. Powell was summoned to the wardroom, where he received instructions to prepare for gun action that evening.

A two-masted schooner was left to continue her journey when sighted at 0930 and an ASDIC contact and a confirmed sighting of three schooners was also ignored at 1155 hours. This was due possibly to the fact that John Stevens did not wish to give away the position of the submarine. Having found a suitable location (39 deg 04 min N 16 deg 56 min E) from which to launch a night attack, *P46* patrolled a line parallel to this location three miles offshore, but ready to come in close with the setting of the sun. The schooners returned at 1330 and were left to pass unmolested.

The boat surfaced at 2000 hours, Stevens being the first on the bridge, followed by Petty Officer Telegraphist Lewis, who began carefully looking around the horizon through binoculars. As there was nothing in sight except for the land bulking dimly in the west, after a few minutes the Captain could be heard down the voice pipe "Officer of the Watch and look-outs up. Standing charge starboard and carry on patrol routine when you're ready Number One!" The orders were repeated back, and all at once the crew began to move about. Telegraphs clanged, and with a few wheezing coughs the starboard engine burst into life. Fresh air came down the hatch and mixed with the stale, sweaty skin it began to put new life into those below. The blood began to flow quicker with each new intake of breath and the brain became clearer, eyelids opened, eyes focused and the laboured effort of breathing became easier. The order to "carry on smoking" was given by Noll.

Having spent 14 hours and 18 minutes in the depths of the Mediterranean, Stanley Powell, the gun layer, and Henry Preece, the gun trainer, immediately went into action by carrying out a number of dummy practice attacks, after which Powell buffed his gun and wiped his oily hands in cotton waste, as no trains passed by until 2130 hours when one southbound train was observed. The lookouts sighted the lights of another southbound train at 2230, resulting in *P46* closing inshore ready to attack. Unfortunately, the boat was unable to get close enough. When it finally reached its best position it remained stationary on the surface, keeping visual and hydrophone watch until a suitable target came into range. The captain tells us "the effective range of the 3-inch gun at night was not more than 1,000 yards". Northbound trains were sighted frequently and the only southbound train to pass was an engine with one or two trucks, which was not attacked.

0205 hours 9th October:

Lieutenant Stevens inform us "a northbound train appeared – we let it pass; then a second and a third. Finally, after all the nerve-racking waiting, the headlight of another southbound train came in sight. The boat opened fire and several hits were seen, the train rolling to a halt half-a-mile down the line. [We felt] that we had at least tweaked Mussolini's tail by giving his soldiers a delayed and uncomfortable return from their weekend. We withdrew to seaward discreetly and Hiles was instructed to add a suitable railway insignia to the Jolly Roger".

Lascelles also remembers the action as a time when "we tried to shoot up an Italian train, the theory being that as the Italians were bombing us in Malta, the train drivers would not like being shot up at night time. Waiting two miles off the coast for a train to go by is a rather anxious [time]. In fact, we had to wait four hours for the train but it was worthwhile in the end".

In total, nine rounds were fired, with two hits being observed. The train comprised eight passenger coaches with hits striking home on the second and third carriages. The rate of fire was very slow due to a breech jamming half open after firing each of the first five or six rounds. The attack conditions were good with a flat calm sea. Stevens says: "While the results of this shoot were disappointing, it is hoped that it had some moral effect."

At 0545 hours Stevens gave the order to dive. The sound of the klaxon echoed throughout the boat, resulting in the deck watch scurrying down the bridge hatch, followed lastly by the captain. *P46* dived to periscope depth and proceeded northward three miles off the coast. At 0700 hours a large

Unruffled under way

The sinking of the Loretto

Timoshenko, the ship's cat

Unloading stores at Malta

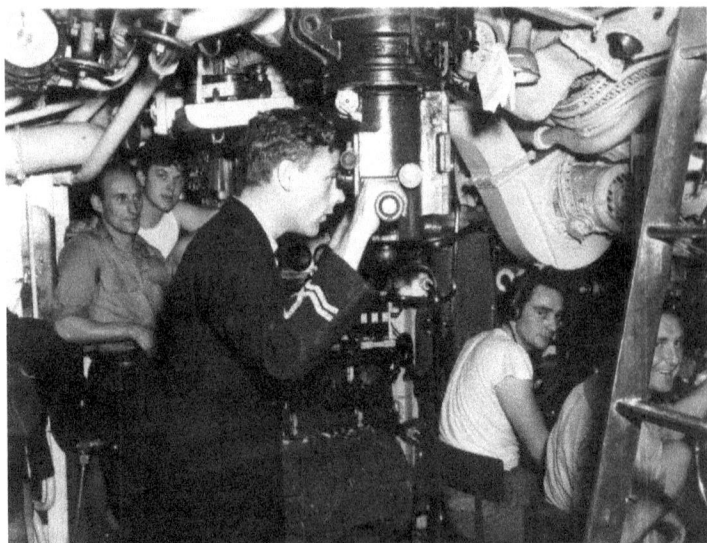

Officer at periscope

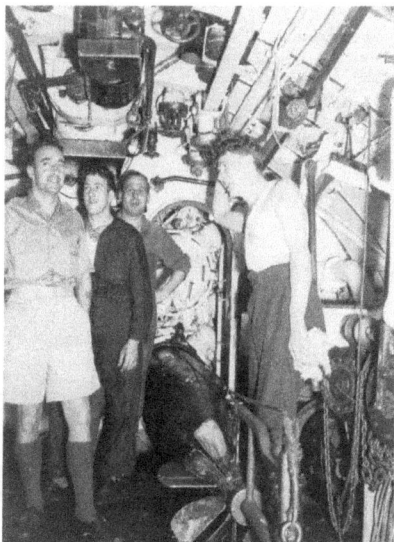
Loading a torpedo

Crew members on the casing

Crew members with the Jolly Roger

HMS Fort Talbot - the Lazaretto

Crew members hoisting the Jolly Roger

Crew attending Colchester celebrations

John Stevens revisits Colchester

schooner with aircraft escort was sighted, but because of the escort the decision was made to avoid any conflict. Those off-watch slept soundly in their bunks or wherever they could find a space to lay, when a two-masted schooner passed at 0855 hours and another two schooners at 1102. An Italian Atlante class tug was sighted at 1135 sweeping for mines, with additional southbound schooners observed at 1310 and 1345. The boat surfaced at 2002 hours, light from ashore signalling unintelligible Morse code to seaward was sighted by the officer of the watch at 2115 hours. Total submerged time: 14 hours and 17 minutes.

0547 hours 10th October:

After a night of heavy air activity, which continued throughout the day, *P46* dived and then re-surfaced at 2002 hours after 14 hours and 15 minutes below the surface.

0235 hours 11th October:

A lookout on the bridge reported sighting a small darkened vessel stopped and drifting and Stevens concluded it was a schooner on anti-submarine patrol. Another was observed at 0423. *P46* dived at 0550 after another active night of patrolling aircraft. At 0710, after sighting another anti-submarine schooner, the submarine dived a little deeper, returning to periscope depth at 0810 hours, when the masts and funnels of a ship was observed. The ship was thought to be proceeding to the west of Capri and, as *P46* was in an unfavourable position, the order was given to increase speed. The vessel was again observed through the periscope at 0840 at a range of 5,000 yards and Stevens ordered an attack to commence.

At 0904 hours Stevens fired three torpedoes from a range of 4,000 yards, allowing for a speed of seven knots. All three torpedoes missed their target, which was estimated to be a 2,500-ton ship with a deck cargo of crates. Stevens continues the description of the event, saying: "Having sighted the bubbling torpedo tracks, she took fright and reversed course to return to Naples. This brought her closer to *P46*, and half an hour later I aimed the only torpedo ready for firing. This hit; she caught fire and sank later. Very soon destroyers and corvettes were sweeping the area with ASDIC, but luck was with us. Slowly, and at depth, we withdrew unmolested."

The target proved to be the 1,400 ton Una of Yugoslav registry. The Patrol Report for this action also states that in position 40 deg 30 min N 15 deg 15.5 min E and from a range of 1,400 yards, the torpedo hit the doomed motor vessel just forward of the funnel after a duration of one minute. The ship burst into flames and for the next five minutes small explosions were heard through the headphones of the ASDIC. *P46* returned to periscope depth at 1035 hours. From his view through the periscope Stevens could no longer see the Merchant vessel, but in its place was a trawler-type vessel which it was presumed had stopped to pick up survivors. Cant aircraft were seen also searching the area.

At 1410 hours, in position 42 deg 22 min N 14 deg 15 min E, the mast and funnel of a hospital ship were sighted and one Climene class destroyer, evidently hunting for *P46*, was observed at 1500 hours. By 1600 another destroyer had joined the hunt, so *P46* went deeper and took the appropriate avoiding action by slowly turning away in the opposite direction at 3 knots. One destroyer closed, sweeping with the ASDIC. She went dead slow ahead, crossing *P46* 3,000 yards astern, but was unable to make contact with the submarine. To the relief of the crew, by 1800 neither destroyer could be seen through the periscope.

The submarine surfaced at 1958 hours and set course for Cape Gallo, with more dummy periscopes being jettisoned in an attempt to confuse the enemy. At 2101 the boat had to crash dive due to the sighting of a small darkened vessel ahead of them. Stevens gave the order to surface at 2140 hours, but due to H/E reporting a fast turbine approaching from the port quarter, Stevens dived the boat once more. With the H/E fading to the north-east, *P46* surfaced at 2235 and proceeded on its way. After spending 15 hours and 27 minutes submerged, the crew were relieved to once again experience fresh air being driven in by the boat's engines. 'Wiggy' Bennett could be heard singing in his galley, preparing hot food which consisted of pea soup for starters followed by a main course of roast veal, roast potatoes and tinned cabbage and finishing off with boiled rice and tinned apricots. Greasy dark brown cocoa was to follow.

0545 hours 12th October:
Having endured a quiet night with no planes sighted or vessel movements, *P46* dived. An uneventful day was to follow with the ship's crew on normal routine and those off-duty either playing games, writing letters, reading or sleeping. The boat surfaced at 2000 hours in preparation for night patrol, with the crew finally able to smoke after spending 14 hours and 15 minutes submerged in their 'tin

can'. Timoshenko also enjoyed the cool air now filtering through the boat.

0425 hours 13th October:

After having encountered aircraft throughout the night, ASDIC reported hydrophone contact of turbines approaching and seven minutes later a green light was sighted. To avoid contact, Stevens dived to 80 feet for ten minutes before ordering the boat to periscope depth. After a good look around they resurfaced at 0455. On final completion of a full battery charge, the boat dived at 0546. Aircraft activity was still heightened, with a sighting of a motor launch at 0720. At 1355 distant depth charges could be heard throughout the boat, resulting in a Cant aircraft, flying at 1,500 feet, being sighted at 1520, zigzagging to the westward.

At 1640 the masts and funnels of a ship were sighted close inshore, resulting in the crew being called to diving stations at 1700 to ensure that everyone on board was ready for the attack. Commencing the attack at 1720, *P46* fired two torpedoes at 1733 directed at an *Italian motor vessel in ballast, which had a gun fitted aft, resulting in one confirmed hit in position 38 deg 14 min N 13 deg 14 E from a range of 1,150 yards. The speed was calculated at 7 knots and the depth setting 6 feet. The vessel sank at 1745, with one boatload of survivors seen drifting in the slight sea.

The second torpedo hit Genmine Island after 1 minute and 56 seconds, enabling Lascelles, the navigator, to get a good fix by range and bearing. Stevens recalls this action by stating: "One more sinking swelled the bag for this patrol; it happened off Palermo. In late afternoon a Cant flying boat was sighted weaving about over the western horizon. This usually presaged an approaching ship, and later masts and a funnel could be seen. Then the ship herself, a seedy old tramp, the Italian Loreto, of 1,000 tons. The flying boat escort caused no concern, one of our last torpedoes hitting right aft, and she settled by the stern and sank."

After 14 hours 37 minutes submerged, *P46* re-surfaced at 2000 hours, immediately commencing a zigzagging course of 20 degrees either side. A message was sent back to Malta at 2139 recording their success. In reply, they received back the signal that the crew had been waiting for – the recall to Malta, which was received at 2210. An intermittent searchlight at 2218 brought everyone back to reality and put the watchkeepers on their highest alert.

*Commissioned by G. Lamy & cie, Caen, the cargo steamship 'Astree' was completed in 1912 at the Sunderland Shipbuilding Co boatyard in County Durham. Designed at 1055 gross ton, 223 feet in length, with a 33 feet beam and a draft of 13 feet 8 inches, this single screw 3-cylinder steam ship was capable of a trial speed of 11 knots. Sold in 1933 to Italian owners and renamed 'Loreto' the vessel was purchased by Lauro Lines, Naples, in 1937.

(Author's note: Within the pages of Dr. Alberto Santoni's study 'Il Vero Traditore' together with Jack Greene and Alessandro Massignani's book titled 'Rommel's North Africa Campaign' references implying that at the time of her sinking the 'Loreto' was transporting one hundred British Indian Army prisoners of war. An Axis signal had been intercepted on the 9th October and re-transmitted as an Ultra warning by the Allies stating 'Loreto will sail from Tripoli at 9.00 a.m. of the 9th, speed 7 knots, and should arrive to

Naples at 07.30 a.m. of the 13th. It will transport 350 POWs'. The reference referred to is sourced from a report of the Admiralty dated 20th November, 1942 which does not have a protocol number and unsigned, titled 'Italian Ships Transporting POW's which says: 'The Mediterranean authorities are always informed of the ships transporting POWs.' Two of these ships were sunk while returning to Italy: Loreto sailed from Tripoli on 9th October 1942 and was sunk by submarine P46 on the 13th October and the information that the ships had POWs on board was signalled to Mediterranean authorities on the 8th. Scillin was sunk by P212 on the 14th November 1942 and the message was transmitted to Mediterranean authorities on 13th November, specifying that the ship was transporting POWs. To avoid such tragedies in the future, the same 20 November 1942 report supplied the names of 29 Italian ships used for transporting POWs between 9 June and 1 August 1942 and 20 November 1942, with the ports, dates of sailing and arrival, and number of POWs on board. This would serve to identify the ships equipped for the transport of POWs, and avoid their sinking. In conclusion, it can be affirmed that it is difficult to abort war missions in progress, especially those of submarine.' Having been unsuccessful in collaborating this signal and details surrounding the prisoners of war as there are no references within the research material, archives or historical accounts, the author leaves the reader to come to their own conclusions. Due to the difficult communication conditions in the Mediterranean, if such a signal was sent, it was possible that P46 did not receive the transmission.

0547 hours 14th October:

P46 dived to a depth of 120 feet and commenced passage through a minefield. Distant depth charges could be heard at 1015 hours. After coming up to periscope depth, a motor vessel was sighted at 1100 hours and there was aircraft activity all afternoon. The boat surfaced at 2000 hours and the crew endured a quiet night, which allowed time for signalman Hiles to add another white bar to the Jolly Roger. Total submerged time: 14 hours 13 minutes.

0530 hours 15th October:

P46 dived after hearing depth-charging in the near vicinity and again at 1740 that afternoon. It surfaced at 1945 after spending 14 hours 15 minutes submerged. The ratings began to clean the boat ready for their entrance into Valletta Harbour.

0500 hours 16th October:

The welcome sight of Gozo was observed through the periscope. *P46* dived at 0730, surfacing at 1600 hours for navigational purposes, then dived again at 1612, having set course to meet up with its escort. *P46* surfaced at 1700 when the escort minesweeper Speedy and *P212* (HMS *Sahib*) were sighted, but had to dive once more at 1728, due to an air-raid over the dock area. Once the all-clear was given, *P46* surfaced at 1806 to follow its escort up the channel, now cleared of mines. The submarine finally docked at berth U4 back at the Lazaretto at 1923 hours, to the delight of Simpson. Total submerged time: 9 hours and 20 minutes. Leave was granted to two-thirds of the crew, who immediately took a bath and had a meal down in the caverns of their new home.

17th-30th October:

The remaining matelots spent the next few days cleaning the boat, which slipped its moorings at 0830 hours on the 20th to load eight torpedoes in anticipation for the next patrol. This exercise was completed at 1630 when *P46* moored at berth U4. During this period, First Lieutenant Gordon Noll exchanged fond farewells with the fellow officers and crew he had served with during the past four patrols. Noll had been recalled to the UK to undertake the CO's qualifying course, the perisher course. This enabled Seaburne-May to succeed him as first lieutenant, after being informed by Captain (S) Simpson "you'd better put up another stripe, it will look better now that you are a 'Jimmy', but I doubt that we can fix the paperwork to get you any more pay for it". Oliver Lascelles became second lieutenant, with a new face - Acting Lieutenant John Fenton (RN) - welcomed on board as the new navigator.

The following day there was even more cleaning and painting of the boat, with the afternoon spent at make-and-mend. Those left on board were also allowed to go to the Lazaretto for recreational and domestic purposes, i.e. washing clothes or visiting the cinema. The crew had exchanged places with their fellow matelots over the last few days, which enabled everyone to have some leave time. This routine continued until the 30th October, when all ratings reported back on board in anticipation of the next patrol.

0830 hours 31st October:

P46 slipped its moorings and proceeded to embark fresh water, which took half an hour to complete. At 0940, during this harbour operation, a berthing wire fouled one of the propellers, resulting in an emergency docking in case a propeller required changing or repairing. Hence, at 1515 *P46* proceeded to Grand Harbour to enter No 1 dock for repair, arriving an hour later.

Unfortunately, the submarine's logs for this next vital patrol are not available from the National Archive and the following daily diary has been taken from the Patrol Report submitted by Lieutenant Stevens to Captain (S) G.W.G. Simpson at the end of the patrol and the patrol report submitted by Captain (S). This fifth patrol took place during the first phase of Operation Torch, the British-American invasion of French North Africa which started on the 8th November, 1942. This armada comprised over 100 warships, transports and cargo vessels under the command of Rear-Admiral H. Kent Hewitt, USN, with the objective of landing troops at Casablanca, Oran and Algiers.

Shrimp Simpson had received orders from Admiral Lord Cunningham, Commander-in-Chief Mediterranean Station, to dispose his submarines to "entrap the Italian fleet should it move to interfere [with] the Torch landings". On completion of the operation, Simpson was ordered to switch his central Mediterranean submarines to their normal but vital duties of preventing supplies reaching North Africa.

Simpson remarked: "At this time I received steady reinforcement from both East (Gibraltar) and West (Alexandria), and my command expanded to 26 submarines towards the end of November. The re-supply position in Malta was very critical in late October and a ruse was attempted by sending two unescorted Merchant ships along the North African coast within French territorial waters, but they were both intercepted and interned at Bizerta."

With the submarine in Grand Harbour undergoing repair, Captain (S) George Simpson wrote on November 1: "*P46* was to have sailed on the 1st November, but due to a rating on the after-casing allowing the stern bow wire to foul the after-planes without reporting it, the wire fouled the port propeller when the submarine went ahead, and *P37*, HMS *Upholder*, commanded by Malcolm David Wanklyn, VC, was sailed instead, since a 24-hour delay was not acceptable in order to reach the original patrol position NW of Cape Milazzo. This incident corroborated the proverb 'It's an ill wind that blows nobody any good'. Divers cleared the obstruction before midnight, enabling the submarine to sail on 2nd November, and take over *P37's* original position."

Fifth Patrol

1000 hours, 2nd November:

P46 slipped her moorings and, in the company of *P44* (HMS *United)* and *P35* (HMS *Umbra),* with 'Speedy' acting as escort, proceeded out of the harbour to negotiate the boom. Following her escort, Stephens opened his sealed orders, directing *P46* to a position three miles from Cape St Vito. This placed the boat at the inshore position in a line of five submarines at ten-mile intervals, the intention being to prevent the Italian Fleet from interfering with Operation Torch. Although Lieutenant Stevens had already been briefed by Captain (S). These necessary orders gave reference to their forthcoming patrol and soon he would inform the crew of the importance of the task that lay ahead.

Lieutenant Stevens recalls in his autobiography: "It was a thrill to open up the Torch Operational Orders to get an idea of that bold plan. At last, after more than three long years of war, during which things had, for the most part, gone well for our foes and badly for us, the Allies were to make a large offensive move. In command of all Torch forces was General Dwight Eisenhower, hitherto little known to the Allied nations, with headquarters on Gibraltar for the assault phase. It was heartening to learn that the Naval Commander of the Allied Expeditionary Force was the redoubtable Admiral Sir Andrew Cunningham, well known throughout the Fleet by his initials A.B.C. The aim of Torch submarines was to attack enemy warships that might interfere with the Allied landings. Enemy supply ships were to be disregarded until three days after the landings." At 1740 hours *P46* parted company with her escort and set course as ordered.

0550 hours 3rd November:
P46 dived to a depth of 125 feet to negotiate the known minefield. Surfacing at 1954, the order "Lookouts to the bridge, patrol routine" was given and Fenton, the navigator, was able to take bearings from Marettimo lighthouse seen in the distance.

0505 hours 4th November:
The signal station on Cape St Vito was observed sending Morse code to an unknown recipient. *P46* dived for the day at 0530 hours. A small merchant ship was sighted through the periscope close inshore at 0745. A Climene class torpedo boat was sighted at 0810 and a Leone class destroyer at

0940. Three minesweepers were also sighted at 1030 steering NW on a heading of 150 degrees. These were seen 20 minutes later turning in a southward direction. At 1430 hours two Abba class destroyers were sighted heading west. Having received orders from 'Shrimp' Simpson to investigate the approaches to Palermo, *P46* surfaced at 1855 hours and proceeded to a position four to eight miles off the Sicilian capital for night watch patrol. By 2108 two darkened vessels were spotted and identified as probable torpedo boats. Stopping engines in a position five to seven miles off Palermo breakwater between the hours of 2130-0030, nothing could be heard on ASDIC, by the lookouts through their binoculars, or seen by the naked eye.

0030 hours 5th November:
Stevens set a new course to assume a patrol position off Cape St Vito, but had to alter course at 0330 following the sighting of a fast motorboat close inshore. Stevens ordered a change of course until the danger was out of sight. The boat submerged at 0518 to begin patrolling the designated area. The sighting of three tugs towing a large dredger and one lighter close inshore at 0605 made a most tempting target, but because of orders, and the specific mission they were on, these targets were allowed to continue on their way unmolested. At 0810 a small motor yacht with Red Cross markings passed close to *P46*'s position. Two Generale class torpedo boats were sighted close inshore at 0944 and two merchant vessels travelling in ballast, estimated to be 3,000 tons, were allowed to pass at 1230 hours. Two MTBs close inshore were observed at 1310. Having surfaced that evening, the process of recharging the batteries began.

Captain Stevens went below when this action was achieved and *P46* remained on the surface with both engines stopped.

0015 hours 6th November:

An Axis E-boat was heard and *P46* dived, resurfacing 17 minutes later when the ASDIC operator reported that nothing could be heard in the surrounding area. At 0658, Stevens was awakened by the call "Captain to the control room" after an Italian U-boat, estimated at 500 tons, was sighted through the periscope by the Officer of the Watch. The Italian submarine was on the surface, speeding westwards and away from *P46*. Due to the sea conditions, an early sighting was not possible and a quick decision was required if an attack was to take place. Calling immediately for torpedoes to be brought to the ready, Stevens changed to the attack periscope and called out a snap course and speed, which was entered into the 'fruit machine' before the torpedoes could be sent on their way. The order to fire was given from a range of 3,000 yards, spread two ship's lengths, on a track of 130 degrees, only to result in the maximum salvo of four torpedoes passing, it was thought, astern of the Italian U-boat. Just two minutes after firing *P46* lost her trim for ten minutes and so the tracks of the torpedoes could not be seen, and by the time Stevens got back up to periscope depth nothing was sighted in all directions. Fenton, the navigator, and Donald Stevens, the ASDIC operator, both confirmed that the Italian submarine had been travelling at 300 revs and a speed of 10 knots.

Although not noted, one can imagine that after this action there was a conversation between the captain and first lieutenant Seaburne-May, who held the ultimate responsibility for control of the boat's trim. Captain (S), an experience submariner himself, in his report believed that "the chance of hitting would have been improved if the ten-minute attack had been shortened to improve the track angle. A track angle of 130 degrees at 3,000 yards gives a poor chance of success".

At 1120 hours a Generale class torpedo boat crossed close to *P46*'s stern and half an hour later a destroyer, approaching bow-on and at high speed, forced *P46* to dive deep and take appropriate avoiding action. At 1218 the hydrophone operator reported that the destroyer was well clear astern and Lieutenant Stevens took the opportunity to come to periscope depth for a quick look around. Normal diving routine continued, with the captain returned to the Officers mess.

At 1240 an Italian Cant aircraft was seen firing red flares to the North of *P46*'s position. At 1300 hours Stevens was again called to the control room when another large unidentified U-boat was sighted travelling on the surface at a range of 6,000 yards. Stevens relates: "We experienced more tantalising frustration when, on the horizon, the bridge top and periscope standards of another U-boat hurrying westwards came into periscope view. I closed her track at full speed at depth for half an hour, but she sped on well out of torpedo range. These proved to be the last Axis U-boats I would sight in the war. To encounter a brace within a few hours without inflicting loss or damage was hard to bear."

Unable to close the distance, *P46* gave up the chase at 1340. An hour and five minutes later, the captain was presented with a dilemma when at a range of 4,000 yards, a 3,000-ton tanker, escorted by two destroyers, came into view. Stevens concluded that he should follow his orders to the letter and so decided not to attack this valuable target, calculating that the priority of the boat was to save torpedoes in case an enemy warship should be encountered during the opening stages of Operation Torch. Simpson wrote: "This was a valuable target to let pass unchallenged but, in view of subsequent events, the decision seems justified."

The only other sighting made that day was two Italian Gregale class destroyers, making high speed close inshore. Having called diving stations to surface and recharge the batteries, the lookouts were extra vigilant, due to the circumstances behind this important patrol, while down inside the submarine the conversation revolved around the subject of the two U-boats, the tanker and future possible action.

0350 hours 7ᵗʰ November:

The officer of the watch sighted, against the beam of a searchlight, the silhouette of a destroyer-type vessel making a southerly course. Whilst dived, a cross Channel-type steamer with a gun on the forward deck was sighted passing close inshore at 0800. Captain Stevens was called to the control room at 0905 after the sighting of one tanker and a 2,000-ton Merchant vessel, escorted by a torpedo boat, passed close. So close, in fact, that *P46* was required to change position and dive deeper.

The torpedo boat acquired ASDIC contact, and the pings were clearly heard inside the submarine. Everyone held their breath in readiness for the possible splash of depth charges hitting the water and the roar of an explosion when they reached their set depth. After five minutes, with no explosions having occurred, the pings faded in the distance. The rest of day was quiet, with only the sighting of aircraft and the movement of the waves being seen through the periscope. At 1855, *P46* dived after a darkened ship, making 185 rpm, was heard by the ASDIC operator. Twenty-two minutes later contact was lost and the boat returned to the surface. Simpson believed this contact to be an unescorted Italian Regolo (also known as Capitani Romani) class light cruiser steering south-westwards. The following day on her return to Palermo, despite being escorted by six destroyers, the cruiser was attacked. Simpson also agreed with Stevens' decision to ignore all north-eastbound traffic viewed during the day. *P46* surfaced for night patrol and the recharging of the batteries at 1947 to the sound of aircraft flying in the distance.

0215 hours 8th November:
The crew received via radio signals the welcoming news that the Allied landings near Algiers and Bone had been successful. A loud cheer vibrated through the boat as they celebrated this significant event and all the talk turned to events taking place on the beaches not too far from their own position. Due to a "glassy swell" which had kicked up following the fresh winds of the previous three days, visibility through the periscope could be described as good.

At 0815, while at periscope depth, the sight of a large ocean-going tug towing a small schooner close inshore was brought to the attention of the captain, who came to the conclusion this target should be left well alone as it was possibly a 'Q' ship unit. (Q-ships were heavily armed ships with concealed weaponry designed to lure submarines into making a surface attack, thus enabling the decoy vessel the opportunity to open fire). At 0953 hours a signal from Simpson reported that one light cruiser and six destroyers were heading towards *P46* from a south-west heading at a speed of 12 knots, with an estimated time of arrival of 1140. Earlier, at 0840, reconnaissance aircraft had reported that destroyers in the Pantelleria area had met up with a Regolo class Italian cruiser from Palermo. This enemy report was promptly rebroadcast from the UK communications centre at Rugby. With this welcoming news, at 0955 Lieutenant Stevens ordered "Up periscope" for a quick look around and immediately identified masts and smoke on the horizon, with aircraft overhead.

Calling for "Diving stations" and giving the order "Down periscope", Stevens allowed four minutes before having another look around through the periscope in high power. This time he spotted the director tower of a cruiser. With the help of the aircraft report received earlier, *P46* found herself in an ideal position for a decisive attack. Stevens continues the story: "The pre-war classic conception of the submariner's art was success against such a force, with its own A/S defence and the capability of high speed with baffling zigzags. Most major exercises involving submariners included that sort of setting and the advance of a peace-time career might depend on a CO's prowess at the periscope. In war, opportunities for training in the techniques were usually non-existent, while actual encounters were rare. I put up a silent prayer that our efforts might succeed. The attack team rushed to its station and all was made ready. We closed the cruiser's estimated track for some minutes; then she was seen to alter course towards us, greatly improving our chances."

At 1005 hours *P46* was 45 degrees off the enemy's port bow, resulting in a large distance off track. Having to go deep in order to close the track, Stevens ordered full speed for a duration of five minutes, returning back to periscope depth in order to have another look at the target through the periscope. Having a quick look, Stevens found that the cruiser had altered course directly towards them, offering him a good attack position. Stevens continues: "I identified the cruiser as one of the Luigi di Savoia class; she was in fact, a Regolo, first of her class, and considerably smaller than I thought. There was no picture of a Regolo light cruiser in the Admiralty intelligence literature supplied; only a fanciful silhouette based on an artist's impression was available. The misidentification caused errors in speed estimation by plotting, as this was based on the target's masthead height."

Due to the calm sea and moderate swell, estimating the range of the intended victim proved to be difficult and, with the attack developing with the enemy up sun, visual estimation of speed was not an easy task. The hydrophone operator reported that the target was making 300 revolutions per minute, but because this would have given this 6-inch gun cruiser a speed of 27 knots, this important detail was disregarded and a final plot speed of 20 knots was accepted. The cruiser and destroyer screen, which was spaced out well clear of the cruiser, appeared to be zigzagging by single turns and there was found to be a convenient gap in the screen on the enemy's port bow, which allowed *P46* to pass through without interference. It was found that three Italian Gregale class destroyers were ahead of the cruiser, with the remainder of the escorts comprising torpedo boats.

Lieutenant Stevens describes the attack:

"Passing between two screening destroyers without molestation, we arrived in position to fire a four-torpedo salvo at 1,500 yards range. With the strong escort, there was no question of staying at periscope depth to watch for a torpedo hit; as soon as the last torpedo was on its way we were on our way to the depths and taking other evasive measures. We heard one torpedo hit a minute after firing. It is probable that due to estimated speed error, three torpedoes missed ahead, while her bow was hit by the fourth."

Indeed, four torpedoes were fired at 11-second intervals, with a depth setting of between 12 and 14 feet, from a range of 2,100 yards, spread over two ships' lengths on an 80 degree track in position 38 deg 14 min N 12 deg 43.5 min E. However, due to an incorrect height of 85 feet being used for ranging purposes, it is probable that the actual firing range was about 1,500 yards. One torpedo was heard by the crew to have hit its target after a duration of 1 minute 17 seconds after firing. Immediate avoiding action was taken by altering course towards the stern of the enemy vessel and going full speed for three minutes, after which slow speed was used. Lieutenant Stevens says: "Three escorts counter-attacked for one and half hours, dropping 40 depth charges, none close enough to cause damage. Meanwhile, we were creeping away, silent and deep, to the west. As we had fired all torpedoes on board, I decided to surface to report to

Captain (S) in Malta, to enable other boats to finish the cruiser off if necessary."

In actual fact, the first depth charge was heard seven minutes after the attack, with 14 more heard in the next hour. It seemed likely that three vessels took part in the hunt, while the remainder stood by the cruiser. The hunting vessels were using ASDIC and appeared to be in good contact on a number of occasions. It was suggested that the time interval between the torpedo hitting its target and the counter-measures used against *P46* was due to the fact that the ship's company was at Divine service, as it was Sunday forenoon and the Italians, as devout Roman Catholics, were attending service.

As ASDIC reported no H/E contact at 1245, Lieutenant Stevens decided to come up to periscope depth for a quick look around. He noticed the destroyers circling and making smoke in the vicinity of where the attack had taken place. He decided to continue on a westerly course, at depth and at a speed of five knots, so that he could make a report to Malta as quickly as possible.

At 1428, after a long look through the periscope, Stevens decided it was safe to surface. Although this was a risky manoeuvre, he believed that it was imperative to get a message sent back to Malta. A smoke screen could be seen on the horizon, close to the scene of the action. He explains: "I decided to surface to report to Captain (S) in Malta to enable other boats to finish the cruiser off if necessary. Through the binoculars I could see mast tops of destroyers circling the cruiser, and laying smoke screens. Aircraft were patrolling the area, but failed to sight us. As our presence was well compromised, it was gratifying that Malta W/T answered our first radio call; it was not unknown for ships to blaze away into the ether at full power for long periods and then to be answered by Bermuda or Whitehall W/T."

The signal read as follows:

'Captain (S) repeated ANCXF from *P46*. Emergency. One hit on a cruiser, now stopped 6 miles Cape St Vito 340 deg. All torpedoes expended. Returning Malta by reverse outward route'.

Stevens continues: "It was frustrating to have stopped and crippled the cruiser without having the means to finish her off. By chance, the officer of the watch in *P44 (United)* ten miles to seaward of *P46* was searching the horizon by periscope on a bearing which gave him a view of the plume of water pushed up by our torpedo hit. He could not see the ships, as they were below his horizon". At 1445 hours *P46* dived and made her way back to Malta as all torpedoes had been expended, although she still had plenty of 3-inch shells stored in the torpedo space.

0515 9th November:

P46 commenced passage through the minefield at a depth of 120 feet. The daily tot of rum tasted that bit sweeter as the matelots were buoyant and in a jovial mood, for it was their first success against an elusive naval cruiser and they were going back to port. Even Timoshenko celebrated by devouring a tin of lobster.

1300 hours 11th November:

P46 docked at Malta after being escorted into the harbour. There on the pontoon to greet their arrival stood a beaming Captain (S) G.W.G. Simpson. In fact, George Simpson had

radioed a message soon after the report from *P46* to Ben
Bryant, commander of *P211*, HMS *Safari*, instructing him
to finish off the crippled cruiser, before she reached
Palermo. *Safari* was able to get inside the screen of the 14
protecting vessels, but these ships were able to cover a good
area and *Safari* was thwarted by their repeated weaving.
From 1945-0100 hours Bryant continually tried to evade the
destroyers, which were just 600 yards from his position.
P44, commanded by Lieutenant Thomas Barlow, also
received instructions to intercept but had already altered
course after witnessing the torpedo striking the cruiser. By
1356 she also sighted the cruiser and proceeded at depth to
enhance her position of attack, and at 1549 fired two
torpedoes from a range of 8,200 yards. Neither torpedo,
however, managed to deliver the fatal blow.

Simpson wrote: "This was a boldly executed and
successful attack on an important enemy unit and is the
sixth success by Lieutenant Stevens since his arrival on the
Mediterranean station in September of this year, and
recommendations for awards are being forwarded under
separate cover." He also added: "Identified as a Savoia class
when, in fact, it was a Regolo class, the masthead height
used was far too great, with the result that the visual plot
also gave too great a speed. H/D reported 300 revs, which
was probably due to double counting, but confirmed a high
speed. One hit occurred at 1 minute 17 seconds from firing,
which was undoubtedly the last torpedo, therefore the
correct range was approximately 1,280 yards."

P46 had, in fact, blown the bow of the Attilio Regolo,
confusingly the same name as the vessel class name. Her
build completion was May 1942, with a deadweight tonnage

of 5,420 tons, 142.2 metres in length and a beam of 14.4 metres. Designed to outspeed any vessel of the French fleet, she had a claimed trial speed of 43 knots, and was armed with eight 135mm guns, eight 37mm guns, eight 20mm guns and eight torpedo tubes, and able to carry 70 mines. Having left Palermo on a mission to set minefields, she returned to Palermo for extensive repairs under her own power. Although these repairs were completed, she never returned to service in the Italian navy and was later given to France and renamed Chateaurenault.

Lieutenant Stevens tells us "reconnaissance reported [seeing] the cruiser, minus 60 feet of her bow part, stopped with tugs around her. Captain (S) repositioned some boats, and there were several attacks in a night melee on the heavily escorted vessel as she was under tow. She docked in Palermo the following day. Attilio Regolo took no further part in the war [the Italian surrender came in 1943]. Twenty years later, at Toulon, I was able to walk from her rebuilt bow to her stern. It was the only anti-Torch sortie by the Italian Fleet surface forces, which at the time were embarrassed by a fuel shortage. The success of the landings and the lack of enemy activity made for a dearth of sensational items for General Eisenhower's first press conference as Supremo at his Gibraltar H.Q. So, in *P46*, we hit the British headlines. 'I'll tell you about the maddest submarine captain in the British Navy,' the General was reported as saying. 'He is Lieutenant J. S. Stevens, who saw an Italian cruiser through his periscope, fired a torpedo and badly crippled her, then prepared to finish her off, but found that he had been fighting so hard that he had run out of torpedoes and ammunition. He then surfaced and radioed his location for other units to take care of her'."

Stevens reminisces: "The British press fastened on to the "maddest" epithet with gusto, and used it for some time to come. General Eisenhower was, of course, using the word in its usual American sense of 'annoyed' or 'frustrated', but the press did not choose to stress this."

Simpson and Stevens headed towards the underground complex at the Lazaretto to discuss the patrol over a quiet drink or two. Stevens reported that the number of vessels sighted in the area was most remarkable in comparison to his previous experience. Whereas small schooners and merchant vessels had been the major traffic, in just four days 20 destroyers or torpedo boats were sighted, either singularly or in pairs. Additional helpful information to Simpson was that a very powerful searchlight, mounted fairly high up near Cape Rosso, was strong enough to illuminate *P46* and a destroyer was observed silhouetted against the beam at least 4,000 yards away. Regarding the recognition of the cruiser, Stevens confesses: "There are only two aids to identifying one Regolo class. They are the drawing in the latest Jane's Fighting Ships and a silhouette issued by the War Vessels Silhouette Identification Book, which had not yet been received on board *P46*. They were both inaccurate, particularly so in Jane's".

When asked about enemy A/S measures, Stevens replied "On the 7th when a single torpedo boat was heard to be transmitting at a very short range, no increase in speed was noticed. After the attack on the cruiser, it is thought that three A/S craft participated in the hunt. Two used 13 K/cs and the third 17 K/cs. All depth charges were dropped singly". He added: "A/S air patrols were observed fairly frequently." Stevens also highlights the inexperience of the

Hydrophone/ASDIC operator by stating "as he had only joined the navy in September 1940, the high standard expected could not be obtained when compared to an experienced operator".

As soon as the order 'Finished with main motor' and the steering became hard, all those from the watches designated first-leave entitlement piled inboard for a hot bath. Those on duty watch began the task of giving the boat a good clear-up and clean, savouring their bath until 1600 hours when, individually, they could take a leisurely stroll to the bath house. Owing to a shortage of meat and a temporary order to conserve the food supplies of the Island, the rations were to be cut yet again. It was hoped that due to the recent success in North Africa this would be only a temporary measure until a convoy could resupply the dwindling stocks. The quantity of *zibeg* (pasta) in vegetable soup, or *minestra*, would be reduced by half. Beans and peas were only available on Tuesdays and Fridays and the portions of tinned fish was cut by a tenth. On the 20th November crowds flocked to the bastions overlooking Grand Harbour to welcome four merchant vessels loaded with essential supplies both for the population and the Services.

12th - 15th November:
The duty watch slipped the mooring and proceeded to load torpedoes, after which they returned to their allotted pontoon to load ammunition, fuel, lubricants, water and food.

Sixth Patrol

1200 hours 16th November:

With all the crew reporting back on board after a recall, *P46* left her mooring bound for the swept channel, escorted by 'Rye', receiving orders at 1330 to sail in the vicinity of Lampion with despatch.

0300 hours 17th November:

P46 had reached a position 12 miles outside Lampion (smallest of the Pelagian Islands) as instructed. Nothing was sighted. By 1800 she surfaced and set a course for the vicinity of Sirte.

At 1400 hours a small unusual floating mine was seen. As it was of an unknown design a drawing was submitted with the patrol report for Captain (S) to refer to when back at Malta.

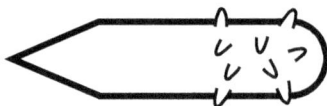

0700 hours 18th November:

P46 arrived at her patrol area, which put them within 20 miles of Sirte.

19th - 20th November:

Due to a heavy swell with gale-force winds up to F5-6, *P46* spent her patrolling time at depth, only coming up to periscope depth for wireless routines and periscope observations. Those officers and ratings who were off duty probably turned to sources of recreation such as uckers, cribbage, chess or dominoes, with the atmosphere becoming heated as they all played off different rounds to decide the boat's champion at each game. Another pastime was the construction of submarine brooches made from plastic toothbrushes. These were carved, using a penknife, to get the plastic to the right shape and then finished off with a nail-file. Finally, a groove was gouged out of the back and a safety-pin glued onto the finished brooch. These souvenirs were often given to visitors or acquaintances who had become friends after a run ashore.

21st November:

The poor weather finally moderated, allowing *P46* to resume its watch near the 20 fathom line off Sirte. Nine motor landing craft were observed at 1600 hours, travelling in groups of three. They had apparently called into Sirte for either stores or instructions as they were still laden on departure. One could be seen flying the Italian flag and had the marking 'MZ.759'. As torpedoes were not the weapon of choice for this type of shallow craft and gun action was thought to have been an unnecessary risk, no action was taken. Upon resurfacing, able-seaman Powell checked his beloved gun, just in case it might be required that evening.

0145 hours 22nd November:

While on the surface the darken shape of a westbound vessel was reported by one of the lookouts on the bridge. This was identified as a small tug and Stevens suggested it would be an ideal target for gun action practice. The conditions for this action were good, with a calm sea, bright moonlight and at a distance of 1,000 yards. Having manoeuvred into a near-perfect firing position, the order 'Fire' was given, only for the 3-inch gun to misfire. It was cleared by re-cocking.

After the first round was fired, the breech had to be hammered open and shut with the flogging hammer, resulting in a 35 seconds delay before the second round could be fired.

As luck would have it, the tug was unarmed and unable to strike back. After the firing of the first round, the tug altered course, zigzagging towards land, which was approximately five miles away. She also increased speed from five knots to ten knots, forcing *P46* to also increase speed to shorten the range.

The breech continually jammed for the next six rounds, reducing the rate of fire to two rounds per minute. Rounds seven and eight became separated from their cartridge cases and caused more serious delay while these were ejected. The remaining rounds were satisfactory as far as the working of the gun was concerned, however, the laying and training became more erratic, due to the failing light conditions and the longer range, with only two more hits being observed. In total, only five hits were registered, causing only superficial damage from a total of 45 rounds fired.

After 20 minutes the action was abandoned, all the flashless ammunition having been expended. The Axis vessel was able to proceed inshore under her own power. Able-seaman Powell muttered expletives as he descended the conning tower hatch, much to the amusement of his colleagues.

P46 dived and remained on patrol, observing the entrance to Sirte (Libya) and at 0900 hours sighted a small tug, which was presumably that which *P46* had engaged during the night. After surfacing at sunset, orders were received from Malta to change location and set a new course for the Burat area.

0430 hours 23rd November:

P46 found herself in her new ordered position eight miles from Burat light and proceeded slowly on the surface, listening for any contact on the ASDIC. From 0500 hours until dawn, *P46* remained in position without any contact or sightings being observed. The boat dived at dawn and it was not until 1155 that a small tug, similar to the one at Sirte, was sighted through the periscope. At 1215 the tug entered Burat anchorage to join another tug, one schooner and three lighters, which were already moored. Having surfaced when the light failed to recharge the batteries, four darkened shapes were reported by the bridge watch, in a northwards direction from the vicinity off Burat light buoy. These vessels were identified as three tugs or trawlers and one motorboat. Stevens began to conclude that an air-and-surface hunt was looking for *P46* when an aircraft fitted with ASV flew overhead at a height of 1,000 feet, forcing the submarine to dive. It later emerged that the aircraft was a British Wellington and the four vessels were just a coincidence, probably a convoy of small craft travelling up the coast.

0120 hours 24th November:

P46 took evasive action when a small darkened vessel was sighted close inshore. As she was either at a dead slow speed or had stopped, probably a motorboat type, it was Stevens' decision to stay well clear of this threat. Having dived, and keeping the harbour under close observation, only the one small tug was present on her moorings.

0430 hours 25ᵗʰ November:
The boat was in a position five miles off Burat light and a mile to seaward of the light buoy. After having dived for periscope patrol, the small tug was observed leaving Burat and heading along the coast. Having received the return call from Malta, *P46* set a course for home.

26ᵗʰ November:
The journey back to base was one of routine, with no sightings or targets being observed. Over the following three days the crew prepared the boat for its imminent arrival.

29ᵗʰ November:
Arrived back at the Lazaretto.

As the submarine logs are missing, a daily report of activities cannot be established. One can only surmise that the usual routine when entering port took place, such as Stevens reporting to Captain (S), the re-supply of torpedoes, leave granted, swimming, painting and cleaning the boat, together with the loading of fresh water, oil lubricants, fuel and fresh supplies.

7ᵗʰ Patrol

1300 hours 10ᵗʰ December:
P46 left Malta escorted by Hythe in company with the supply submarine *N75, Parthian*. Both parted company to go their separate ways at 1554. *N75* was to return to Malta two days later with a serious defect, which required her to be dry-docked and repaired. At 1730 hours *P46* passed a convoy of merchant vessels being escorted by HMS Orion, a

light cruiser of the Leander class, and destroyers bound for Malta.

Known as Operation Quadrangle, the convoy consisted of the two merchant ships American Packer and Ozarda, both of which had sailed from Port Said and were escorted by the minesweepers Boston, Cromarty and Whitehaven, to be joined by the destroyers Dulverton, Hurworth and Paladin from Alexandria, the destroyer *Belvoir* from Tobruk and the destroyers Orion, Croome, Aldenham, Exmoor and Hursley from Malta.

11th December:

The boat proceeded at a depth of 120 feet through the minefield on her way to the patrol area.

0100 hours 12th December:

After surfacing and reaching their designated patrol area at 37 deg 42 min N 10 deg 50 min E, *P46* identified an aircraft, possibly a Cant flying boat, through the search periscope at 1305, with apparent smoke coming from underneath the fuselage, and two camouflaged trawlers deceptively engaged in an A/S sweep. At 1515 there was an intermittent sighting of a large motor vessel escorted by three torpedo boats. The incident immediately brought the klaxon into operation and the call for the crew to diving stations. Though *P46* pursued the vessel, contact was lost 44 minutes later due to showery weather and a large swell. Two motor boats in line and eastbound were sighted at 1656 and then a torpedo boat, approaching ahead, forced *P46* to dive at 2025 until she had passed and cleared. At 2320 H/E reported a contact, confirmed by the bridge lookouts, as a destroyer passing to the north east. The captain ordered a change of course and speed, and with the help of Fenton, the navigator, a change in course was set for a new patrol area.

0217 hours 13th December:
P46 dived due to a destroyer closing her position. The rest of the day was quiet, with aircraft activity being described as 'slight'. At 1952 hours the submarine was forced to dive after two E-boats were seen closing their position.

0045 hours 14th December:
The only activity seen whilst surfaced was a twin-engine aircraft flying at height overhead. Having dived, and after taking a land fix through the periscope, a re-adjustment of course was ordered at 0700 hours when it was discovered that they were ten miles from their patrol position. The force of the easterly wind was not fully appreciated and had not been allowed for when calculating their position. The officer of the watch, First Lieutenant Seaburne-May, and navigator Fenton set a course along the Bizerta convoy route which would lead them back to their designated area. Timoshenko became agitated, pacing the boat and mewing.

At 1106 a circling aircraft raised hopes that this might indicate an approaching ship and an alteration of course was ordered. Stevens was summoned to the control room just as several distant explosions could be heard over a duration of four minutes. This was followed at 1116 by a heavy explosion that vibrated throughout the boat, followed by a smaller one.

Stevens, still in the control room at 1300 and calling for diving stations, sighted through the periscope the funnel of a motor vessel escorted by three aircraft overhead and he immediately ordered a change of course and an increase in speed in an attempt to intercept. Fifteen minutes later he identified a convoy of two merchant vessels in line ahead escorted by two torpedo boats bound for Tunis. The second merchant ship was identified by Lieutenant Stevens as the most suitable target and an attack commenced. This convoy consisted of the lead ship, Italian merchant vessel Honestas (built 1920 and 4,960 grt), the Italian tanker Castelverde (built 1921 and 6,666 grt) escorted by the Partenope-class torpedo boats Ardito and Fortunale together with several aircraft, including JU88s and ME110s. Stevens describes the action: "Early December found us patrolling in the Gulf of Tunis. Having sighted weaving aircraft, indicating ships below them, we ran at medium speed to intercept. A convoy of two supply ships in line ahead was sighted. A destroyer escort was stationed on either bow. The attack plan developed. 'Stand by number one tube,' I ordered from my position at the periscope. Up went the periscope again. 'Put me on to red 10 degrees and hold it there,' I instructed the young telegraphist, who was the periscope bearing reader. This was the final thing to be done before the target crossed the sighting graticule and the torpedoes were launched on their way. Out of the corner of my eye, on the edge of the periscope lens, I saw a plume of water rise up on the far side of the leading ship and a moment or so later the clunk of a torpedo hit was heard, then came the report 'Torpedoes approaching' from the ASDIC operator. I ordered a depth of 90 feet, and cancelled out attack for the present. The torpedoes passed harmlessly overhead; then we returned to periscope depth.

"The leading ship, which had been struck by a torpedo from *P212,* was losing speed and swinging off course, while the escorts were hunting *P212* on the far side from us. The second ship made an evasive jink, which was towards us, and soon three torpedoes were on their way. I saw one strike her amidships. The escort then turned their attention to us, but could not inflict more than superficial harm. After we had shaken off the escorts I sighted, both ships stopped. I fired another torpedo at our target, which had the escorts milling around her, but was encouraged to go deep before seeing the result by an aircraft flying towards us and firing a Very's light.

"The torpedo was heard to hit and the ship sank. After dark there was a very heavy explosion, which was *P212's* target blowing up."

At 1351 hours the lead ship Honestas, bound for Tunis and carrying 1,000 tons of ammunition and 50 vehicles, was struck amidships on the port side by a single torpedo from a salvo of five fired by *P212,* HMS *Sahib*, commanded by Lieutenant J.H. Bromage DSC, RN. It was hoped that by firing five torpedoes, one would overlap and strike the second merchant ship. Honestas swung off to port and immediately drifted as though the engines had been stopped. On board *P46*, the hydrophone operator reported a torpedo running on red 40 degrees and, as the bearing did not alter very quickly, *P46* dived to 40 feet until the bearing was heard to be growing aft and it was safe for the captain to order periscope depth. At 1359 a loud explosion was heard and believed to be a torpedo exploding at the end of its run.

At 1403 Stevens fired three torpedoes spread over one-and-a-half ship lengths, from a range of 2,000 yards, with a firing interval of 26 seconds and a depth setting of 14 feet. Stevens had allowed for a speed of seven knots and aimed each individually torpedo at just ahead, funnel and astern.

As the torpedo boats and six aircraft were busy concentrating on the attack of *P212*, Stevens decided to remain at periscope depth to watch the results of the salvo, only to witness his third torpedo break the surface and veer to port due to a servomotor failure. At 1405 the second torpedo hit just abaft of the funnel on the starboard side. Castelverde turned to port and immediately began to list to starboard. *P46* altered course towards the enemy's stern and dived further down into the depths in order to avoid any retaliatory action. According to Italian sources the Fortunale reported a sonar contact and was ordered to hunt for the submarine while the Ardito, which reported what appeared to be a possibly faulty sonar, picked up survivors. Fortunale carried out four depth charge runs and then returned to help pick up survivors. Ardito saved 174 sailors from the cold sea and the Fortunale 96. Two bombs were also reportedly dropped from an R.S.14 Italian aircraft. The first pattern of depth charges started at 1428 hours when four 'tin-cans' descended into the blackness of the sea and exploded fairly close to the fragile shell of the submarine, but not close enough to do any damage. The subsequent hunt that followed lasted 21 minutes, with 27 depth charges being dropped. This resulted in a few light bulbs having to be replaced. *P212* was not counter-attacked. By 1533, the Fortunale returned to help pick up survivors and Stevens ordered the boat to periscope depth, none the worse following the attack.

Stevens noticed that "both ships had stopped. I fired another torpedo at our target, which had the escorts milling around her, but was encouraged to go deep before seeing the results by an aircraft flying towards us and firing a Very['s] light. The torpedo hit, and the ship sank". This action happened at 1553 when, from a range of 6,000 yards, one torpedo, set at a depth of ten feet and aimed at the foremast, was fired at the Castelverde. Two minutes later, on observing an aircraft firing three red and one white star Very light along the torpedo tracks, *P46* went deep and took the appropriate avoiding action. At 1557 the sound of a torpedo hitting its target could be heard throughout the boat, followed two minutes later by the noise of the ship breaking up. At 1600 hours the first of nine depth charges over a period of 47 minutes was dropped, but none was close enough to cause concern amongst the crew. Periscope depth was ordered at 1720, when Stevens noticed that the ship he had torpedoed was no longer there and the last remaining merchant vessel was still burning fiercely. A loud and very violent explosion reverberated around the inside of the submarine, at 1735, when finally, the Honestas blew up and settled on the sea bed. *P46* surfaced at 1917, setting a course for her original patrol position and taking the opportunity to recharge her batteries.

John Stevens saw it this way: "This Axis convoy had left Italy with three supply ships; *P228 (*HMS *Splendid)* had sunk one before the remaining two came our way, so the result was a total loss for the enemy".

0640 hours 15th December:
Some time after having dived for the night the H/E operator

reported contact on the port quarter and, upon coming up to periscope depth, the officer of the watch looked out upon two destroyers passing close astern. Heavy distant explosions were heard at 0926, with the crew relieved that it was not their time to endure another attack. At 1050 an aircraft was sighted circling on a bearing of 50 Deg. *P46* changed course to intercept the position, as this sighting might have indicated a convoy under escort. Suspicions were soon vindicated when at 1240 two merchant vessels were seen on a heading bound for Bizerta. On closer inspection, Stevens conveyed to those in the control room that he was looking at one Italian merchant vessel of approximately 4,000 tons, one medium size tanker and two torpedo boats acting as escort. Above them could be seen an escorting aircraft. The ships were sailing in line abreast, with the escorts disposed either side of their bows. The tanker was on the far side of *P46*'s position and therefore the merchant vessel was chosen as the target. Later she was reported to be the Italian merchant vessel Sant'Antioco, 4,994 gross tonnage and built in 1919.

In a position of 37 deg 32 min north 10 deg 39 min east and at 1330 hours, Stevens fired four torpedoes from a range of 2,000 yards, allowing for a seven-knot ship speed, depth setting at ten feet and aimed half-a-length ahead just abaft of the stem, just forward of the stern and half-a-length astern. *P46* was travelling at a speed of two knots.

In the control room the scene was tense – everyone was still, some standing, some sitting, others crouching, all silent, unblinking and tight-lipped, straining to catch the sound of a torpedo striking the target. Two and a half minutes later two explosions, 22 seconds apart, could be heard and a loud cheer echoed throughout the boat. Smiles, a sense of pride, triumph and back-slapping congratulations erupted through all departments as the roar of the first and second torpedoes striking home brought forth evidence of another victim. After the sweet smell of success, the crew prepared themselves for the anticipated backlash to ensue. They did not have to wait long – in fact it took only 90 seconds before the first depth charge was launched. Stevens ordered "Group down, slow ahead together", taking *P46* immediately deeper into the depths until she reached 150 feet whilst simultaneously turning towards the enemy's stern. The ventilation and cooling systems, together with all other pieces of machinery in the boat, except for the compass and the slowly revolving main motors, were stopped. Orders were passed in whispers and all unnecessary lighting was doused.

At 1336 the counter-attack began in earnest with the sound of an 'ash-can' being dropped into the water, followed by a sharp metallic click, which came from the firing mechanism, followed half-a-second later to a sound similar to Krrrump! as the depth charge exploded. This was followed by a pair and then another single at two-minute intervals. The torpedo boat used ASDIC to locate the submarine's position, then launched a pattern of ten depth charges, which exploded fairly close, shaking the boat without causing any damage. At 1406 hours, with the crew able to clearly hear the 'pings' created by their pursuers' ASDIC and the screws turning to pass very slowly overhead, everyone held their breath, many wondering if they would see their loved ones again, some offering a silent prayer, some cursing. But not a sound was made or spoken. The 'pings' worked their way towards the stern of the boat until a pattern of 12 depth charges dropped very close, causing a shower of cork to rain down upon the crew, light bulbs to shatter and a few small leaks to develop. Those responsible for the repairs were at least distracted from the continued bombardment from above as they busied themselves replacing and repairing. It was fortunate that the depth charges had been set too shallow.

More splashes were heard as even more depth charges were thrown into the sea, followed by the explosion and the sound of rain as tons of water, thrown up by the charge, fell back into the sea. This time the patterns were becoming more distant but, no matter what alterations *P46* made, they were unable to shake off their pursuers. Another torpedo boat joined in the attack at 1700 hours but fortunately, rather than helping his expert consort, it seemed to hinder its endeavour in locating the submarine as only five depth charges were dropped this time. At 1830 hours all hydrophone activity ceased, 62 charges having been dropped in this counter-attack.

Stevens recalls this action as follows: "Within twenty-four hours another convoy approached. A tanker and a supply ship with two escorts and aircraft were en route to Bizerta. Two hits were heard from our torpedo salvo, and later intelligence assessed the result as severe damage to the tanker, which had, however, survived. A skilful counter-attack was carried out by one of the escorts. She was deliberate in her attacks, making several runs overhead, without dropping any charges; only when she appeared to be in very certain contact did she use ammunition. She hung on to us for over five hours, and dropped 65 depth charges.

One pattern of 12 fell very close, but perhaps too shallow, lighting went off and broken glass from all sorts of fittings showered down, but we were able to keep control. Hopes of shaking off this persistent non-friend after dark were upset when the ASDIC operator reported hearing a second vessel approaching.

"In the event the newcomer was a benefactor; she passed overhead once without dropping anything. The second ship seemed to put the first one off her stroke. This counter-attack was most efficient and accurate and must have been a nerve-racking experience." At 2008 hours *P46* rose to the surface to withdraw to the north-east and set course for Malta as all torpedoes had been expended.

0100 hours 17th December:

P46 sighted one, or possibly two, unidentified small vessels off Limosa. The crew, still shocked by the duel with the motor torpedo boat, thanked the heavens and looked forward to a quiet voyage back to Malta, giving them the opportunity to clean up the boat in anticipation of some well-earned leave.

1130 hours 18th December:

P46 tied up at the Lazaretto in Malta, proudly flying her 'Jolly Roger' with two newly-sewn white bars on both sides of the flag, and was greeted by Captain (S) Simpson, who summed up the patrol as "a very valuable patrol, carried out with fine dash and judgment, which cost the enemy two ships full of vital war supplies". Stevens, in his report to his commanding officer, reported: "Armadas of twenty-five to thirty large troop carriers were sighted three or four times daily ferrying between Sicily and Tunisia". He went on to describe the ASDIC operation as "generally satisfactory, though, as ever, there was little assistance during attacks. In the first attack no revolutions were forthcoming, and in the second the revolutions given were obviously too high. However, the HSD was of the greatest assistance during the counter-attacks, and on two occasions at night H/E of approaching vessels was reported before sighting". On arrival at Malta, the ship's cat, Timoshenko, was tethered to the casing with a collar of ribbon. He was in a highly nervous state, thoroughly disapproving of the depth-charging, and on release immediately took 48 hours' patrol leave.

December 18th- 29th:

The crew enjoyed a well-earned break. Tight rationing was still in force, leading to shortages of all material goods except for the bare necessities, so, understandably, there was only limited festive cheer. But life carried on. The usual routine was in place and the matelots made the most of their leisure time. Unfortunately, by the time they were to sail again, it had been announced that an outbreak of poliomyelitis, or infantile paralysis, had broken out throughout the stressed Island. As a result, all public places, including the bars, were out of bounds.

Lieutenant Stevens renewed old acquaintances when his previous boat *Thunderbolt* arrived in Malta from the UK with a number of her original crew still on board and Crouch, his old captain, still in command. Together they discussed events that had taken place over the past 18 months and the variety of experiences and success of both submarines. Crouch briefed Stevens on the new large cylindrical pressure-tight containers, 25 feet long and five feet in diameter, placed forward and abaft of the conning tower. These had been installed to her uppercasing to house a number of 'chariots', as the new manned torpedoes, with a two-man crew, were known.

On the 20ᵗʰ December 1941 the battleships Queen Elizabeth and Valiant were sunk by Italian manned torpedoes – 'human torpedoes' - inside Alexandria Harbour. Winston Churchill wanted to know why the British lagged behind the Italians in such an effective weapon. The Prime Minister wrote to General Ismay, Chief of Staff's Committee on the 18ᵗʰ January, 1942, asking: "Please report what is being done to emulate the exploits of the Italians in Alexandria Harbour and similar methods of this kind. Is there any reason why we should be incapable of the same type of scientific aggressive action that the Italians have shown? One would have thought we should have been in the lead."

Using a captured Italian human torpedo flown back to the UK, it fell upon Captain W.R. Fell, assisted by Commander G. Sladen, to develop a British version, and this resulted in the 'chariot'. By September, 1942 a chariot with a crew of two arrived at the Lazaretto for testing in Mediterranean conditions. After successful trials, seven chariots with operational crews, arrived in Malta on board parent submarines. First to arrive was *Trident,* under the Command of Geoffrey Sladen, with two chariots, followed by *Thunderbolt*, under Lieutenant-Commander C.B. Crouch, with two chariots, then *Trooper*, under Lieutenant J.S. Wraith, with three and, finally, *P311*, under Lieutenant-Commander P.D. Cayley, with two.

Stevens was to learn that *P46* was to act as a recovery vessel for 'Operation Principal', the first mission in which chariots were to be used in action. The plan was for the chariots to be launched from their mother ships, with *P311* and *Trooper* attacking the last two Italian 8-inch cruisers at anchor in the Strait of Bonifacio, by attaching explosive charges under the hull of the cruisers. Upon completion, the crews would sink the chariots and make for a wooden shelter at the Eastern shore and a folbot (canoe) from the rescuing U-class submarine would recover them under the cover of darkness.

Thunderbolt was to attack Cagliari, where a convoy was at anchor, preparing to set sail for North Africa with instructions to attack Palermo if the convoy had sailed. As the parent submarines were clumsy, and judged to be non-operational and very vulnerable, their duties were restricted to the outward passage and the launching of their chariots, so that small U-class submarines could be used as recovery vehicles to the chariot crews. *Unbending* (Stanley), *Unison* (Daniell) and *Unruffled* were to be sent as the recovery boats.

President Roosevelt's Christmas message to Malta, broadcast on the 30th December contained the uplifting words: "The mighty blows which you and your ships have struck the enemy during the past week have been an inspiration to the people of the United States of America and their armed forces. The last war had its Verdun. The present conflict brought us Stalingrad and the epic struggle of the battle of Britain. Now Malta, after endless months of sacrifice and valour, strikes back with [the] devastating power of your sailors and aviators to bring us a complete victory in North Africa." 'The Times of Malta' newspaper, proclaimed: "The year 1942 will live in history as the year in which the Axis lost the war".

P311 sailed on the 28th December, followed by *Thunderbolt* and *Trooper* the next day.

8th Patrol

30th December:

P46 sailed from Malta with orders to patrol off Palermo and assist the crews of the chariots. The crew was informed of its forthcoming mission and another new chapter opened for the matelots. Soon the talk was about who would sleep where when the pick-up was achieved and how much they all looked forward to conversations surrounding the exploits of the chariot crew members when on board.

31st December:

Another routine day passed. Negotiating the minefield at a depth of 150 feet, the crew looked towards another new year, the thought of loved ones back home being very much in their minds. Crew members mustered in their relevant compartments, whilst Auld Lang Syne was sung throughout the boat. On reaching their patrol area off Palermo, and in readiness for the expected pick-up of the chariot crews, the Matelots awaited in anticipation for the allotted time to arrive.

0001 hours, 1st January, 1943:

The lookouts on the bridge sighted flak over Trapani and Palermo at 0010 hours. Aircraft were spotted throughout the early hours, particularly from 0450, indicating the presence of shipping in the area. *P46* dived at 0556 hours, sighting 18 southbound troop-carrying aircraft at 0905. Aircraft continued to be active for the rest of the day. Having spent 12 hours and 37 minutes submerged, *P46* surfaced at 1833 and the lookouts began their shift in the knowledge that Operation Principal had been put back by one day.

0010-0115 hours, 2nd January:

Intense air activity was witnessed over Palermo and along the western coast. The boat dived at 0557 hours and nothing of note was spotted within *Unruffled*'s patrol area, but there was frequent air activity. After 12 hours and 31 minutes submerged, *P46* rose to the surface at 1828, recharging the batteries to seaward. Operation Principal had begun. However, air reconnaissance warned that there was considerable anti-submarine activity west of Marettimo Island, indicating the sailing of the convoy from Cagliari. The unnamed *P311* signalled its position at 0130 hours on the 31st December before passing through the mined area in the Eastern Approaches to the Strait of Bonifacio.

This was to be the last communication to be received from *P311,* as all contact was lost. It is presumed she hit a mine and that this gallant submarine was lost to the sea. The attack on Palermo took place on the night of 2nd-3rd January, which was dark and blustery with an offshore wind. All five chariots got away before midnight. Chariot XXII, led by Lieutenant R.T.G. Greenland and leading signalman A. Ferrier from *Thunderbolt*, reached the new light cruiser at the innermost wharf of the harbour, detached their chariot bow containing 400Ib of explosives and placed it against the hull, then placed limpet mines under the Italian destroyers Gregale, Ciclone and Gamma. Chariot XIV, led by Sub-Lieutenant R.G. Dove and Leading Seaman J. Freel from the submarine *Trooper*, placed the main charge under the 8,500-ton merchant transport vessel Viminale. Three chariots failed to penetrate the harbour, the crew of one was rescued and one member of each of the other two died. All four chariots were abandoned and sunk and a total of six men taken prisoner. The main charge under the transport vessel Viminale exploded, but the limpet mines, after a search by Italian divers, were located and removed. At 0800 the charge set under the cruiser Ulpio Traiano went off and she sank. *Thunderbolt* and *Trooper* returned safely to Malta.

0130 hours, 3rd January:
The lookouts were particularly vigilant due to the expected arrival of the chariot crews. The chef brewed up fresh cocoa and hot food in readiness for their visitors. Because of A/S transmission, *P46* was forced to dive at 0211 and, due to frequent activity, had to remain underwater until 0300. The lookouts spotted a light at 0425 and Stevens called for group up, (full speed) rescuing two chariot crew at 0439. Once inside the submarine they were given dry clothes, a cup of cocoa and hot food. Stevens described the event as follows: "Chariot XXIII, manned by my namesake, Sub-Lieutenant H.L. Steven RNVR, and Chief Petty Officer Buxton, suffered a breakdown which caused them to abandon their attack. They made their way towards us, and had a lucky escape as the feeble light of their torch being flashed to seaward was

barely visible. As it was, we finally recovered them 90 minutes after the deadline time when we should have started a dived withdrawal".

Between 0515 and 0535, explosions could be seen coming from the vicinity of Palermo. The boat dived at 0554 and another explosion was heard at 0715. Stevens explains: "The explosions caused by the charioteers had alerted the enemy, but he had been taken by surprise and did not immediately appreciate what type of attack he had suffered. We were not harassed by patrols, as had been anticipated, and thus had a quiet start to an uneventful return passage to Malta." Aircraft activity during the day was relatively sparse and *P46* returned to the surfaced at 1826 hours to begin charging the main batteries and start the nightly bridge watch. The crew was able to smoke and the garbage was weighted down and thrown over the side. New friendships were cemented between the 'charioteers' and the crew.

0535 hours, 4th January:

After a quiet night the boat dived, resurfacing at 0658 to transit Ustica, then submerged again at 0712. A quiet day for all, enabling the crew time to catch up on letter writing and playing games. The boat surfaced at 1826 for the routine of night patrol. Total submerged time: 12 hours 45 minutes.

0057 hours, 5th January:

The weather was relatively calm with an F2 wind from a southerly direction. Five aircraft were spotted during the watch period, with *P46* diving at 0535 when an aircraft came to close for comfort. At 0900 an Italian Cant aircraft, flying at 2,000 feet, was observed and an armada of 22 planes (G12s) recorded at 0915. Between 1022 and 1300 heavy concentrations of aircraft were sighted, ranging from a lone Cant aircraft to squadrons of bombers and fighters. This led up to an aircraft troop carrier being sighted at 1235. Heavy air activity continued throughout the afternoon until *P46* surfaced at 1826 hours. Total submerged time: 12 hours 31 minutes.

0200 hours, 6th January:
Marettimo light was sighted bearing 191 degrees, leading to a small light in the sky suddenly going out at 0259 and presumed to have been from an aircraft. At 0300 Stevens sounded the klaxon, resulting in the submarine diving when an aircraft dropped two red and two green flares close to the submarine's beam. Four distant depth charges were clearly heard at 0730, and one Cant aircraft and two bombers were sighted between 0835 and 1025. By 1245, two troop-carrying aircraft, northbound, could be seen through the periscope crossing the horizon, with another six southbound at 1300 hours. Another 20 aircraft transports were identified at 1515. The on-duty H/E operator reported a contact at 1825, resulting in three torpedo boats passing *P46* at 1905 and a further two at 1935. Once these had passed, the commander gave the order to surface at 1958. Total submerged time: 16 hours 58 minutes.

0043 hours, 7th January:
After sighting two bow waves, *P46* dived and resurfaced at 0110. When bow waves were again sighted at 0525, but no

H/E, she dived again and at 0545 the sound of one distant depth charge was heard. Three Italian fishing boats and one motor ship was observed at 0928, and H/E being heard at 1210, which was presumed to be *P35*. Two troop-carrying aircraft and two fighter planes were observed at 1525. *P46* surfaced at 1830 into a F3 wind and clear visibility. The H/E operator reported a contact at 2118, forcing the submarine to dive at 2125 and two motor torpedo boats passed to the west. Upon re-surfacing at 2143, an air raid on Pantelleria was observed. Total submerged time: 13 hours 5 minutes.

0100 hours, 8ᵗʰ January:
Sighted a bright light beyond the horizon, which was assumed to be a fire burning. The crew continued to clean the boat ahead of the return to Malta. Gozo was sighted at 0510 as the weather began to decline, the wind increasing from F7 to F8 with a sea swell of ten feet. After picking up its escort at 1304, *P46* docked at berth U4 at 1455. Awaiting to greet them, 'Shrimp' Simpson welcomed back Lieutenant Stevens and the returning passengers for the last time, as the Captain (S) was due to hand over command and leave the Island. Leading them to the underground safety of Port Talbot, this final de-briefing was discussed over a gin or two. The submarine was moved at 1600 hours to berth U3.

Stevens and Buxton, who crewed chariot XXIII, participated in another chariot operation just a few weeks later, launched from *Thunderbolt* off Tripoli. Having entered the main harbour entrance and approaching their main target within 150 yards, two explosions shook the chariot and their main target, the Giovanni Bassista, sank before them. Switching to their second target, Giulio, they successfully attached limpet mines before sinking their own chariot. The limpet mines exploded, sinking the Giulio.

Stevens and Buxton were captured and sent to Rome as prisoners of war. After being separated some months later, they met up again at Campo 50. After the fall of Mussolini they managed to obtain Italian uniforms from a friendly guard, who advised them how to reach the Vatican. Following forcible ejection after lengthy prayer, it looked as if the Italian police might turn them over to the German authorities when, much by chance, a British diplomat from the Vatican arrived and conducted them past the Swiss Guard into the Holy City. They remained there until Rome fell to the Allies in July 1944.

0830 hours, 9th January:
With Seabourne-May in command, a third of the crew was employed cleaning the boat, the remainder having been given leave. After lunch, make-and-mend gave some crew the opportunity to take a swim or visit the Lazaretto.

0830 hours, 10th January:
The boat slipped its mooring to disembark four torpedoes, returning to berth U3 at 1530 hours.

0830 hours, January 11th:
After waving a fond farewell to Captain (S) G.W.G. Simpson for the final time, *P46* departed its mooring and entered Grand Harbour half-an-hour later, securing to No.1 dock and finally being dry-docked at 1700 hours. One of the reasons for the dry-docking was the fitting of binocular sights on the 3-inch gun. One can also assume that the

boat's hull was cleaned and painted, and any other outstanding problems were addressed. This was also a good opportunity to disinfect the boat.

0830 hours, 12th January:
Hands were employed in all departments, a process that continued throughout the next four days.

0900 hours, 16th January:
The flooding of the dry dock began and was completed at 1130 when *P46* made her way back to her berth at U3 in front of the Lazaretto. By 1400 the storing of the boat began in readiness for another patrol.

0800 hours, 17th January:
The mooring was slipped and the boat proceeded to the torpedo loading berth where an additional four spare 'fish' were loaded into the torpedo room. Having arrived back at berth U3 at 1130, the hands were employed painting the boat.

0830 hours, 18th January:
The cleaning of the boat and make-and-mend was the order for the day.

<h2 style="text-align:center">9th Patrol</h2>

0830 hours 19th January, 1943:
All hands were employed storing the boat with food and supplies. At 1258 *P46* left her mooring and proceeded unescorted via the swept channel bound for an area in the

Gulf of Hammamet, north-east of Tunisia and just south of Cap Bon. At 1425 *P46* was overtaken by HMS Javelin and HMS Kelvin, who were part of the K Force Flotilla. The boat dived for a trim test at 1451 and returned to the surface at 1505 where it remained until it reached the designated patrol area.

0006 hours 20th January:
The lookouts on the bridge reported a darkened object approximately 11 miles off Limosa light. Stevens order a change of course to intercept, only to find that the vessel appeared to be a submarine moving very slowly in an easterly direction. As *Una* and *P44* were eastbound for Malta at this time, it was considered that the object was one of them. However, at 0020, and after one of the objects had altered course towards them, *P46* decided to err on the side of caution and dive. All attempts to exchange identification by SS/T were unsuccessful and at 0122 *P46* resurfaced and resumed her course.

The boat dived again at 0522 hours after a build-up of overhead aircraft brought expectations to a higher level. At 1042 the order was given to change course to investigate another unknown object, and at 1057 it was shown to be an aircraft. At 1833 hours *P46* surfaced to recharge the batteries and Stevens established his patrol area in the vicinity of Ras Mahmur. Whenever weather permitted, Baden Powell would clean the 3-inch gun chamber, first with emery paper and then with grease, a process that was continued throughout the patrol. Total submerged time: 13 hours 55 minutes.

0022 hours 21ˢᵗ January:

The first of many aircraft passing overhead was observed and Stevens gave the order to dive the boat at 0615. Fifteen distant explosions could be heard at 0945, with a group of six, similar to a depth charge pattern, echoing throughout the boat at 0950. One torpedo boat passed within 3,000 yards inshore northbound at a speed of 15 knots, leaving no ASDIC transmission, much to Stevens' annoyance. No sightings were observed during the rest of the day and at 1832, having surfaced in a slight sea swell, the crew was given the opportunity to 'light up'. Total submerged time 12 hours 17 minutes.

0613 hours 22ⁿᵈ January:

Stevens dived the boat and, after a routine, non-active day, it surfaced at 1831 hours.

0230 hours 23ʳᵈ January:

Stevens was forced to dive the boat when an aircraft flew close overhead and re-surfaced 22 minutes later. At 0319 a lookout reported seeing a darkened shape, and the order to 'close' was given. As the distance was reduced between the two, the shape was identified as two small vessels. One was a tug and the other an 'F' boat (Flak-Lighter). Stevens came to the conclusion that they were not suitable targets for gun action and at 0349 hours *P46* dived. Because of their shallow draft and efficient gun armament, which made them practically immune to submarine attack, the Flak-Lighters were being frequently used by the Axis forces.

Looking through the periscope on what was a good bright moonlight night, Stevens decided that the tug was not worth a torpedo. The boat surfaced at 0422 and set a course three miles from the shore, along the north coast of Hammamet. The boat dived at 0614, but it was not long before the crew was called into action. Stevens was awoken from his slumber at 0915 when the masts of a schooner were identified. He decided to call for gun action and immediately the crew organised a shell-loading train, while the gun-layer and gun-trainer waited patiently in the control room ready to clamber up the ladder and send away the first shell. The boat surfaced at 0954 and Stevens describes the event which followed:

"We sighted a smart-looking motor schooner chuffing along the coast. Surfacing on her quarter, we were soon hitting her with 3-inch shell. As she lost way, her three-man crew lowered a boat and pulled for the shore. We came under fire from shore batteries and some near misses encouraged me to dive. Some minutes later we surfaced close to the schooner on the seaward side with the idea of scuttling or setting her on fire, but the guns from shore opened up again with uncomfortably heavy and accurate fire. We made a spectacular stern-first dive to avoid ramming the schooner. This resulted in a claim, broadcast to British listeners by Lord Haw-Haw from Germany, that an Allied submarine had been sunk by fire from shore batteries.

"The schooner, of about 1,500 tons, was still very much afloat, and although of wooden construction, was not burning. We had taken her ensign and it seemed wrong to let matters rest there. I aimed one torpedo set to four feet depth at her; this hit with impressive results. She vanished in a cloud of smoke, dust and flame. She might well have been carrying cased petrol or explosives."

P46 had fired 29 rounds from her 3-inch gun, with ten hits, including one that severed the mainmast halfway up, from a range of 2,000 feet for a duration of approximately six minutes. After the first ten rounds the shore batteries opened fire and, as they increasingly gauged the range, Stevens ordered the boat to dive. It resurfaced at 1026, but a minute later, due to the accuracy of the shore batteries, was compelled to dive again. Firing one torpedo from a range of 1,000 yards at 1048, the Amabile Carolina (39 gross tons) disintegrated.

At 1100 hours the boat set a course south-west five miles off the coast to continue its patrol. Another small ship was sighted at 1247. Thirteen minutes later it was identified as an Italian naval drifter, which Stevens left alone. After sighting the Tunisian town of Susa at 1730, *P46* surfaced to recharge the batteries, beginning night patrol at 1828 and setting course for Ras Mahmur, which seemed to be the best focal point for traffic. Total submerged time 12 hours 47 minutes.

0615 hours 24th January:

After an uneventful night *P46* dived. At 1100 hours she sighted a naval drifter and an hour-and-a-half later she spotted two fighter planes. At 1315 hours the boat changed course to avoid fishing boats. Fast hydrophone contact was made at 1600 hours and ten minutes later two E-boats, close inshore and similar to the silhouette below, were identified.

The boat surfaced at 1843. Total submerged time 12 hours 28 minutes.

0611 hours 25th January:

P46 dived for periscope patrol. Having received a radio report at 0930, Stevens increased speed to 3.5 knots to investigate the sighting of a small merchant vessel in a stopped position west of their own position. This action took place at 1100 hours, with the crew being brought to diving stations at 1229, when a 300-ton tanker, in ballast, was observed anchored off Hammamet. Stevens manoeuvred the boat into a very favourable position some 1,500 yards from the target and fired one torpedo aimed amidships at a depth setting of four feet. The torpedo fired at 1302, was seen to run under the foremast and was heard to continue its run for some time until it presumably buried itself in the mud. Luckily, no one ashore or on the vessel had noticed that a torpedo had, in fact, passed beneath them. Stevens repositioned the boat and 22 minutes later fired one torpedo from a range of 1,850 yards, with a depth setting of four feet and aimed at the bridge, which was located towards the stern of the vessel. The torpedo hit the engine-room of the vessel, which turned out to be the Teodolinda, of 361 gross tons. She sank stern first, the bow protruding out of the water at a steep angle, thus indicating she had broken her back. Stevens remarks: "I had estimated her size as 1,000 tons; in fact she was a 300-ton water carrier and had been built by Philip and Son, of Dartmouth in 1931. She had been on the stocks when I was a cadet at the R.N. College."

The shore batteries opened fire at 1345, possibly due to the sighting of the periscope protruding out of the water. *P46* surfaced at 1841 and yet another white rectangular symbol was added to the Jolly Roger.

0227 hours 26th January:

Sighted a darkened vessel and with the klaxons giving the call to diving stations, the crew members immediately went to their designated positions with the expectations of some action. Stevens ordered a change of course, putting the boat in an attacking position. Through the periscope Stevens could make out a heavily-laden cacique (local fishing boat) and immediately reached the decision to surface for gun action. With the gun-crew and shell-handlers quickly but efficiently prepared for the forthcoming shelling of an enemy ship, hearts began to beat faster, bodies sweating and the adrenalin pumping. At 0322 *P46* surfaced and the captain, followed by Baden Powell, Henry Preece, William Reed, Seaburne-May and two lookouts, went through the hatch. In position 36 deg 21 min north 10 deg 38 5 min east, *P46* opened up with the 3-inch gun, firing 14 rounds that resulted in nine hits. The crew of the cacique, the 46 grt Italian Redemptory Z90, abandoned ship almost immediately after smoke began to rise aft of the engine-room, though this was rapidly extinguished as the ship began to flood.

Due to a sighting of an approaching darkened vessel, the order 'Check, check, check', was given and once more the gun-crew made its way below. Stevens ordered the boat to dive to periscope depth and with this achieved he immediately had a good look around using the high-powered telescope. Nothing could be sighted and, at 0337 hours, with H/E reporting that nothing could be heard, Stevens ordered the boat back to the surface to re-commence with gun action. Having climbed onto the bridge, Stevens decided that the best course of action was to board the ship, the crew having abandoned her, ensuring that ammunition would not be wasted. Lieutenant Lascelles and Acting Petty Officer W.J. Bell boarded the stricken vessel and found that, although the upper deck was awash, she refused to go to the bottom of the sea. After removing the Italian flag from her mast and with an increasing north-easterly wind, Lascelles concluded that the vessel would be blown ashore and wrecked. He confirmed, too, that she was fully laden with cargo. On returning to *P46*, the first lieutenant reported his findings to Stevens, who ordered five or six shells from the 3-inch gun to be fired at the stern, thus ensuring that the flooding of the engine room would continue. The order was carried out at 0415, and *P46* withdrew to the west.

This was not to be the last time the crew came across the Redemptory. Diving at 0615, with the intention of patrolling three miles offshore, they passed her again, still afloat, at 0730 hours, but it was decided to leave her to her fate. Stevens now set course to ascertain the demise of the tanker they had torpedoed the previous day, only to discover that she still had her bow out of the water at a steep angle with the top of the bridge clearly visible.

Setting a new course for a destination three miles off the coast of Kuriat Island, Fenton, the navigator, anticipated arriving at their new patrol area at 2300 hours that evening. While at the periscope, the officer of the watch noted floating driftwood at 1000 hours. The boat closed to investigate, but no satisfactory conclusion was reached as to its origin. A passing British Mosquito aircraft, at a height of 1,500 feet, was identified at 1120, and at 1453 the captain was called to the control room when an unidentified small ship off Herkla (Hergla) was sighted. As this was too far to give *P46* any chance of catching her up, it was decided to allow the vessel to continue on her way. At 1845, after an eventful day, *P46* surfaced, allowing the cook to begin preparing a meal, the opportunity to freshen the air in the boat and the crew to light up a cigarette after spending 12 hours 39 minutes below the surface.

0609 hours 27th January:

After a quiet night, with only seven aircraft being heard, *P46* dived for the rest of the day. The boat received orders from Malta to proceed to a new patrol position three to four miles off the coast in the vicinity of Ras Kapudia, as several reports had been received of ships entering and leaving the northern end of the Kerkenah Channel, but nothing was seen or heard for the next 12 hours. At 1845 hours *P46* arose from the depths to begin bridge watch. Total submerged time 12 hours 36 minutes.

0610 hours 28th January:

Three Italian torpedo boats were sighted close inshore. After surfacing at 1845 hours, the crew was ordered to diving stations at 2332 when the boat was forced to dive due to an approaching E-boat. Total submerged time 13 hours 3 minutes.

0038 hours 29th January:

The boat surfaced to resume patrol. A large aircraft, at height, crossed the bow of the submarine at 0535 and Stevens ordered the boat to dive for periscope patrol at 0603. The captain was ordered to the control room at 0950, when four tank landing craft (TLC), flying the German ensign and travelling southbound, were sighted, three of which were numbered 477, 479 and 846. As these were not deemed to be suitable targets, *P46* continued on its way until at 1040, when the TLCs were seen heading below the horizon. At 1722 hours Stevens was again called to the control room after H/E reported a contact. Nothing, however, could be seen through the periscope. By 1740 it was assumed to be background noise and the captain, unconcerned, returned to his bunk. *P46* returned to the surface at 1855 hours. Total submerged time 13 hours 30 minutes.

0042-0608 hours 30th January:
Twenty-one aircraft were either heard or seen during the night, raising hopes that a convoy might be making its way close by. Between 0550 and 0600 four aircraft passed close to *P46*'s bow and at 0510 two more crossed its stern. At 0608 it dived, an increase in aircraft activity being noted throughout the day. At 1000 hours three tank-landing craft, with air cover, were sighted through the periscope and at 1945, an hour after surfacing, all those on the bridge witnessed one red flare and three green flares being fired at distant, followed by the same combination five minutes later, and a vivid red glare coming from the direction of Tunis, some 100 miles distant. This was described by Lascelles as "if lit by a distant explosion". On this clear night with faint starlight, ASDIC reported a contact at 2321, bearing 130 degrees, which was identified four minutes later as three or four 'F' boats heading northbound. Stevens ordered an alteration in course to keep these torpedo boats astern of the submarine until such time as they had disappeared from view. Total submerged time 12 hours 27 minutes.

0510 hours 31st January:

Allied aircraft reports indicated that a medium-sized merchant ship and one destroyer were making their way for Sousse at a speed of eight knots. *P46* was still positioned off Ras Kapudia and Fenton advised Stevens that, in order to reach their objective by 1000 hours, they would have to remain on the surface at full speed. Stevens explains: "Conflicting air recce reports referred to a southbound ship plus one ship as escort near Cape Bon. One report indicated Sfax as her probable destination, while the other implied Sousse. Sousse seemed to be more likely and by moving at full speed on the surface until four hours after daybreak we were in a position to cut her off."

At 0709 a further Allied aircraft report showed the two vessels in approximately the same position at a speed of eight knots. This suggested that they were bound for Sfax, and the decision had to be made whether to cover the Sousse or Sfax route to intercept. Stevens decided to select the Sousse route for the following reasons: Firstly, two reports indicated an approach to Sousse and, while the third report was more up-to-date, there seemed to be no sound reason for a navigational alteration of 50 Degrees; secondly, the BBC news had reported heavy air raids on Sfax; and, thirdly, during four days at the entrance to the Kerkenah Channel the only craft sighted were torpedo boats, and there had been no air reports of merchant shipping moving in or out of Sfax.

It is remarkable, and a case of good fortune, that when on the surface in good visibility no aircraft were sighted. Having reached their destination at 1008 hours, *P46* dived to the safety of the depths, only to find no ships were in sight. Had they made the right decision? Was the ship heading for Sfax after all? The crew could only wait.

At 1145 the crew's morale was boosted when flak was sighted. "Our spirits revived three hours later when AA shell burst was seen to the northwest," said Stevens. Shortly afterwards, seven explosions were heard, thought to be the result of an air attack on the two ships. *P46* continued to close the coast at a speed of four knots. The captain sighted a supply ship with its air cover and escort through the periscope at 1358, finally confirming the sighting to be a torpedo boat and merchant vessel close inshore at 1405. On being called to diving stations, the crew settled in for action in anticipation of another symbol being added to the Jolly Roger. Due to the air activity and a close encounter with one aircraft, *P46* was forced to dive deeper at 1428. The hope was that they had not been seen and that the element of surprise was still in their favour. Seconds later Stevens commenced the attack. The merchant vessel, of approximately 2,000 tons, continued on a straight course, despite the torpedo boat zigzagging on her port bow. A speed of eight knots was calculated after the timing of the ship's length passing a point on the land had been taken and checked. At 1502 four torpedoes spread over two ship's lengths at an estimated speed of eight knots and at a range of 6,000 yards had been fired using the data from the 'fruit machine'. Although no aircraft could be seen at the time of firing, it was decided to go deep at speed to avoid any retaliation from the escorting torpedo boat.

In the control room the stop-watch was started and the crew began its own countdown to the approximate time when the torpedoes should strike home. All was silent in the boat as the seconds seemed to turn into hours as they awaited the sound of a torpedo hitting home. Reluctantly, after six minutes and 11 seconds, it was decided that as this suggested a running range of 8,200 yards, they must have missed and the sound was of the torpedo reaching the end of its run. Stevens recalls: "The glassy calm sea, shallow depth, and white sandy sea bed did not favour us, but we sent three torpedoes on their way, unobserved, from an estimated three miles range. It seemed that we had missed, when the clunk was heard after a time, indicating a torpedo running range of four miles.

We returned to periscope depth at 1515 hours for a cautious peep through the periscope, which showed the ship (German SS Lisbon, 1800 tons) to be stopped, afire and sinking. The escort corvette was rushing about, dropping depth charges at random, it appeared, and she was easily evaded."

In fact, two depth charges had been dropped at 1517. Judging by the small splash produced, they had been set fairly deep, with the depth of water available to *P46* being 160 feet. As three aircraft were now in the vicinity, *P46* again went deep at 1525. The torpedo boat continued the hunt for an hour, during which time she dropped two single depth charges but never got close. At 1650, *P46* rose to periscope depth and observed grey smoke emanating from the stricken vessel. At 1725 dense black smoke was seen coming from the merchant vessel, and this continued until dark. A large, heavy explosion was heard at 1820, which could have been the death-throe of the Lisbon. Much to the delight of the crew, *P46* set course for Malta on receiving her recall. Not only could they add another white bar to the

Jolly Roger but they were homeward bound. What could be better?

P46 surfaced at 1900 and at 2008 a large explosion was heard over Tunis, although nothing could be seen. The batteries began their recharge at 2200, allowing more time to distant themselves from the scene. In his patrol report, Stevens highlighted the fact that three torpedoes, set to four feet, all ran correctly. Although attention was drawn to the fact that sea conditions were flat calm, it is stressed that depth settings of a target in ballast should be sufficiently shallow. Total submerged time: 8 hours 52 minutes.

0355 hours 1st February:

P46 dived and the day passed without incident, enabling the crew time to prepare for some welcome leave. Thoughts of a bath and the tales to be told at the Lazaretto uplifted the crew's spirits and they were delighted to get some fresh air when the boat surfaced at 1845 hours. Total submerged time: 12 hours 47 minutes.

0425 hours 2nd February:

H/E reported contact, but nothing was sighted. Zigzagging was increased to 60 degrees either side until 0839 when, having entered the cleared channel, they met with their escort, Rohaval, and secured alongside *P42* (HMS *Unbroken*) at berth U2. Stevens was the first to leave the boat, heading for the Lazaretto and reporting to Captain (S) George C. Phillips DSC, Simpson's replacement, having handed over the reign on the 23rd January. Captain Phillips, an ex-submariner, had previously been with the 3rd Flotilla at Harwich. Half the crew was given leave.

0815 hours 3rd February:
The remainder of the crew began the routine of painting the boat in the morning and make-and-mend in the afternoon.

0815 hours 9th February:
The embarkation of stores began.

0815 hours 10th February:
Ammunition was brought on board.

10th PATROL

0815 hours 12th February:
All hands fell in on board the newly named *Unruffled* in readiness for the first official patrol following the decree by Winston Churchill that all submarines should be named. Though the crew had been told of the name allocated to *P46*, there was still much debate and argument below deck as to the final choice. At 1040 hours the crew was called to harbour stations, preparations were made for another patrol, and at 1104 the boat was untied from the pontoon and made its way unescorted out of Marsamxett Harbour via the swept channel.

A test dive was achieved at 1305 in order to check and adjust the trim, and at 1452 *Unruffled* resurfaced, Fenton setting a course for the patrol area off Hammamet, Tunisia, at an engine speed of 340 revs. Total submerged time: 1 hour 47 minutes.

0549 hours 13th February:
Having remained on the surface since leaving Malta,

Unruffled dived for periscope patrol. Due to a north-westerly gale, periscope depth could not be maintained, and this forced the boat to dive deeper. At 1857 hours it resurfaced to begin recharging the batteries and carry out a routine night surface patrol. Total submerged time: 13 hours 2 minutes.

0343 hours 14th February:

Unruffled dived and commenced periscope patrol, and at 1200, the boat was patrolling to the south-east of Ras Mahmur, in the Gulf of Tunis, before resurfacing at 1900 hours to maintain bridge watch and start the battery charge. Total submerged time: 15 hours 15 minutes.

0543 hours 15th February:

Following a night in which there was a slight increase in aircraft activity, *Unruffled* dived to proceed to a position 3,000 yards offshore. At 0800 hours the wreck of a schooner was identified two-an-a-half miles off the Tunisian coastal town of Hammamet, south-east of the northern peninsular of Cape Bon. This wreck had not been sighted on the previous patrol so clearly it had only recently been sent to a watery grave. One shell splash was heard ahead of the submarine at 0954 at a distance of one cable. It was judged that this had been fired by a shore battery which had sighted the periscope out of the water. A British Mosquito aircraft, heading eastbound, passed overhead at 1345.

A noticeable increase in air activity brought the crew to diving stations at 1720 hours in the hope that a convoy was on its way but, after a lull in the frequency, the boat surfaced at 1858. At 2030 hours the boat received orders direct from Malta to proceed to the convoy route north-west of Pantelleria, the Italian island in the Strait of Sicily 60 km east of the Tunisian coast, and Fenton was instructed to set a new course in order to arrive by dawn.

After sighting a darkened vessel close inshore at 2245, Stevens ordered the submarine to close the position for a better look, only to discover a large schooner being escorted by three E-boats. He quickly assessed that as an attack on this target was unlikely to succeed it was best to resume their original northerly course.

0145 hours 16th February:
Unruffled passed a floating mine and spotted two white flares at 0150 hours and one more at 0205. The submarine arrived at its new patrolling position at 0310 hours and at 0437 another white flare was seen, followed by another at 0545. As they came from the expected bearing from which a convoy would approach, it was concluded that they could be nothing other than a convoy. At 0559 the order was given to dive. Nothing was seen that morning, but at 1225 three distant explosions were heard, followed by two more at 1240, three more 27 minutes later and two heavy explosions at 1412.

The crew, expecting to be brought to diving stations at any moment, prepared for action, but at 1859 the boat resurfaced and a disappointed crew's main thoughts switched to the forthcoming night bridge patrol and *Unruffled*, so as to comply with order 1046A/16 sent from Malta, set course to patrol the vicinity of Ras Mahmur.

0057 hours 17ᵗʰ February:

Unruffled dived at 0557, taking up a position 3,000 yards off the coast, and at 1859 surfaced and set a course for Ras Mahmur. A hawk-eyed lookout identified two darkened ships, possibly schooners, crossing the horizon at 2153 and the order to 'Close' was given. After one hour seven minutes, Stevens thought his luck had changed when, without warning, the two vessels turned towards *Unruffled* on an intercept course. Thirteen minutes later, with the two ships still advancing on *Unruffled's* position, Stevens reverted back to his original course, suspecting that the two unidentified ships were an anti-submarine patrol. Total submerged time: 12 hours 21 minutes.

0435 hours 18ᵗʰ February:

Seven F-lighters' advanced close inshore steering north-west and the decision was made to allow them to pass unmolested. At 0553 *Unruffled* dived to assume periscope watch and at 0700 hours sighted a large schooner in ballast escorted by eight F-lighters, one of which was towing the schooner. As *Unruffled* was not in a position to make up the required distance, the small convoy continued its journey, unaware that it had been sighted by a hostile submarine. Five F-lighters, flying the Italian flag, came into view at 0800 but were not considered to be a justifiable target.

At 1335 hours the masts of two schooners were sighted lying alongside a jetty off the village of Neboel (Nebeul), north of Hammamet. Stevens immediately attended the control room, relaying the order to change course and speed in preparation for an attack. Coming to diving stations at 1357, the control room readied for action, with data updated into the 'fruit machine' every few minutes. Stevens brought the periscope out of the water for a few seconds and then, as quickly as it had risen, it was withdrawn.

The shore batteries, having seen the tip of the attack periscope protruding above the waterline, opened fire and the resulting explosions were clearly heard throughout the boat. The No 2 tube, with a depth setting of six feet, was at 1418 hours fired at the left-hand schooner. While explosions were still being heard around the boat, a second 'fish' was fired from the No 1 tube one and a half minutes later, this time aimed at the right hand side of the schooner's stern. The first torpedo ran under the stern of the schooner and then ran up the beach without exploding. The second torpedo missed just astern and, possibly due to insufficient allowance for drift, exploded in shallow water. The crews of the two schooners, having been alerted, rapidly abandoned ship and made for the beach in skiffs. There appeared to be approximately ten men on board each schooner.

After this disappointment, *Unruffled* withdrew, but after further consideration Stevens decided to try again, this time with a torpedo depth setting of four feet to allow for the rising wind from the north-east, though the lee of the land kept the swell from building. The state of the sea was considered satisfactory for the shallow depth setting. At 1425 *Unruffled* closed in to attack, with diving stations called at 1459. Once again the shore batteries, having spotted the attack periscope protruding above the water, had an aiming point and so opened fire. A torpedo from the No 3 tube was sent away at 1513, aimed at the right-hand side of the schooner's stem. Unfortunately, to everyone's surprise, the torpedo broke the surface and ran three degrees to port before finally exploding in shallow water. The only effect of this sudden explosion was to cause panic among those on the beach, and they were seen scattering in all directions.

Stevens explained the action thus: "Returning to the Hammamet area, two schooners were sighted at anchor off Neboel. They appeared to be laying cables. One torpedo was fired at each of them without success; then another, which also missed. I decided that this scale of torpedo expenditure was too expensive and so withdrew to seaward. This was not before the startled crew had been seen abandoning ship as the torpedoes ran up the beach. The wind was now blowing almost gale force and the unmanned craft was swept ashore. Later, the wreckage was observed high and dry on the sand. Although the schooners were lost to the enemy as an indirect result of our action, the incident demonstrates the difficulty of torpedoing small stopped vessels. Imperceptible rates of tidal streams or current during the torpedo's running time can suffice to cause a miss."

A curious incident concluded this unsatisfactory afternoon's work. At 1528 *Unruffled* was still swinging to starboard to steady on a course of 180 degrees at periscope depth when the H.S.D. operator reported a torpedo running on bearing green 120. The submarine was taken to 60 feet, the H.E. of the torpedo closed until heard all round at 1530 hours and then rapidly faded. Stevens thought he heard a whirring noise at the same time as H.E. was reporting all-round sound and the noise in the headphones of the H.S.D. was heard two or three feet away by Joseph Lewis, the Petty Officer Telegraphist. The conclusion was that a torpedo had been fired by another submarine and aimed at *Unruffled* from an approximate bearing of 270 degrees somewhere in the open sea.

Ten minutes later the submarine returned to periscope depth for a quick look round. Nothing was in sight except for the shore and the two schooners. Stevens ordered the continued withdrawal to the south. By the time the submarine had surfaced at 1858 the wind had increased to gale force, leaving those on the bridge windswept and soaking wet. The old proverb 'an ill wind' was very much in everyone's mind as this put the two schooners in a precarious position off a lee shore and with no crew on board. Examination of the area on the 22nd February showed two newly-wrecked schooners ashore. As the crew had not officially sunk these vessels, no addition bars could be added to the Jolly Roger.

0544 hours 19th February:
Unruffled dived and patrolled at depth as because of the gale, periscope depth could not be maintained. After spending 13 hours and four minutes underwater, they surfaced at 1848 hours into a heavy swell.

0538 hours 20th February:
Dived and remained so for a total of 13 hours and six minutes. The heavy swell, combined with the mist, reduced periscope visibility to 3,000 yards. The boat surfaced at 1858 after an order received from Malta instructed it to patrol the convoy route north-west of Pantelleria by dawn on the 21st. A change of course was set accordingly.

0550 hours 21ˢᵗ February:

After an uneventful night *Unruffled* dived, the slight sea and heavy swell making periscope observation difficult. H/E reported a contact at 0742 hours, resulting in two merchant vessels being sighted through the periscope by the duty watch officer. Calling the captain to the control room, Stevens observed a convoy comprising two medium merchant ships escorted by two torpedo boats, fighter planes, seaplanes and reconnaissance aircraft. The merchants were 3,000 yards apart, with the escorts each disposed abeam on the outward sides of the convoy.

Orders were issued to manoeuvre the boat into a more prominent position and two minutes later the klaxon was sounded throughout the submarine and the crew assembled in readiness for confrontation. At 0751 two explosions, from an unknown origin, were heard throughout the boat. Aircraft activity increased as Stevens positioned the boat into an attack position. Four torpedoes were launched at 0814 over a firing interval of 16 seconds from a range of 4,000 yards and spread over two ships lengths at a depth of 10 feet. The majority of the crew crossed their fingers and rum tots were placed as bets on the result.

After two minutes and fifty-seven seconds of silence, there was one loud explosion, followed 12 seconds later by a smaller explosion, which echoed through the boat. A loud cheer and an increase in chatter could be heard inside all departments, followed by silence as the prospect of a reign of terror descending from above in retaliation suddenly developed in the thoughts of every man on board.

The noise of the German merchant vessel Baalbek (a former French vessel of 2115 gross tons) breaking up could be heard and then, four minutes and 57 seconds after the first torpedo had been fired, there was another loud explosion. Stevens ordered the boat to take avoiding action by proceeding at full speed for three minutes on the reverse of the enemy's course and then continuing slow at 150 feet. At 0824 hours one torpedo boat commenced the hunt for *Unruffled* and 18 minutes later a pattern of five depth charges were dropped and exploded moderately close, but no damage was reported. The torpedo boat was never heard to be in contact and at 0930 hours when the boat rose to periscope depth, Stevens could see nothing but just one enemy craft far in the distance.

The torpedo boat did, however, close the distance at 1000 hours, but was easily evaded and by 1115 hours had been lost completely. Twelve explosions were heard at 1055, all at distance and of no real concern to the crew. However, aircraft now became more troublesome and at 1135 an unidentified aircraft flew close, with further air activity continuing until 1400 hours. Two E-boats were sighted through the periscope at 1235, and closed to within 4,000 yards. However, after listening for ten minutes, they sailed away. *Unruffled* took avoiding action by slowly withdrawing and there were no further incidents.

Aircraft activity continued during the afternoon and *Unruffled*, after spending 13 hours and seven minutes submerged, resurfaced at 1857 hours. Stevens sent a wireless transmission to Malta, via Whitehall, reporting the situation and that he had exhausted all but one torpedo. Another additional white bar was added to the Jolly Roger.

0544 hours 22nd February:

With the swell now having disappeared, *Unruffled* dived
and set a course for Hammamet and Neboel. Aircraft
activity was busier than usual and at 1010 hours an
explosion ashore was logged. A close reconnaissance of the
two areas showed that a new jetty was under construction
at Hammamet and the jetty at Neboel appeared to be being
rebuilt. Stevens concluded that these targets were not
practical to damage by torpedo. Having surfaced at 1846
hours, the recall back to Malta was received and a new,
homeward course set.

0547 hours 23rd February:

The submarine dived. Three distant explosions echoed
through the boat at 1520 hours and five minutes later a
floating body could be seen in the water, so *Unruffled* closed
to investigate. Another three bodies were sighted, but could
not be identified as either Allied or Axis personnel. The boat
surfaced at 1858 and continued their voyage back to Malta.

0255 hours 24th February:

Sighted Gozo and entered the swept channel at 0845 hours
astern of HMS *Thunderbolt* and their escort 'Hebe'. The
submarine moored alongside *Thunderbolt* on berth U4 at
1045 hours and Stevens headed for his meeting with
Captain (S) George Phillips. Two-thirds of the crew headed
for a hot bath; the remainder had to wait until 1315 hours.

0815 hours 25th February:

Half the ship's company was given shore leave, giving those
ratings left on board the opportunity to clean the boat. At
1500 hours the boat was shifted to berth U2.

0815 hours 27th February:

All hands reported on board and the remainder of the ship's company went on leave.

(*Author's note: Unfortunately, the submarine logs for the next submarine patrol are missing, so all information has been taken from the patrol log.

11th PATROL

1500 hours 6th March:

Unruffled left Malta and proceeded unescorted to her designated patrol area.

0922 hours 7th March:

Twelve distant explosions were heard and the thoughts of the crew turned towards those on the receiving end. The submarine surfaced at 1750 hours and five practice rounds were fired from the 3-inch gun.

P.M. 8th March:

A patrol area to the north-east of the Tunisian city of Sousse had been established and, upon surfacing, *Unruffled* withdrew to seaward in order to recharge the batteries and to escape the three powerful searchlights sweeping the sea in the vicinity of Sousse.

1930 hours 11th March:

Unruffled was ordered by Malta to relieve HMS *Unseen* in the northern patrol area. No shipping had been sighted in the Sousse area.

0522 hours 12th March:

The boat dived after sighting a small darkened vessel. A fast diesel H/E was heard, but the noise soon faded. It was thought that this was probably an E-boat on passage from Pantelleria to Cape Bon. A patrol line was established, but this was changed after a message was received from Malta to concentrate in the north-east corner of the patrol area.

0657 hours 13th March:

Twenty-two distant depth charge explosions were heard throughout the boat over a period of 31 minutes.

0820 hours 14th March:

Five distant explosions were heard.

0815 hours 15th March:

After observing smoke on the horizon through the periscope, *Unruffled* changed course and increased speed to close the distance. At 0822 hours the smoke disappeared over the horizon and was not seen again. No aircraft were in sight, but a floating mine was seen in position 36 deg 44 min N 11 deg 33 Min E.

0600 hours 16th March:

Unruffled proceeded southwards, two miles clear of the coast from the vicinity of Kurba (Korba) on the east shore of Cape Bon. Upon sighting a barge at 0730 hours, the submarine changed course and speed to intercept and take a closer look. This was later identified as a tank lighter. At 0945 a party of Arabs was seen boarding the lighter from a small boat and begin looting the contents. As *Unruffled* was too close inshore to surface, Stevens decided to deal with the lighter after dark. At 1436 hours the shore battery sighted *Unruffled*'s exposed periscope 3,000 yards offshore and opened fire with three rounds, one of which sounded like a close call. This testifies to the alertness and vigilance of the coast watches. It was also noticed that the pier at Neboel had been completed and was estimated that one lighter could be berthed either side of the pier. After surfacing at 1930 hours, a course was set to find the lighter sighted earlier in the day. At 2012 *Unruffled* located the intended quarry and went alongside.

Lieutenant Fenton and Petty Officer E. Holmes boarded the lighter with the intention of setting charges. The lighter consisted of a cylindrical tank with a bow and stern riveted on. The bow and stern compartments acted as buoyancy chambers and were fitted with watertight hatches. The after-hatch was jammed shut. Four one-and-a-quarter pound charges were placed in the forward compartment. The only fitting in the compartment was a semi-rotary pump with a suction leading to the bottom of the tank. The discharge hoses and other gear had doubtless been removed by the Arabs.

Fenton reported a strong smell of petrol in the compartment. Eight minutes later the fuse was lit and the demolition party re-embarked the submarine, which set off to seaward. The charge exploded at 2032 hours with a flash of flame, after which the lighter settled by the bow and floated vertically with two feet of her stern out of the water. She sank shortly afterwards and a symbol representing a demolition charge was added to the Jolly Roger that evening.

0600 hours 17th March:

Whilst *Unruffled* proceeded westwards along the coast towards Hammamet, it was confirmed that the construction of the stone and rubble jetty west of the old fort in the town was still in progress. Having received the return-to-base signal, a course was set for Malta at 2000 hours.

0600 hours 18th March:

Fourteen single explosions were heard at varying intervals through the day, lasting until 1800 hours and giving the impression of heavy explosions a long way off.

1230 hours 19th March:

The boat tied up in Malta. Stevens reported to Captain (S) that air activity was light and that a rotating framework on a mast, thought to be from a radar station, was found on the coast one-and-a-half miles north of Sousse. Only one power-propelled vessel was encountered, giving no value to the A/S ratings in terms of practice. Stevens then went on to celebrate his 27th birthday in the best fashion that Malta would allow.

Unfortunately, bad news was to follow when it was announced that *Thunderbolt* was overdue from her patrol and was to be considered lost. Stevens was very much saddened by this news, commenting that the submarine's commander, Captain Cecil Crouch, "had bid me *au revoir* when we sailed for Tunisia, as it had been planned to change *Thunderbolt's* base from Malta to Algiers after her ill-fated last patrol. 'See you in the UK when we get back for the next refit, I expect,' he had said. His loss and that of other fine and experienced submariners on board was a blow to the submarine branch".

As the Allied conquest of North Africa neared completion, the number of merchant vessels sailing from the Italian mainland became less frequent, therefore targets for the 10th Submarine Flotilla became scarce. There was, however, another role for the versatile U-Class submarine to act out.

Stevens, however, offers a glimpse into future operations when he is quoted as saying "Captain (S) G.C. Philips introduced me to Lieutenant N. McHarg. We were to see much of one another in the next two months. Mac was in charge of a Combined Operations Beach Party (COPP); they had been formed to make clandestine surveys of potential assault beaches in future operations against the Axis. Embarked in *Unruffled*, Mac's COPP was scheduled to examine the south-east Sicilian beaches. Before we sailed with the COPP for Sicily, there was a training period in local Malta waters.

"Each COPP was commanded by a specialist navigating officer or hydrographic officer; he was supported by two naval officers, a Sapper officer, with expertise in assessing beach exits for use by armoured vehicles and other military aspects, and two other naval ratings. For *Unruffled*'s crew, the training centred around perfecting a slick drill for getting the canvas canoes and crews from the torpedo compartment to the casing, and thence into the water and away in double quick time. When they returned, an equally fast re-embarkation was required. In this way, the parent submarine was at risk by lying stopped with the large torpedo hatch open for a minimum of time".

Codenamed 'Party Inhuman' and known as the Coppist, the COPP team undertook submarine periscope surveys, as well as examination of the beach area, noting the gradients of underwater approaches, sand bars, obstacles, mined areas, beach exits, rocks, land surfaces, beach defences, beach consistency, natural hazards, gun emplacements, lookouts, sentry posts and enemy positions. These details would have been mapped out and charted for the invasion troops. At the time of the invasion the Coppist would return to the beach and guide ships by using torchlight.

The procedure for the submarine pick-up of the COPP team allowed for a period of 30 minutes before the folbot was expected back to flash 'K's on the R.G. (a signalling disc and shutters that could be operated and read using a periscope) towards the shore for one hour or until the folbot returned. The COPP team was to return the signal by the letter 'M' if practicable. If the folbot had not returned after one hour the submarine dived and would take up a position six miles offshore, waiting until 0600 hours, when she would wait on the surface.

According to Stevens: "The daylight hours were used by the COPP team for resting, photography and sketching through the periscope, as well as noting details of defences sighted. In the moonless part of the night two canoes would be launched from three miles offshore. Using double paddles, the two-man crew, clad in rubber suits, would move close inshore. There, one crewman from each crew would get into the water, equipped with simple aids such as a soil sampler, compass, underwater slates, pencils and a torch. Walking around, with only his head and blackened face above the surface, he would record the information required to map the beach gradients and other details.

"I was full of admiration for these brave people. On

occasions they would be paddling or walking around close enough to hear Italian soldiers guarding the coast, or singing 'O Sole Mio' to while away the tedium of night watches. The gymnastic feat of leaving and entering the canoe without capsizing required skill and patience; it was certainly not without risk. While the canoes were inshore, *Unruffled* would withdraw to seaward, hoping to charge the batteries without interruption. Four hours after the canoes had set off, *Unruffled* would be at the rendezvous for recovery, three miles from the beach. This was always a nerve-racking time for the canoeists and myself. The canoes were supplied with a signal lantern covered by an infra-red shade, from which the filtered light could be seen only through special binoculars or spectacles. Even with these lanterns, it was easy to miss a rendezvous.

"One canoe (not from *Unruffled*) got left behind, and paddled 120 miles from east Sicily to Malta. The crew arrived tired, sore and sunburnt, but otherwise unharmed".

20th March-3rd April:
Training commenced with the COPP team.

*(*Author's note: Once again there is no ship's log for the forth-coming patrol.)*

12th PATROL

1600 hours 4th April:
When *Unruffled* sailed unescorted from Malta destined for its pre-arranged patrol area, the submarine had three guests on board. Lieutenant Neville Townley McHarg DSO,

Lieutenant George Sutherland Sinclair DSO and Leading Seaman Thomas Reilly DSM, all from the COPP Party IV, had embarked with their equipment to carry out clandestine operations. The standard issue COPP equipment included a wetsuit; Chinagraph pencil attached to the suit by a short line; matt white slate for underwater writing; revolver in holster that had to be stripped and cleaned after every sortie; waterproof torch with blue lens; fighting knife in scabbard; fishing line on a reel attached to a foot-long brass rod used for measuring distance; waterproof compass; infra-red signal lamp; grenade for use as a signal underwater explosion (SUE); auger tube for taking core samples; and a 'bong stick', which was a metal box containing a mechanical hammer operated by a rotating handle attached to a rod.

Unbeknown to *Unruffled*'s crew, Party IV COPP had already suffered losses amongst the team while undertaking reconnaissance of the Sicilian beaches on the 26th February and the 9th March, 1943. From January to March 1943, the COPP teams suffered five Coppist missing, presumed dead, and seven out of 16 captured.

2230 hours 5th April:
The folbot was launched for a practice run and at 2315 hours, having recovered the craft and crew, a change of course was made for Sicily. This practice run was deemed to have been successful as the folbot homed onto the submarine from a range of one-and-a-quarter miles, though R.G. transmissions were not sighted, probably due to the slight swell.

0120 hours 6th April:

Stevens began the reconnaissance of the beaches, surfacing at 2015 hours. After discussion with the COPP party on board it was decided to postpone folbot action because the moderate swell made boat operation difficult. An examination of the coast was made and leading landmarks were noted.

0825 hours 7th April:

Unruffled continued periscope reconnaissance and sighted a tug towing practice targets for the shore batteries, which had engaged at a range of 6,000 yards. At 1145 hours the tug stopped and commenced shortening the tow rope and, on completion at 1200 hours, left the vicinity heading towards Syracuse. When *Unruffled* surfaced at 2030 the weather was suitable to launch the folbot, so Stevens ordered the submarine to dive in preparation of the COPP operation.

The Coppist team changed clothes, gathered their equipment together and mentally prepared themselves for the mission to come. Once *Unruffled* had surfaced at 2230 the folbot was launched. The wind, it was noticed, had changed direction to the north-west, so Lieutenant Sinclair, a member of the COPP party in charge of the folbot, was instructed to see what the sea conditions were like before proceeding inshore. The COPP team personnel returned at 2315 due to the adverse weather conditions and, once they had been retrieved, the folbot was put as quickly as possible back through the torpedo hatch. The barometer continued to fall rapidly and the weather deteriorated, making any further attempt too dangerous.

2030 8th April:

Unruffled surfaced but, with the wind gradually increasing from F4 to F5, the weather conditions were unsuitable for any type of operation. At 2225 hours, while charging batteries ten miles offshore, the shore batteries near Avola, Syracuse, carried out gunnery practice at a target illuminated by searchlight.

2030 hours 9th April:

The submarine surfaced into a strong north-westerly wind, which proved unsuitable for any kind of boat work. It was therefore decided to set course for the Catania area of Sicily. Breakfast that evening consisted of bacon, beans and coffee, and, as there was not enough room to seat everyone around the table at the same time, it was taken in relays by the officers and Coppist members. It was noted with some amusement that during the meal the guests struggled to prevent a swarm of cockroaches from stealing their bread. Any offensive action taken to brush away the unwelcomed visitors resulted in the creatures scurrying, with amazing speed, over the edge of the table, with only their eyes and antennae visible. As fast as one was exterminated, another appeared.

0700 hours 10th April:

A reconnaissance patrol was carried out at periscope depth in Catania Bay. At 0830 hours the boat withdrew to the south-east and upon reaching Cape Santa Croce, near the Sicilian village of Campolato, at 1325 hours, sighted the funnel and the bridge of a torpedo boat close inshore. After surfacing at 2030 and setting course for Malta, it was decided that, due to the unfavourable sea conditions, any further attempt to launch the folbot would be dangerous.

1030 hours 12th April:

Arrived safely back at Fort Talbot, Malta. Stevens and McHarg both reported to Captain (S) that no patrol ships had been encountered and very few aircraft were either heard or seen. Unusually, they reported, no aircraft were heard at night.

Lt McHarg also suggested that the success of future operations depended on more accurate navigation by the submarine rather than the use of R.G. signalling. This required good leading marks being visible at night for the folbot to steer by and to assist the submarine in maintaining position. Stevens agreed with McHarg's observations.

A new R.D.F. (Radar direction finder) was fitted on board the submarine, and described by Lieutenant Stevens "as a device that warned when an enemy radar set was in contact. It caused some anxious moments until it was appreciated that a powerful airborne radar, 100 miles away or more, could trigger the search receiver if it was pointing in our direction. There was such a mass of radar emissions all around us that we decided to keep the search receiver switched off".

The quality of food had begun to improve as more convoys resupplied the island of Malta. The ratings also enjoyed better facilities ashore, although there were still limited supplies; a beer could only be purchased at the right price. On the 2nd May a football match between the Royal Navy Malta Force and the 1st Coast Regiment RMA took place at the Empire Stadium, Gzira, and attracted an appreciative 14,000 spectators.

13th PATROL

1500 hours 28th April:
Unruffled motored from the pontoon off the Lazaretto to participate in operation SOX (Submarine Observation Exercise). As well as the three-man crew from the COPP team IV, surgeon Lieutenant A.F. Crowley R.N.V.R. had volunteered to come on the patrol. This was because Lieutenant Stevens had an ulcer on this leg that required frequent medical attention While on board he also dealt with one case of gastroenteritis, one ulcerative stomatitis (an infectious disease of the mouth) and a minor, and not unsurprising, common cold epidemic.

There were now seven officers on board, which caused additional difficult overcrowding problems, and the claustrophobic experience was described by one as a position "of extreme discomfort".

Unruffled proceeded at 1715 hours to her planned patrol area and a practice run of launching the folbot was undertaken at 2135, with the successful recovery of the canvas kayak at 2220 hours.

29th April:
A routine day, with no aircraft or ship sightings.

30th April:
Details of the beaches and coastline were noted through the periscope during daylight hours but, after surfacing, a rising wind prevented boat operations during the night.

0001 hours 1ˢᵗ May:

With a persistent strong north-easterly wind, boat operations were once again postponed. An all-round flashing lamp high upon the shore was seen transmitting Morse code for approximately ten minutes in the vicinity of Avola. The only readable word was 'Augusta'.

0101 hours 4ᵗʰ May:

Unruffled was forced to dive in a position of 36 deg 45 min N 15 deg 21 min E as H/E reported a contact, and one minute later the approaching bow wave of an E-boat was identified, passing the submarine close to the port side at 0115. The submarine continued to recharge the batteries some ten miles offshore.

5ᵗʰ-7ᵗʰ May:

Due to low visibility and inclement sea conditions, all inshore operations were cancelled.

2330 hours 8ᵗʰ May:

Having surfaced and completed the recharging of the batteries some five to six miles offshore, it was agreed finally to attempt to launch of the folbot and *Unruffled* made her way to the launch position. Having seen the Coppist team safely disembarked *Unruffled* dived as R.D.F. activity from the shore stations put everyone on alert.

Patrolling close to where it had dived, *Unruffled* remained in the vicinity of the rendezvous point. The powerful beam of the searchlight on Cape Murro di Porco, on the edge of the Peninsula della Maddalena and six miles away from the launch position, swept round 15 minutes after the launch.

0208 hours 9th May:

Both the pre-arranged signals, two underwater charges at a half-a-minute intervals, were heard, indicating that the folbot had returned early and required the submarine to close the rendezvous and re-embark the crew. At 0215 hours *Unruffled* surfaced and the order was given to bring the H.G. lamp to the bridge. At that moment, however, the folbot was sighted and a few minutes later retrieved.

Just as the canoe arrived alongside, the beam of the shore-based searchlight crossed the path of the submarine, swept along the shore before reversing its path. This was a stressful time for the crew, for the submarine could have been spotted at any moment and attacked by the shore batteries. Fortunately, they avoided detection and five minutes later, with the Coppist safely down below deck, *Unruffled* withdrew seaward to charge the batteries.

Because the folbot had been unable to find the beach when inshore during the night, a course was set in daylight, at 1300 hours, close inshore. At the same time two E-boats passed astern, though this minor incident did not cause the crew undue alarm. At 1500 hours it was found that the periscope wire was badly stranded and was replaced. *Unruffled* surfaced at 2100 hours, only to discover that the strong south-westerly wind was unsuitable for any folbot operations. As this was the last night of suitable moon conditions, Stevens decided to return to Malta.

0430 hours 10th May:

A signal was sent to Malta with an E.T.A. (Estimated Time of Arrival) at Malta.

1100 hours 11th May:

Unruffled secured alongside at the Lazaretto. Together with Lieutenant McHarg, Stevens went ashore to make his report to Captain (S), highlighting the disappointment of the poor local weather conditions. Inshore fog was the most frequent problem. It was difficult enough to locate the canoe in clear weather, let alone in fog, which could so easily have jeopardised the missions. Stevens also reported that the searchlight on Murro di Porco had not been sighted when they had previously been in the area and that it swept four or five times at intervals of not less than an hour, illuminating the submarine as it swept past.

He also reported that air activity in the area had been on an extremely low scale and that throughout the patrol only two aircraft had been sighted. There was also no evidence of any surface ships within the vicinity. As to the R.D.F. set, many contacts were reported, chiefly from shore stations, and a few from aircraft. In no case was a contact followed by an attack. It was considered that until the ratings responsible for the operation of the set had become more skilled, there would be a certain number of false alarms.

During this short reprieve Stevens was confronted with an unusual problem: "Our sister vessel, the Polish O.R.P. *Dzik*, had arrived from the UK to join the flotilla. The genial [Lt-Cmdr Boleslaw] Romanowski was in command and he had introduced a special initiation procedure for guests before they became socially acceptable in the submarine's hospitable wardroom," recalls Stevens. "A full tumbler of neat gin, or [fruit brandy] slivovica (slivovitz), would be provided; a liberal addition of red pepper was stirred in. The guest, or rather, victim, was required to drink the mixture 'straight down the hatch'. This fearsome beverage was known as 'gindzik'."

14th PATROL

1715 hours 25th May:
Unruffled, escorted by Hebe, left Malta for a patrol area in the Tyrrhenian Sea with an important extra person on board. After an hour the boat was forced to dive because of an air-raid warning, but surfaced at 1835 hours and at 2045 parted company with Hebe.

The special additional crew member was 23-year-old Lieutenant Jack Bitmead DSO, one of the youngest naval officers to be awarded this decoration. He was on board *Unruffled* as part of his special training for submarine command. Lieutenant Bitmead earned his DSO in May 1942 whilst serving on the destroyer HMS Forester, which had been escorting the light cruiser HMS Edinburgh back to Murmansk after she had been torpedoed by a German submarine. The crippled vessel and her Russian convoy escorts were attacked by the German destroyers Z24, Z25 and Z7 Hermann Schoemann. HMS Forester attempted to attack Z25 with torpedoes but was hit by shells and disabled. Twelve crewmen were killed, including the captain, and nine wounded.

With HMS Forester lay stopped less than two miles from the enemy and the captain dead, Bitmead assumed command. At one point the enemy came so close that Bitmead feared HMS Forester might be boarded. He then watched helplessly as two torpedoes raced towards the destroyer, only to pass beneath her and continue on towards the helpless HMS Edinburgh. Fortunately, the engineers on board the Forester managed to repair her fractured steam pipes, enabling her to get underway, and she eventually joined the other British warships.

Bitmead then decided to use the ploy of drawing enemy fire, tempting the Germans to make HMS Forester their chief target. During this sortie, the destroyer endured several heavy attacks while at the same time continuing to adopt the tactic of producing smokescreens, resulting in one German ship being sunk and another badly damaged. After sailing back to Russia for repairs, Bitmead retained his command and returned to Britain before continuing on escort work, this time involving another cruiser, HMS Trinidad. When she was attacked and set on fire, Bitmead was first alongside and, despite coming under fire from German bombers, and with fires burning fiercely and ammunition exploding, he managed to evacuate 30 stretcher cases and other casualties.

Having distinguished himself, he was ordered by the Admiralty, along with three others, to report to Blyth, Northumberland, for submarine commanding officer training as part of a fast-track experiment. Bitmead undertook a total of four war patrols, but found it "interestingly unpleasant" to be depth charged. He persuaded the Admiralty that the project would not work and reverted back to general service. John Stevens reported: "I think the patrol was of greater value to him as he was to see things going wrong and the steps taken to remedy them."

0440 hours 26th May:

Unruffled, after having continued its journey at a depth of 60 feet, the instruction was given to maintain periscope depth in order to collect the wireless telegraph routines. A/S transmissions where reported at 1410 hours, which were determined to emanate from HMS *Trident* (N52), which was expected to pass on a reverse course at this time. A single loud explosion, probably a bomb, was encountered at 1851 hours, resulting in the crew looking towards the heavens for one fleeting moment and expelling expletives the next.

0300 hours 27th May:

In position 37 deg 22 min N 2 deg 47 min E another submarine was sighted on an opposite course to *Unruffled*. This was probably *Dolfijn* (*P47*), but so as not to take any chances, the klaxon sounded for diving stations and Stevens slipped the boat below the surface. *Unruffled* resurfaced half an hour later and continued on the surface for the remainder of its night patrol. A single aircraft, at a height of 300 feet and carrying out a surveillance sweep, came close to the port side at 2205 hours, and the horizontal searchlight near Cape St Vito, north-west Sicily, was seen to be sweeping the area. A message from Malta revising the patrol area was received at 2330 and *Unruffled* changed course accordingly and proceeded on the surface.

1340 hours 29th May:

The submarine arrived at a patrol area off the Cape of Tindaro and at 1415 hours an F-lighter passed overhead, an incident which, according to Stevens, indicated that these lighters were being used to supply Sicily. At 1600 hours it was decided to inspect the shoreline, so a slow, creeping course was set in order for a better look. Stevens identified five or six boats with men on board and appearing hard at work either laying cables or undertaking repairs.

On closer inspection these barges looked like long mooring lighters. Stevens chose to ignore these targets and the workman continued with their labour, unaware that they had been watched through a submarine periscope.

After an hour the submarine withdrew to deeper water. *Unruffled* was forced to dive at 2153 hours, three minutes after the ASDIC operator had reported H/E contact. Shortly afterwards a white light appeared, fairly high up, as though a lamp was being used, and turbine transmissions could be heard by the H/E operator giving a turbine of 140 revs. This contact faded after ten minutes, but 40 minutes later an irregular series of bangs was heard similar to 'hull tapping', giving the crew an anxious moment, and Stevens issued the order to "Diving stations". *Unruffled* surfaced, at 2247 and the "terrible tappings" were lost in the water noises.

0900 hours 30th May: The boat established a patrol area off Cape Vaticano, in the Municipality of Ricadi in Calabria, Italy, but apart from several transiting aircraft being sighted, no ships or naval targets were either sighted or heard during the day or when surfaced that night.

0430 hours 31st May: In glassy calm weather conditions, and having dived for the day, a patrol area six miles off Cape Vaticano was established and Stevens considered it to be impracticable to patrol close inshore.

Smoke was sighted at 1440 hours, with a lone Cant

Z.501 aircraft zigzagging overhead, suggested to Stevens that a convoy could be approaching from the north. The order to commence closing to intercept was given and the crew was brought to diving stations.

Having closed to a range of 6,000 yards, at 1500 hours Stevens observed through the high-powered periscope a small merchant vessel escorted by a Generale class torpedo boat. Commencing the attack, Stevens soon became aware that the merchant vessel was hugging the coast and it was difficult to observe against the background of the land.

The escorting torpedo boat was stationed well aft on the seaward quarter, clearly with a view to punishing any submarine that made an attack rather than to try and prevent a strike being made. No transmission was reported and the speed of the Axis vessel was achieved by her passing a point of land. This speed was estimated to be 11 knots and, as this was higher than she looked capable of steaming, Stevens adjusted accordingly for entry into the 'fruit machine'. The attack failed due to the enemy's constant change of course and *Unruffled*'s inability to get into position, so no torpedoes were fired. Stevens admitted: "I now realise that the position off Cape Vaticano was ill-chosen, and that a straight stretch of coast is preferable when operating against coastal traffic". At 2130 hours the submarine proceeded northwards

0430 hours 1st June:
The boat dived and set up a patrol area three and a half miles off Cape Suvero, Italy, but only a fishing craft, one E-boat and one or two small craft close inshore were sighted throughout the day.

0600 hours 2nd June:

After being forced to dive deep in order to clean the high-powered periscope, which was badly fogging, the submarine returned to periscope depth at 0730 hours, only to find that the condensation that caused the fogging was on one of the upper lenses and, therefore, could not be cleaned.

Two Axis merchant vessels, both in ballast and escorted by a single torpedo boat and a seaplane, were seen to be passing inshore while *Unruffled h*ad gone deep, but were now out of range. Stevens was later to tell Captain (S) back at Malta that "it was tantalising, to put it mildly, to see the second worthwhile target in two days slip through our fingers in such a fashion. During the day the fogging of the high-powered periscope got worse until it was useless". One distant explosion reverberated through the submarine at 2052 hours.

1100 hours 3rd June:

Six distant explosions were heard and, due to a rising swell during the night, a patrol line was maintained two miles off the coast of Cape Suvero. A single southbound vessel, escorted by a torpedo boat, was sighted at 1510 hours at a range of 5,000 yards. Diving stations was ordered and the crew quickly and efficiently stood by for an attack. No air escort was seen, which was not surprising because the high-powered periscope was out of action and the only available attack periscope did not have sky-search capability.

Stevens identified the Axis vessel as the 10,000 gross tons former French medium-sized tanker Henri Desprez, while the escort was thought to be a new class of torpedo boat. Stevens continued to relay plot information and tactical data to enter into the 'fruit machine', resulting in four torpedoes being launched at 1531 hours.

From a range of 1,100 yards and the escort close astern of the submarine, the first deadly 'fish' took just 47 seconds to reach its target. Three hits were heard and the tanker blew up and sank. *Unruffled* dived deep, ready for the inevitable retaliation. This took only eight minutes to arrive in the form of 15 depth charges being dropped in two patterns of three, with the remainder dropped singly. No damage was caused and Stevens decided that the best tactic was to slowly approach close inshore near the steep cliffs, but he confused both himself and the hunting escort, as he explained. "Noises as if of more hunting vessels were reported by the ASDIC operator. These noises were, in fact, generated by surf breaking on the rocks near to us. When this little problem had been solved we were able to withdraw unscathed."

The submarine was brought up to periscope depth at 1745 hours and Stevens was able to confirm that there was nothing in sight except for one Cant Z.501 floatplane withdrawing to the west. This was to be the largest prey of *Unruffled*'s commission, resulting in another white bar for the Jolly Roger.

0930 hours 4th June:
After having received the recall signal from Malta, *Unruffled* set a course for Port Talbot. That evening the klaxon sounded for diving stations and the submarine rose to the surface to begin charging the batteries. The cook began to prepare breakfast and the inside of the submarine soon began to assume a more pleasant atmosphere, the flow

of air to the diesel engines through the conning tower hatch having the effect of cooling and ventilating the boat.

0225 hours 8ᵗʰ June:

On the approach to Malta an aircraft dropped two flares one mile astern of the submarine. *Unruffled* fired three red star grenades, which was the wrong signal, as the grenades used were only for inter-ship identification. At 1100 hours *Unruffled* tied up and the order to 'Stop motors' was given. When Stevens reported to Captain (S), he highlighted a number of notable observations regarding radar and listening stations on the mainland and on the island of Sicily.

He also raised certain issues regarding *Unruffled* and the equipment on board: "It is a matter for concern, that with calm weather conditions becoming prevalent, I have no confidence in being able to carry out an attack firing by ASDIC, should it be impossible or inadvisable to use the periscope. My H.S.D. is a keen rating, who does his level best, but due to lack of experience, he cannot produce good results.

"On a quiet patrol, he is lucky if he hears H.E. for a total of two hours and therefore his capabilities are liable to get worse, and every effort should be made to give a thorough training in A/S practice submarines before sending them to an operational boat."

He also went on to list the number of defects encountered on board the submarine, including the 'Q' tank which, although blown (emptied of water) when at periscope depth, was found to flood (fill up) again. The high-powered periscope had three carbon lamps placed in the well and left for three days in order to empty the moisture out of the upper lenses.

Although this worked, it would only prove to be a temporary cure. The steering was leaking on the port side, but after a running repair job by the engineers the defect was made good. Battery ventilation flooded on diving for trim due to the valves seizing, a task that would require repair in the dockyard. The Vickers tele-pump had to be bypassed due to a screw working loose and the toilets (heads) had been causing great concern. This was proving to be not only a major defect but a source of general annoyance and inconvenience to the crew.

15th PATROL

9th June-5th July, 1943:
All records relating to this historically important period are inexplicably missing. One can only presume, therefore, that submarine defects that had been reported by Stevens were acted upon and finally the boat was dry-docked in Valletta for repairs. Stevens gives us a partial account of the following six weeks in his autobiography 'Never volunteer'. He writes: "We were required for COPP work again. [Lieutenant] McHarg's team had moved on, and this time we took a COPP commanded by a piratically-bearded and forceful character, Ralph Stanbury."

Lieutenant Ralph Neville Stanbury DSO was in charge of COPP V, a team consisting of ten specialists. Stanbury selected three Coppists to accompany him. They were Captain Peter D. Matterson MC, Royal Engineers, leading-seaman A. Thomas, bar to DSM MiD, and Lieutenant Kent

Douglas Thomas, bar to DSC, a volunteer RNVR expert on combined operations.

Matterson is described by Stanbury as follows: "... difficult to find someone [as] completely painstaking or conscientious as Peter, or anyone whose judgment was so sound. He was always immaculately dressed, from the forage cap perched on his rather round head to his shrewd brown eyes and clipped brown moustache right down to his army boats, which he personally polished for at least an hour each night. He was also the eldest of the party, and by far the most patient."

Describing Lieutenant Kent Thomas, who was 23 years old and apparently married with a baby on the way, Stanbury tells us that he was "at times embarrassingly frank and outspoken. He had a boyish face, rosy cheeks and round blue eyes, and was as courageous as a lion". He was also "miserable unless he was in the thick of the fray". The last member of the team was leading-seaman Thomas, who was "always a pillar of strength and a fund of humour. He had passed up a commission so as to be with me in this job, and I was extremely lucky to have him".

The two folbots used for a total of eight excursions into enemy territory were named 'Karol Anne' and 'Old Faithful', especially chosen earlier by Stanbury and his team. Explained Stanbury: "I thought at the time that 'Karol Anne' must have had some connection with the reminiscent twinkle that would often light up in Thompson's (leading-seaman Thomas) eye." He was single, while the other two were married men.

"As regards 'Old Faithful', Thompson said he thought I [in particular] ought to name her, as she was going to be our 'number one' [kayak]. "Oh, just call her 'Old Faithful'," I said absently. "I expect I shall spend most of the coming months 'roaming the range' in her!"

Unruffled was docked in Malta on 20th June, the day King George VI arrived from Tripoli on HMS Aurora for his historic ten-hour visit to mark the raising of the Siege. Around 6,000 British and US naval servicemen and more than 1,000 merchantmen welcomed the King, who made a special visit to the island's submarine base. Though there are no records available, it is inconceivable that Stevens and the crew of *Unruffled* did not play some part in the celebrations.

22nd June:

Lieutenant Stanbury refers to *Unruffled* sailing on this day with a team of four Coppists, describing life on board and how: "Kent and I, being the two naval officers on the passenger list, were billeted in the ward-room. Matterson, the engineer of our party, was farmed out to the Engine Room Artificers, while leading-seaman Thomas had part-share in a bunk with three petty officers. Matterson, however, would come into the wardroom for his meals.

"The first lieutenant (Seaburne-May) would organise a supply of eggs at the Maltese black market price of one shilling and sixpence each, and we used to boil these in a kettle and consume two each for tea at four o'clock in the morning."

Lieutenant Stanbury also, like so many on *Unruffled*, admired one very important crew member, Timoshenko the cat. Stanbury reckoned that Timmo certainly lived up to the fame of his gallant namesake. "Nothing seemed to shake him out of his serenity," he noted.

25th June:

Just after dawn *Unruffled* arrived off the east coast of Sicily. The Coppists had been tasked with investigating three beaches and the work had to be completed in a short period of time. By 1800 hours Lieutenant Thomas and Matterson had inspected all three beaches through the periscope and familiarised themselves with landmarks so as to make them easier to pinpoint at night.

Lieutenant Stanbury decided to take Kent Thomas ashore with him that night. The pair couldn't wait to set off, for "the air inside the submarine was as stale as last year's gorgonzola, and [the temperature] about 120 degrees Fahrenheit". The klaxon for diving stations was sounded at 2100 hours, slowly surfacing, and the two men, dressed in wet suits, climbed up the conning-tower ladder and onto the bridge. A cool breeze greeted them, with dancing wavelets on the surface of the sea.

Lieutenant Stevens wished his guests good luck and the two daring Coppists lowered themselves into the folbot, which had been brought up on deck through the torpedo compartment hatch, and the party soon disappeared into the darkness. Stevens ordered *Unruffled* to dive, heading out to open sea so that the process of recharging the batteries could be achieved. After the close, humid atmosphere of the interior of the submarine, the cool air and the sudden increase in the supply of oxygen began to have the effect of drunkenness upon the pair. Stanbury felt an intense desire to stand up in the canoe and sing, feeling free of the confines of the submarine, where they had been under strict instructions not to exert themselves in order to conserve the precious air. Stanbury and Thomas found it invigorating to be able to swing a paddle and dig it deep into the water. Approaching the coast with the low cliffs, the sound of waves washing ashore was magnified by the silence of the night, conjuring up the vision of an inhospitable, rock-girt coast, where the breakers would seize the frail canoe and carry it to destruction. Three hundred yards from the shore they stopped paddling to look for the small beach (Beach 45) which had to be examined. "Damned if I can see it" Stanbury said, before surveying the area through his binoculars. "There's our beach, directly opposite us. You can also see the northern limit, where the gorge of the Cassibile River emerges, and it appears very dark. We've made it first time".

Lieutenant Thomas whispered in reply "Yes, but look over there". He pointed to the northern end of the beach, where a horn of steep, rugged land jutted out into the sea. Stanbury saw a small building midway along the horn, clearly silhouetted on the skyline. As he looked, a door opened, letting out a stream of light, and the sound of men's voices, raised in laughter and song, drifted out – a sentry hut!

They swung the canoe round to a more southerly position, and it was decided that Stanbury would swim to the shore. At 2300 hours, the Coppist leader extracted himself from the canoe after instructing Thomas, "Wait for me at the other end of the beach, where we first came in. I'll swim out and flash my torch for you. OK?"

The water was dark and turgid, enveloping him like treacle, leaving Stanbury feeling utterly alone and deserted. Fear of the unknown, with the cold-blooded suspense was the most frightening thing Stanbury had ever experienced. He looked at his watch, and saw that time was getting short. Ashore there were lights moving, and men's voices.

Suddenly his right foot touched the ground. With only his head and shoulders showing above the waterline and his feet touching sand, he found, after closer inspection, that the sand would not harm tanks in the assault, whereas shingle of a certain size posed a danger of getting trapped in the tracks and doing greater damage. He crept forward to the water's edge, crawling on his belly, feeling carefully every inch for mines or trip-wires. When the depth of the water was about six inches he felt shingle. There was a sudden movement on the beach above him, and a pebble rolled down the bank and plopped into the water close to his head. Time passed and he looked at his watch again, fully expecting hours to have passed, whereas in reality it had only been minutes. Attached to his belt was a reel, carrying a hundred and fifty yards of fishing-line with a stake at the end. He dug the stake into the sand, then, swimming silently away from the beach on his back, paid out the line. Every ten yards he trod water and took the depth with a thin lead-line. From these two factors – depth and distance – he could work out later exactly how far each type of landing-craft would beach from the water's edge. This task took an hour.

Earlier through the periscope, he had noticed a thick hedge running along the back of the beach, but was unable to estimate its height or thickness. It was an obstacle which required further investigation. Stanbury was unable to crawl over the shingle bank, which could very well be mined, and he reached the conclusion that there might be a way round via the gorge of the Cassibile River as it made its way into the sea. He was right; crawling up the gorge until he was level with the hedge, his knee struck against a projecting rock, instantly causing excruciating pain. To make matters worse, at that moment the door of the sentry-hut opened, letting out a beam of light that gleamed on the bushes round him. Stanbury waited until the light was extinguished and headed for the hedge. After careful haste he examined the hedge, retraced his steps, re-entered the water, and swam out to where Lieutenant Thomas should have been waiting. Two hundred yards from shore, he took out his torch and gave a Morse signal, but was unable to get a reply. He began wondering if Thomas had lost his bearings, an easy thing to do in the darkness while waiting off a strange coast.

Then, faintly at first, the growing defined shape of the canoe came into view. As he was cold and stiff after his long period of swimming, Stanbury found it difficult to clamber back into his seat, a task which seemed to take an age. The canoe headed out to sea, with an hour to cover the two miles to their rendezvous point with *Unruffled*. The Coppists found themselves paddling at a faster rate as the thought of a warm meal and a bunk in the submarine spurred them on.

0200 hours 26th June:

Some five hours later, having collected the required information, Stanbury and Lieutenant Thomas made for the rendezvous point with *Unruffled*, Stanbury flashing his narrow, shaded beam torch, in the direction *Unruffled* was supposed to be, as the signal for the pick-up. It was too dangerous for *Unruffled* to reply by displaying any light landwards, so the two canoeists simply had to listen out for the faint murmur of the submarine's diesel engines. Stanbury recollects "All we could do was sit and wait, and I think the suspense of those minutes of waiting added years to my life".

Fortunately, they were reunited without a problem and were delighted to be greeted with a cup of hot cocoa and a nonchalant comment from Stevens enquiring if they had "had a pleasant trip". *Unruffled* dived once more, maintaining a position close inshore, in anticipation of their visitors' return to the periscope for further observations.

0800 Lieutenant Stevens shook Stanbury from his sleep, informing the Coppist that *Unruffled* was in position at the next beach to be examined. Stanbury awoke to find his wetsuit had been removed and he was wearing new dry trousers, "though I couldn't remember it, someone had changed my clothes". Rubbing the sleep from his eyes, he took over from the Officer of the Watch at the periscope and began the complicated task of identifying strong points and objects of interest and pinpointing their positions. The enemy had cleverly camouflaged the pill-boxes and obstructions from aerial photography, but had not considered observation from a more horizontal vantage point on the sea. Throughout the day periscope observations were taken and sketches made of the next beach to be examined, but the beach looked far too steep for tanks or vehicles to climb, except at two points where gullies, overgrown with thick vegetation, led inland. It did not look too promising. On Casino d'Avola, (Beach 47) at the southern end of the beach, stood a large building with two pillars on a small, rocky escarpment which separated this beach from its neighbour to the south.

At 1730 hours COPP V was ready for another run ashore, Stanbury and Matterson having carefully prepared a timetable for the night's work. "The difficulty in concentrating [in the submarine] was enormous" said Stanbury. "The air was again beginning to become foul and humid, so that we could only breathe in short pants that racked the lungs with pain. It was so weird and grotesque to be methodically setting out in black and white a programme for a nocturnal perambulation on a hostile shore that my mind would suddenly stop in its tracks and wander off onto some more conventional and less ridiculous subject."

At 2200 hours, finally, the klaxon sounded and the crew scuttled away to diving stations in preparation for surfacing. In the torpedo room the folbot was lifted to the correct level with the torpedo hatch ready to be manhandled onto the casing upon surfacing. There was a sudden cessation of pressure on the ears as the conning tower hatch was opened, the built-up pressure in the submarine was released and the two men clambered up the conning-tower ladder, onto the bridge and into the bobbing kayak before paddling away. *Unruffled* dived, making to seaward, resurfacing to recharge the batteries and wait for the appropriate pick-up time, the crew restless in their thoughts as to their visitor's predicament.

Heading directly towards Casino d'Avola, Stanbury and Matterson became aware of a humming sound in the air, emanating from the large building. Matterson whispered into his colleague's ear "Dynamos!" Stanbury checked his kit was all in place and once again entered the water, heading for the inky blackness of the beach. The sentries were evidently alert, lights flashing at the back of the beach and voices calling to one another in the dark. The beaches had been heavily mined. Stanbury examined the gullies and hedges and the bank at the back of the beach, noting the depth and distance measurements of the sea approaches. Having gathered the necessary information, he headed for his pick-up point with the folbot.

Fifty yards from the beach, he glanced down at his left foot and there, fastened on to it, was a large, luminous object. "I quickened my stroke and tried to shake the thing off my leg" Stanbury tells us. "But the ghastly creature still kept pace with me, and every moment I expected to feel sharp teeth crushing on the bones. I thought, with horror, of the strange aquatic monsters that attracted their prey by an eerie, ghoulish light they shed".

It suddenly occurred to him that his waterproof torch, which was pointing downward in his left hip-pocket, had sprung a leak and shorted and was continuously shining on his left foot. Wrestling to retrieve his torch, he found it was no longer able to flash Morse, and moments later it flickered and died. So on reaching the arranged pick-up point, he put Plan B into operation – to imitate the call of a bird. "Try as I might, I could not think of anything except the "quack" of a duck, or the "cluck" of a hen," he said. Luckily, he managed a few squawks vaguely similar to a sea-gull.

The next moment he heard Matterson's voice in his ear. "Feeling sick, old man?"

"I don't do this for pleasure," answered Stanbury.

"I saw your torch just before it went out" replied Matterson.

27th June:

Having gathered the required information, the Coppists headed for the rendezvous position and once in place gave the appropriate signal. Worryingly, there was no response and after 20 minutes when there was still no sign of *Unruffled*, the pair began to suspect that the submarine had perhaps run into trouble. After a brief discussion, they even considered actually paddling the 80-mile journey back to Malta, which would have taken around three days.

It was only then that Stanbury, despite the obvious danger, decided to take a gamble. He unclipped the shade of his powerful lantern and directed the beam across the surface of the sea. Much to his relief, the distant murmur of *Unruffled*'s diesels could finally be heard making a steady course towards them.

Stevens also remembers the occasion well, commenting: "There were no problems with the COPP drill until the last night when Ralph and his mate could not be found at the rendezvous [point] and we searched around for some time after the deadline time for withdrawal. As dawn began to creep in we sighted a powerful unshaded lamp flashing inshore of us. In minutes we had recovered them, without enemy interference, had dived, and set course for Malta".

Having climbed onto the bridge, Stanbury was greeted by a relieved Stevens, who exclaimed: "Thank god you're safe! We were on just on our way back to Malta to break the sad news that we'd lost you when we saw your lantern."

The final beach was observed through the periscope during the day, with no hazards being sighted. According to Stanbury, "It looked, in fact, just the sort of beach one would choose for a picnic". Intelligence received from Allied Headquarters gave the impression that they were quite content with the quality of information they had obtained as regards this beach and due to the insistence of

Lieutenant Kent Thomas and leading-seaman Thomas on participating in the night's excursion, a plan was conceived.

The well-practised drill of launching the folbot went without a hitch, but as soon as the two men had paddled away Stevens hastily pressed the klaxon for diving stations and the boat submerged, an unusual decision that did not escape the notice of Lieutenant Thomas and leading-seaman Thomas. Stanbury asked Stevens what the matter had been and Stevens explained: "We had been picked up by two radar beams from the shore. I wouldn't mind if it had been only one, but if two reports of contact are sent to their control then they'll realise that there must be something out there and they'll sweep for it with a searchlight."

Once dived, Stevens raised the periscope to the level of his eyes and commented: "They [the Italian shore defences] are having a grand time lighting up the sea over our heads." For most of the night and early morning *Unruffled* continually dived and surfaced due to heightened enemy activity, recharging the batteries in short bursts and replenishing the stale air, whilst maintaining a suitable distance for the inevitable pick-up of the folbot.

28th June:

After having safely recovered the folbot with its occupants, *Unruffled* set course for Malta. Lieutenant Thomas reported to Stanbury that the beach was a death trap. "How did everything go?" asked Stanbury.

"Pretty grim" came the reply. "Look at this swimsuit. It's practically cut to pieces by underwater rocks. I tell you, Ralph, I've never known anything that could look so lovely to the eye and yet be so perfectly foul when examined closely. It took me half an hour to wade over those rocks and reefs. No landing-craft could have got closer than two hundred yards to the beach, and the soldiers would be drowned or shot to ribbons before they could land."

"Thank heavens you found that out. Anything else?"

"Yes. I shipped a lot of water into my swimsuit clambering over the rocks, and it gave me bad cramp in my legs and stomach. It's a large flat beach and I could see there was no one around. So I slipped off the swimsuit and was standing just as I was born, massaging my limbs on the water's edge, when the blighters [Italians] went and turned a searchlight on to me!"

Stanbury whistled and asked "Do you think they spotted you?"

"Good heavens, no. It was you they were looking for. But it was certainly somewhat embarrassing."

Matterson typed out his report on the reconnaissance of the beaches ready for dispatch upon arrival in Malta, from where, within six hours, it was taken by plane to Alexandria to be studied by Army Intelligence.

2nd July:

Unruffled, a thankful crew and guests, arrive at the Lazaretto, immediately noticing the hive of activity and expectation surrounding the port area. Assault ships, Liberty ships and grey tank and infantry landing craft clustered in the areas around the various creeks. Leave was not granted, as the crew busily preparing the boat and replenishing supplies for 'special duties'.

4th July:

Stanbury was told by Captain (S) G.C. Philips that he was to assume additional responsibility for three small motor launches tasked with guiding the main prongs of the east-coast assault to positions opposite the main assault beaches. Lieutenant Thomas was delegated by Stanbury to handle this job. Each launch was to collect a landing craft after it had been lowered from the assault ship and taken to the separate positions one mile offshore where they would see the beach markers. This would give Stanbury the opportunity to lay beacons from the submarine, and after discussing the matter with Stevens rehearsals of drill and equipment were carried out. This gave the crew the opportunity to learn about the new radio beacons and practice launching the folbots. The crews of the motor launches were also able to follow the submarine and rehearse the vital role they were to play later.

6th July:

The siege now lifted, Malta was now buzzing with activity ahead of the planned invasion of Sicily, known as 'Operation Husky', with Grand Harbour and its adjacent creeks gradually filling up with ships and landing craft. Valletta, especially, was again bursting back into life, the availability of goods, food and rations being at its highest for months. It was a particular source of delight for thirsty matelots that beer was freely available in the local bars.

Admiral Sir Andrew Browne Cunningham, Commander-in-Chief of the Royal Navy in the Mediterranean, and affectionately known as 'ABC', had already arrived back on the island, and he was followed shortly by the Allies' Supreme Commander General Eisenhower and the Deputy Supreme Command General Harold Alexander.

"There was plenty to do before the Sicily invasion date," says Stevens. "We were to take Stanbury's COPP to Sicily and land them just before the assault and *Unruffled* was to act as a navigational beacon. In the few nights available there were more rehearsals of drill and equipment and we had to test and learn about some new gadgets, including radio buoys, bonglers [a device for making easily heard noises underwater] and a special radio beacon retained on board [a new type of radio direction finder that was portable for use on the bridge]."

Captain (S) summoned Stanbury and Donald Andrews, a pseudonym for a fellow COPP team leader, to his office, where he informed them that he would be handing the responsibility of piloting and marking the chosen beaches for the British and Canadian assaults to their sole command.

16th Patrol

7th July:

The COPP team V now comprised Stanbury, Matterson, Lieutenant Thomas, Leading Seaman Thomas and a newly arrived Corporal, Ronald A. Williamson, Royal Scots. Once all were safely on board and stores and equipment loaded, *Unruffled* sailed from Malta, destined for the beaches of Sicily.

A total of 15 submarines took part in Operation Husky. Five British submarines were stretched on a patrol line across the entrance to the Gulf of Taranto in case Italian battleships came out, though this threat never materialised. Three more submarines were placed north of the Strait of Messina and seven more patrolled opposite the landing beaches to act as navigational beacons, both for the incoming convoys and the actual landing craft.

8th July pm:

Before the boat surfaced to recharge the batteries, Stevens summoned everyone involved in bridge duty to the control room to offer a few words of warning and advice. He stressed that their role would be similar to that of a lighthouse in that *Unruffled* would be guiding the Allied forces in towards their respective landing places and, as such, those submarine crew members concerned would be in the thick of it and should be ready to expect the unexpected. Once surfaced, the main instruments on the bridge were tested, including the new portable RDF set and the Aldis lamps, which were visible only to those with a special pair of binoculars designed to spot the signal light.

No records are available for this patrol, only the personal recollections of Stevens and Stanbury. But in remarks taken from a recorded interview after the war, as well as extracts from 'Never Volunteer', Stevens explained: "We sailed with Stanbury and his team to arrive off the beaches before the planned time of the assault in the early hours of 10th July. We surfaced [the following day] before the assault to lay three radio beacon buoys under the cover of darkness. The beacons had a special mechanism, controlled by a time clock, which sank them to the sea bed. Shortly before zero hour they would float to the surface and their signals would help guide in the special navigational minelayers, which were to lead the assault fleet to its anchorage."

Stanbury also remembers that night vividly and reflects that "there was a quiet, tranquil setting as *Unruffled* headed out for open sea until a great roar and a huge black shadow swept over the submarine. This was followed by another and yet another until all the stars above were blotted out and the heavens torn asunder by the noise".

Minute after minute they passed over *Unruffled*, squadron after squadron. Nothing but bombers. In the direction of Syracuse and the coast opposite them rows of flares were floating down to earth, while streams of bright red tracers leapt up to meet them.

On the bridge, Stevens turned to Stanbury and commented: "They're getting it tonight all right. I suppose this is part of the softening up for tomorrow's invasion."

A dull red glow could be seen emanating from the direction of Syracuse, indicating that the city was burning. The weather began to change, the wind increased and storm clouds began to develop overhead.

10th July:
The weather deteriorated and by midday the wind was at gale force. As zero hour approached to signal the invasion of Sicily, the crew began to experience a strange feeling of awe, apprehension and excitement, with countless scenarios and possible consequences being discussed among individuals. They were soon to discover the reality of the situation. Stevens recalls: "To us, it seemed doubtful that the smaller landing craft in the assault fleet could keep going in such conditions. Postponement of the landings for

24 hours became a distinct possibility. Ralph was rather gloomy and cursed as he gazed at the angry seas through the periscope. His party had laid the radio buoys and were due to launch two folbots that night. They would mark the limits of the northern assault beach and their crews were to give on-the-spot advice to the first officers and men ashore… by 2100 hours the weather conditions could only be described as unpleasant, but no signal had arrived to suggest a postponement of the landings, so the first kayak was launched from half a mile offshore."

Stevens underplayed this decision, for in truth it was by no means an easy task. In fact it was a highly risky manoeuvre on two counts, the first being the close proximity of the shore, which, while giving the two-man folbot team of Matterson and Corporal Williamson a far better chance of success, left *Unruffled* in a far more exposed position. Even Stanford remarked that he felt the submarine would be compromised in the bright moonlight, but Stevens responded: "You needn't worry, these craft are hard as hell to see in broad daylight, and I'm keeping her end-on to the shore."

The second risk factor was the launching of the folbot in this particular position, with angry sea conditions and a slippery fore-casing. "This was a nervous time for those involved and many a silent prayer was offered," admits Stevens. "We moved north some miles and launched the second folbot [Lieutenant Thomas and leading seaman Thomas], which benefited from getting more of a lee from the gusty wind. Then it was time for *Unruffled* to pinpoint herself as the marker for the northern 'Acid' group of beaches. Ralph dashed up and down the conning tower as he checked our position on the bridge compass from bearings taken of dimly visible land features, and advised on the necessary manoeuvring to keep ourselves in the right place.

"As it approached midnight we heard, and on occasions saw, heavy bombers flying in to soften up defences. Then came the transport planes, flying low and slow as they towed the gliders to their release points. The bungler went over the side, making its noises, and the electrician switched on the shaded beacon light, which flashed a coded letter to seaward [the phonetic letter F, dit-dit-dah-dit, continually repeated].

"By midnight the sky had cleared and there was a dim starlight. Soon a dark shape could be discerned to the south-east. It grew larger and there was a blurred confusion of other dark outlines behind it, but it was forbidden to challenge or reply by light for recognition. Fortunately, we had sighted a destroyer leading in a group of ships detached from the main convoy. They included many famous ocean liners, which were being used as assault troop ships. They loomed nearer, until we were surrounded by large, silent and stationary vessels. On this occasion, instead of being spooky, their unchallenged presence was comforting indeed. All this time, apart from sporadic anti-aircraft fire as the bombers, para-transports and gliders swept in, there had been an uncanny lack of enemy reaction. To seaward, there was no shell splashes or sweeping beams of searchlights and the defenders of Sicily seemed unaware that a vast armada of transports, landing craft, and their supporting warships, were now stopped and in position two miles off their coast.

"Just before dawn, the small assault craft went in. From

Unruffled's bridge the lack of enemy response appeared to continue. Soon after daylight a boat arrived alongside us; it was to take Ralph to H.Q. ship Bulolo, where he was to report to [Thomas Hope] Troubridge [Rear Admiral Combined Operations].

"We took leave of each other on the casing, and Ralph set off in the boat. The sun was shining, and only a trace of swell remained to remind us of the previous day's foul weather. The vast force of ships, which stretched over the southern horizon, was a magnificent sight.

"Small landing craft could be seen scurrying between their parent ships and the beaches as though the occasion was a goodwill visit rather than an opposed amphibious assault. A few bombs were dropped from very high-flying aircraft without effect, otherwise Allied domination of the scene was total.

"At 0800 hours a small minesweeper approached *Unruffled*, detailed to escort us to Malta. Obtaining permission to proceed by signal from the naval force commander, we pointed south and followed the sweeper as she threaded her way through the vast floating assembly."

Admiral Cunningham [Commander-in-Chief] praised all those who took part in the landing and made special mention of the submarine and COPP service when he wrote: "We were much indebted to the gallant young men of the COPPs, who landed and reconnoitred the landing beaches beforehand in folbots sent in from submarines. Then there were the submarines themselves, the *Unruffled, Unseen, Unison, Unrivalled, Seraph, Shakespeare* and *Safari*, which served as inshore beacons guiding the flights of landing craft to their beaches in the dark and early morning of July 10th."

This patrol also proved to be the last trip for first lieutenant Seaburne-May as he was ordered to return to the UK to undertake the perisher's course. Lascelles was promoted to No 1, with Fenton becoming No 2. Sub-lieutenant Brian Richards joined the boat as navigator, taking over from Fenton.

17th Patrol

2200 hours 27th July:
Unruffled proceeded through the eastern channel on its way to the new patrol area in the Gulf of Taranto, southern Italy.

1744 hours 29th July:
While on the surface two Cant floatplanes were encountered and *Unruffled* was forced to dive.

0600 hours 30th July:
When the submarine reached its designated patrol area, still submerged, it was noted that two destroyers, travelling at 10 knots, passed overhead at 0735 hours. At 2345 hours, *Unruffled* changed course to comply with new orders that the boat should enter the Adriatic Sea and patrol within 15 miles of Brindisi, on the Italian eastern shore south of Bari.

2237 hours 31st July:
After a quiet, routine day a large two-funnelled hospital ship passed on a course of 140 degrees.

0400 hours 1st August:

A patrol line six miles off Brindisi, which for a short period during the war was the temporary capital of Italy, had been established and at 0622 hours a large grey drab-looking three-funnelled vessel loomed out of the heat haze, and *Unruffled*'s crew was immediately placed on diving stations alert.

Stevens was professional and honest enough to admit that "sighting a three-funnelled vessel was extremely rare, and such an unusual apparition in the periscope seemed to unnerve me". She was at a range of 8,000 yards, travelling at a speed of 13 knots, and on a steady course – just the answer to a submariner's prayer.

After closing to 1,000 yards and running on a parallel but opposite course, *Unruffled* turned to an 80-degree track. The range was now down to 800 yards, but as Stevens admitted: "Unfortunately I made the elementary mistake of missing the direction angle and, due to being too close, I was unable to turn to a broader track in time to fire."

Then at 0639 hours and, despite having returned to a more favourable firing position at a range of 2,500 yards, *Unruffled* did manage to release one torpedo, but it missed its target. Stevens described the failure as "most depressing" and "disappointing", but decided to continue patrolling the approaches to Brindisi Harbour. At 1115 hours one E-boat passed at speed and 30 minutes later two small merchant vessels, sailing in ballast and escorted by a torpedo boat, passed northbound. At 1540 hours one small merchant vessel towing two schooners entered Brindisi harbour. The harbour area itself was busy, with small craft and schooners being sighted throughout the rest of the day.

1000 hours 2nd August:

A vessel was seen to be approaching from the south and Stevens sounded the klaxon to call the crew to diving stations and begin an attack. As the submarine approached the vessel, it was identified as an old tramp of 1,000 tons and in ballast. A decision was made to call off the attack and the tramp steamer was allowed to continue unmolested. At 1945 hours a tug towing two gunnery targets was seen leaving Brindisi.

0545 hours 3rd August:

The submarine sighted one large floating crane, towed by two tugs and escorted by an AMC of the cross-channel packet type, but Stevens decided that this was not a worthy target and allowed the small convoy, making on a steady course at a speed of five knots, to continue on its way. At 1035 hours a large vessel, at a range of 8,000 yards, appeared out of the mist. Preparing for an attack and closing the vessel, Stevens at once recognised her as the same three-funnelled ship encountered just days earlier. Checking the silhouette in the 'Talbot Booth Silhouette' book, he came to the conclusion that she was of similar construction to the French S.S. Providence, an ex-immigration liner which, before the hostilities, was routed between New York and Continental Europe. She was unescorted and heavily laden with passengers and was on a steady course at a speed plotted at 14½ knots.

At 1054, in the position 40 deg 44 min N 18 deg 05 min E, *Unruffled* launched a salvo of four torpedoes from an estimated range of 1,000 yards, resulting in three hits, the first only 39 seconds after being launched. The whole of the ship, except for the bow and foremast forward, was seen at 1056 hours to be covered by dense smoke and flame. She was settling by the stern and one minute later disappeared, stern first, below the waves.

Stevens recalls seeing "about 100 survivors in the water clinging to wreckage or swimming. These were probably saved by two minesweeping schooners, which closed them".

The excitement amongst the crew intensified in the belief that they had sunk an important large ship comparable in size to the Queen Mary. Unknown to the crew at that time, *Unruffled* had, in fact, sunk the Italian merchant vessel Citta di Catania, a cross-Adriatic ferry of 3,355 gross tons which had in 1941 been used as a troop carrier but at this time in 1943 was chartered to Adriatica for a Brindisi-Durres service. She was inbound from Durres when hit in an action that cost 256 lives.

Unruffled dived to the depths and maintained a speed of six knots for 20 minutes in an evasive manoeuvre to escape any counter-attack. Coming back up to periscope depth for an all-round look through the periscope, Stevens identified one Abba class torpedo boat closing in from the east, at a range of 4,000 yards. He gave the order to dive to 120 feet and withdrew slowly from the scene. A counter-attack of nine single depth charges caused no damage to the submarine.

For the next 24 hours *Unruffled* took the precaution of keeping clear of the scene of the attack. Air and sea search continued until dusk and at 2330 hours the shore batteries of Brindisi opened fire to seaward, but there seemed no explanation for this.

4th August:
A quiet day, as expected, as the Italians had been put on alert that an Allied submarine was patrolling in the area. However, there was a sighting of four minesweeping schooners, with a gunboat acting as escort.

2115 hours 5th August:
Because of the disturbance outside the harbour entrance caused by the sinking of the Citta di Catania, *Unruffled* was redirected to patrol the southern approaches to Valona (Vlone), a coastal town in the principality of southern Albania.

0430 hours 6th August:
Unruffled dived to patrol five miles off Cape Garlovez, on the Albanian coast, keeping outside the 200-fathom line. At 0740 the masts and funnels of a three-funnelled destroyer were seen approaching Valona anchorage. It would appear that the destroyer was acting as escort to three schooners and a trawler. At O900 two schooners left harbour, then swept round in an arc before returning. The masts of another schooner anchored off Saseno Island, eight km from Cape Garlovez, could be seen through the periscope. Between 1800 and 1830 hours a Cant flying boat was seen searching the area.

0500 hours 7th August:
Unruffled was given instructions to set course for Malta. The boat continued on its way on the surface, but was forced to dive after spotting an aircraft.

8th-9th August:

An excessive load appeared on the port motor which, after being stopped and reversed, reverted back to normal at 0045 hours. The cause was put down to a piece of rope being caught round the shaft. This incident apart, the trip back to Malta was uneventful.

1200 hours 10th August:

Unruffled arrived back at Malta and Stevens immediately reported to Captain (S), explaining that one of the main features of the patrol was the weather, particularly early in the morning when they were often hampered by poor visibility due to mist.

An interesting postscript was Stevens' report on the good health of the crew. He pointed out his surprise that "despite the adverse conditions of long hot diving days, no cases of sickness occurred". But he added "a dehumidifier would have been welcome under these conditions".

During the routine inspection it was discovered that one of *Unruffled*'s main generators was defective. The nature of the repair meant that the submarine would have to remain in the dockyard for two weeks, which gave the shipyard the chance to fumigate the boat and either overhaul or replace other essential items.

Captain (S) told Stevens that he ought to take the opportunity of a well-earned break and, with Malta still experiencing a siege economy, albeit an improving one, he suggested that with Lebanon now emerging as an independent state, then the capital, Beirut, would be an ideal choice. This idea appealed to Stevens who, from previous experience, remembered Beirut as "abounding in fleshpots of all kinds and cosmopolitan glamour". During a week away touring the cabaret and night spots of Beirut, Stevens put on eight pounds in weight. Meanwhile, the ratings took the opportunity to revisit many of their old haunts on the island.

18ᵗʰ PATROL

1430 hours 22ⁿᵈ August:
With Timoshenko safely below deck, *Unruffled*, escorted by B.Y.M.S. 28, left her mooring heading for Brindisi with two guests, who were to be dropped off at the Greek island of Cephalonia (Kefalonia) in what was given the codename 'Operation Seaman'.

24ᵗʰ August:
In a position off the Axis-occupied island a watchful eye was kept through the periscope to determine the lie of the land and locate a suitable point on which to disembark these unusual passengers. Understandably, as the day wore, the two strangers became restless, especially as they spoke no English, and no one on board was able to translate. One, in fact, had been born on Cephalonia and was due to be reunited with his family but, even so, the crew of *Unruffled* had a difficult time trying to keep up the spirits of the pair.

2045 Hours 25ᵗʰ August:
In the launch position 230 degrees Cape Vlioti two miles offshore, 'Operation Seaman' was executed without any complications. Two Greek Army officers, F. Simopoulos and A. Galiatstos, had embarked *Unruffled* prior to the

submarine departing Malta. They brought with them an RAF inflatable dinghy, a supply of demolition stores and radio equipment weighing a total of 300 pounds, with orders to make their way onto the mainland and sabotage German activities.

Conditions that night have been described as ideal, with a slight sea swell and an inky darkness. Even so, loading the dinghy alongside the submarine proved an increasingly more difficult task than had been anticipated. Because the craft was so light the slightest wave threw the boat about, and it took an agonising 45 minutes to transfer it from the open hatch to the moment the crew waved goodbye to the occupants.

Lieutenant Stevens remembers the pair fondly. "They were brave men," he said. "If captured in German-occupied Greece they faced penalties [too] horrible to contemplate. We fervently wished all would go well for them, [but] we never heard the outcome of their efforts.".

At 2134 hours *Unruffled* set a course for her original patrol area off Brindisi, and at 2134 hours encountered a four-engine aircraft which, although flying directly overhead while *Unruffled* was on the surface, showed no interest and disappeared into the distance.

0305 hours 26th August:
Other than reporting the success of 'Operation Seaman', via Whitehall, nothing of note took place this day.

0935 hours 27th August:
Timoshenko became agitated and a Cant aircraft was sighted circling northward. As this was always a good sign

of future action, the officer of the watch gave the order to close the position and inform the captain. Stevens was now in the control room, from where at 0955 hours he identified the masts of a merchant vessel, which turned out to be the Italian merchantman Citta di Spezia, of 2,474 gt, en route from Valona to Brindisi. Diving stations was ordered and the attack commenced. Upon closer inspection Stevens was, through the periscope, able to see a medium-sized merchant vessel of a modern design with some passenger accommodation.

The vessel, unescorted, was well off *Unruffled*'s track and so an increase in speed was ordered to achieve a better firing position. The sea was flat calm and Stevens was able to observe that the target was not making any smoke. He came to the conclusion, therefore, that this was a diesel-powered vessel, capable of a much greater speed than the eight knots she was making. Nothing could be heard on the hydrophones.

At 1038 hours, and in a position of 40 deg 36 min N 18 deg 37 min E, four torpedoes with a depth setting of eight feet were launched at intervals of 12, 13 and 17 seconds, aimed half-a-length ahead, foremast, mainmast, and half-a-length astern, from an estimated range of 4,200 yards. One minute later it was believed that *Unruffled*'s position had been identified when a Cant aircraft flew over the torpedo tracks between the submarine and the target. Fortunately, the aircraft continued on its way.

Three minutes and three seconds after the firing of the first torpedo, a hit was seen abreast of the foremast. This was followed by two further strikes, which caused the Citta di Spezia to list sharply to starboard and begin to settle. Due to the sighting of another aircraft, Stevens decided to dive deep and withdraw. Two more explosions were heard on the seven-and-a-half minute and nine-and-a-half minute mark. The first explosion was probably a bomb, while the second was most likely *Unruffled*'s remaining torpedo reaching the end of its run.

When the submarine returned to periscope depth at 1150 hours a floatplane was identified close to the scene of the attack and four or five pieces of wreckage could be seen in the vicinity. *Unruffled* withdrew without any further incident. Stevens rejected the idea of calling for gun action and surfacing to attack the Cant aircraft as being "unnecessarily inhuman". Between the hours of 1345 and 1543 a total of nine explosions was heard and at 1850 hours a convoy of small craft consisting of two schooners, two trawlers and one gunboat was observed heading for Valona.

28th August:

No shipping was sighted in the approaches to Brindisi, which was not surprising, and the day passed uneventfully, giving time for another white symbol to be sewn onto *Unruffled*'s Jolly Roger.

0255 hours 29th August:

Those on the bridge witnessed an air-raid on Brindisi. Two torpedo boats passed to seaward at 0735 hours and again at 1030, and one torpedo boat passed inshore. At 1555 hours two torpedo boats were identified passing close inshore. Due to a strong north-westerly wind (Bora of the Adriatic) vision through the periscope was impaired and depth-keeping became a problem.

30th August:
Due to the continuing strong wind the only shipping sighted was two F-lighters, which entered Brindisi at 1700 hours.

0835 hours 31st August:
The Bora faded and two minesweepers, making volumes of smoke, were seen sweeping the channels, which took most of the day. One torpedo boat was observed patrolling two miles east of Brindisi. At 0900 hours an additional torpedo boat was seen to leave the harbour and link up with a second before sailing off into the distance.

Destroyers and torpedo boats left Brindisi at 1125 hours and patrolled in pairs two miles outside the harbour entrance. They returned to harbour at 1315. White smoke was observed over Brindisi at 1145 and it seemed likely that the destroyers had, due to an air-raid, evacuated the harbour. At 1515 hours two explosions rang through the submarine a few seconds apart and further distant explosions, either singly or in pairs, continued until 1820. *Unruffled* surfaced at 2045 hours and set course for Valona.

0300 hours 1st September:
The port generator was stopped, as it was too noisy, and it was found that five adjacent segments of the armature were about a quarter-of-an-inch proud at their after-ends. This had stripped some of the brushes, which required in-house repairs. The boat continued to patrol the area south of Valona for the rest of the day, without incident.

2nd September:
After having received the recall signal (S10's 291102), the boat set a new course for Malta.

5th September:

Unruffled arrived at the Lazaretto after an uneventful passage. Stevens reported to Captain (S) that the stern glands had been leaking badly and were in need of repair. He also reported that the forward compressor had been fitted with new glands whilst on patrol, but was now in need of repair.

He also stated that one of the crew had a temperature of 105 degrees and several of the crew were troubled with sore throats and had a slight increase in temperature. Stevens also mentioned that the windy beans supplied to the crew were "most unappetising". These were the American Seca brand, which were mainly very hard beans in a thin watery sauce. Stevens suggested that "something nearer the Heinz specification would be welcome".

Three days after their arrival back in Malta the bells rang out across the island with the news that the war with Italy had reached a conclusion. Command-in-Chief Admiral Cunningham reported to the Admiralty that he was "pleased to inform their Lordships that the Italian fleet now lies at anchor under the guns of the fortress of Malta".

Celebrations took place all over the Island, and while the men of *Unruffled* would doubtless have been delighted to have joined in with the festivities, it is more likely their focus would have been on more personal matters, the news having been passed down through the ranks that *Unruffled* was soon to return to Blighty for a refit.

24th-25th September:

After having loaded stores and personal items on board the submarine the crew looked forward to the time they were due to sail back to home waters.

19th PATROL

0930 hours 26th September:
When the submarine, once again escorted by B.Y.M.S 28 (J.R. Clark RNR), left Malta for what was to be its last patrol in the Mediterranean, the boat was accompanied by one of its sister ships, HMS *Unshaken (P45),* under the command of Lieutenant Jack Whitton.

0230 hours 27th September:
Apart from being overtaken by a convoy of large Allied liners while *Unruffled* was still on the surface, there were no incidents reported and by 1830 hours, after having completed the transit of the Scillian channel, *Unruffled* parted company with the escort ship and *Unshaken,* which proceeded to its own patrol area off the Isle of Elba. Stevens then followed the orders received from Captain (S) that *Unruffled* was to dive by day and resume a war patrol status and set a course for the Axis-held north-eastern Corsican port of Bastia.

2100 hours 30th September:
By the time *Unruffled* had reached its patrol area to the north-east of Bastia, the weather had deteriorated. Visibility was poor and there was intermittent lightning and rain squalls.

0645 Hours 1st October:
As the rain began to clear, two vessels were sighted about four miles east of Bastia. *Unruffled* closed to investigate and identified one as an escorting German U J boat (U-Jag

boote/submarine chaser). The other was a small coaster with heavy AA (anti-aircraft) armament and a radar array on its masthead. Stevens believed this to be a flak ship as both vessels were patrolling, with constant alterations of course. At 0700 hours six landing craft were sighted heading for the open sea and at 0715 the flak ship and its escort headed for the shore. Although visibility was variable throughout the day due to the rain squalls, it was noticed that various types of landing craft appeared to be evacuating Bastia and several transport aircraft were observed throughout that night.

2nd October:

With the weather conditions improving it was evident that the evacuation of Corsica had gathered speed dramatically and a larger number of barges and landing craft appeared to be loading across a considerable expanse of the coastline. Several aircraft flew close overhead once darkness had fallen.

0150 hours 3rd October:

The boat was forced to dive when a low-flying aircraft directly overhead turned to attack, but on resurfacing at 0212 hours several landing craft were spotted arriving and departing Bastia.

At 0555 hours *Unruffled* noticed what appeared to be a merchant vessel, though it was difficult to positively identify because of the glare as dawn broke. The submarine changed course and accelerated to full speed to close and identify the ship, which was a three-island tramp, flying two barrage balloons, and of approximately 2000-3,000 tons. Landing craft could be seen vaguely to the south of the vessel.

At 0619 hours, and in a position of 42 deg 43 min N 09 deg 31 min E, Stevens fired four torpedoes set at six feet, spread over two ships' length, using an estimated speed of eight knots and at a range of 4,500 yards. Stevens admits that this was a long shot, but with the fall of Bastia imminent, this was probably the last ship that *Unruffled* was likely to see in the area. All torpedoes missed, but six minutes later a red and white pyrotechnic signal was fired from near the target and a fast boat was seen approaching the submarine.

As no aircraft could be seen in the vicinity Stevens decided to remain at periscope depth. He witnessed the oncoming torpedo boat drop eight depth charges in eight minutes, none of which was closer than 3,000 yards. It was noted that the swirl of one depth charge dropped close to the stern of the submarine indicated a shallow depth setting and shortly after this the torpedo boat hurried back to shore. At 0820 hours *Unruffled* headed for the shore to see where the merchant vessel had anchored.

Ten minutes later a sloop was sighted patrolling the coast using ASDIC and was clearly aware of the presence of a submarine. Stevens decided to withdraw from the scene, but noted that several fires were burning in Bastia. Later in the day an exchange of gunfire could be heard in the town and in the surrounding hills, and splashes caused by shells were seen exploding in the sea.

In the afternoon there were several explosions in the town and through the periscope it was seen that many landing craft, motor boats and barges were carrying out an evacuation, so *Unruffled* decided to repeatedly go deep to avoid a possible collision with the increasing amount of traffic.

At 1730 hours a number of masts and some smoke were sighted close inshore to the north-west and immediately the submarine's klaxon called the crew to diving stations. It turned out to be a small freighter of about 1,000 tons and *Unruffled* closed to within 4,000 yards. However, Stevens decided that, because of the uncertainty of the ship's speed and the distance of a torpedo run, the chances of success were limited, so he allowed the vessel to continue her journey. At 2100 hours a signal from Captain (S) Malta was received ordering a new patrol line routed across the Gulf of Genoa to Leghorn.

4th October:

Although nothing was sighted all day between the hours of 0742 and 1100, several distant explosions were heard. At 2030 hours a new northerly course was set.

0729 hours 5th October:

A northbound vessel, flying two balloons close to the shoreline, was spotted through the mist and *Unruffled* commenced to close at speed. The vessel was, in fact, soon recognised to be a convoy of three ships, escorted by three torpedo boats. The largest of the three vessels, which had a squat funnel and a cruiser stern, was approximately 5,000 tons. She was of modern design and was low in the water. The vessel was accompanied by a small tramp, which was further inshore, while a medium-sized vessel, which had no funnel, brought up the rear. The three escorts were one ahead and one either side of the trailing ship. The small convoy was on a steady course, with the escorts continually zigzagging. The convoy's speed was calculated to be 'very slow', plotted at just three-and-a-half knots, with the largest vessel travelling at four knots.

At 0810 and in a position of 44 deg 13 min N 09 deg 18 min E *Unruffled* fired four torpedoes, spread over two ships' lengths and aimed at the larger of the escorted vessels and the overlapping tramp. The estimated firing range was 3,500 yards. The torpedoes were each aimed individually. *Unruffled* then dived to a depth of 120 feet and reversed course for five minutes. No hits were recorded and there was no counter-attack.

The sea state was slight and Stevens was surprised that the six-boat convoy appeared not to have noticed anything. "It was incredible that the tracks should not have been sighted," he wrote. Half an hour after the firing of the torpedoes *Unruffled* came up to periscope depth and Stevens could see that the biggest vessel was zigzagging violently, but that no other vessels were in sight. A disappointed Stevens had been confident of some success and remarked: "While the bad workman blames his tools, it seems of interest to note that this was the first salvo to be fired using CCR pistols set to contact."

At 0845 *Unruffled* retired from the vicinity of the attack and, with a relieved crew on board, proceeded to Algiers.

6th October:
Stevens was unable to contact Malta direct and, after some difficulty, sent his contact report via Whitehall.

9th October:
After arriving alongside HMS Maidstone at Algiers, Stevens renewed acquaintances with Captain (S) George Fawkes

and, within his report, explained that the forward compressor had become defective after running for 24 hours and that the Chernikeef Log (an instrument used to measure nautical speed and distance travelled) also had a defect.

To the frustration of the crew, Algiers proved to be an anti-climax compared to Malta. However, despite the town being plagued with mosquitoes and not smelling too pleasant, it did offer other benefits. Having bathed, and drawn their pay on board HMS Maidstone, ratings who planned to go out for the night would, due to the large number of brothels in the area, be issued with a warning regarding venereal disease. Particularly, they would be advised that if ratings did intend visiting a brothel then they should select a better class of house, and preferably one examined regularly by doctors, a procedure carried out in an effort to keep cases down to a minimum.

It would have also been the duty of the officer of the watch to warn crew members that the infamous Casbah was out of bounds and that all leave for ratings was to end at 2200 hours, and for chief and petty officers at midnight. Local beer, wine, champagne, cocktails and spirits were plentiful in Algiers, but because of the nuisance caused by beggars and peddlers it was impossible to sit outside for very long. There was a rest camp about an hour's drive away at the Algerian coastal town of Sidi Fredj (Sidi Ferruch), and the fine beaches, attractive village and small bar would have proved an appealing contrast to many ratings after the cramped and restrictive life on board a submarine.

Because there was no available accommodation in Algiers, HMS Maidstone was to be home for the crew, who for the next week would have to sling their hammocks in the allotted mess. The mess decks were unbearably hot, so ratings usually slept on deck. Sunbathing and swimming were the main activity and a football pitch could be found opposite the HMS Maidstone mooring.

In the shops, such items as French face powder, lipstick, nylon and silk stockings, hair nets, hair grips, white towels, local wine in four litre jars and, in particular, Muscatel wine, were widely available. The menu on board the depot ship included kippers, haddock, roast beef, fried potatoes, onions, fresh vegetables, fruit and melon. Tea, coffee and buns were a popular treat. Timoshenko was not privy to the lecture from the officer of the watch and enjoyed local feline company whilst on leave.

16th October:

The storing and loading of torpedoes, ammunition, fresh fruit, vegetables and tins of pilchards was completed, spare parts for Gibraltar were brought on board and every available space was crammed with personal cartons and packages ready for transit to the UK.

CHAPTER SEVEN

HOMEWARD BOUND

17TH OCTOBER 1943 - 21ST NOVEMBER 1943

—⊰∞⊱—

20th PATROL

1300 hours 17th October:
Unruffled slipped its mooring at HMS Maidstone, having been wished *bon voyage* by Captain (S) George Fawkes, and proceeded on the surface destined for the UK, except for a scheduled stop-off at Gibraltar for a short break and the opportunity to do some shopping.

18th October:
The boat surfaced during daylight hours, but the passage was devoid of incident, with only the occasional fishing craft and Allied vessels being sighted.

1315 hours 21st October:

Unruffled entered Gibraltar Harbour and at 1330 hours secured to berth 38 next to the USS Mayo, a 1620-ton Benson class American destroyer, the crew of which over the next four days proved extremely hospitable neighbours. Meanwhile, *Unruffled*'s personnel were accommodated in HMS Cleopatra, "whose bakers should be congratulated on supplying [us] with excellent bread," Stevens says. HMS Cleopatra, a 5450-ton Dido class cruiser, was in Gibraltar undergoing temporary repairs after being badly damaged in a torpedo attack by the Italian submarine *Dandolo* on the 16th July, 1943.

The initial plan was for *Unruffled* to stay in Gibraltar for a two-day shopping and rest period before leaving for the UK on the 26th October. However, anti-submarine and air surveillance was stepped up when a group of German U-boats attempted to encroach into the Mediterranean, and reinforcements were detailed to track them down. As it was considered dangerous for Allied submarines to risk leaving the protection of Gibraltar, *Unruffled* was assigned to this hastily-prepared support force.

Four days of A/S training were carried out with various vessels of the Gibraltar Command, and Stevens allowed the first lieutenant to carry out a dummy attack on targets zigzagging at speeds of up to 20 knots. Within 24 hours of *Unruffled* being involved in exercises, there was a successful confrontation when HMS Fleetwood, a 990-ton sloop under the command of Commander W.B. Piggott DSC, sank a U-boat by ASDIC attack.

"This visit to the Rock turned out to be tough on our livers," says Stevens. "Knowing that we would soon be in heavily rationed Britain, it was tempting every night to have just one more go at the sherry, and perhaps a Spanish omelette at the Victoria Hotel, or a short run into Spain in daylight."

On several occasions Stevens also visited the operations room buried deep inside the Rock to inquire when *Unruffled* might be heading home, but his request invariably received the same answer: "Soon, but not just yet."

The ratings, now getting short of money and clearly anxious to return to home waters as quickly as possible, could only pass the time as best as they could, most simply relaxing and sun-bathing.

3rd November:

Having disembarked the torpedoes ashore and taken on board a large supply of bananas, which had been in short supply in the UK for four years, together with enough stores and provisions for the journey home, the boat was filled to capacity with a selection of duty-free goods and presents.

1145 hours 4th November:

The moment arrived for *Unruffled* to leave its mooring and head out into the Atlantic. The mood, however, was sombre, for one important member of the crew was absent without leave, Timoshenko having jumped ship two hours earlier. Some of the crew regarded this as a bad omen and murmurs of 'We'll never make it without Timmo' spread through the boat. The boat's much-loved cat had possibly preferred to remain in the back alleys of the Rock, from which he had joined the submarine some 16 months earlier.

The boat's patrol report stated: "The call of his

birthplace was evidently too strong for him. He had been on board for every patrol". Vic Preece, the gun trainer, is also quoted as saying: "He probably found it nice that the lady cats spoke his native language and decided to settle down after living through all those times when his world went bang and oxygen got short."

However, a most credible explanation for Timoshenko's non-appearance was the decision to set sail before noon; 'Timmo' was usually back on board by 1700 hours.

Unruffled was ordered to proceed on the surface and the boat passed two United States destroyers at 1530 hours, the Georges Leygues, a French destroyer, at 1550, and a troopship convoy at 1610. All were heading in an easterly direction.

5th November:

The boat dived to periscope depth but, apart from sighting a few Spanish vessels, the day passed peacefully and normal routine was resumed.

1400 hours 9th November:

Unruffled entered 'home station' and proceeded via route 'brown'.

11th November:

Exceptionally bad weather conditions forced *Unruffled* to dive deep, returning only occasionally to periscope depth for the officer of the watch to have an all-around look. The talk amongst the ratings revolved around Timoshenko's disappearance, which in the minds of many could still bring them bad luck, even though they were closer to home.

The recorded barometer reading of 1049 was unusually low for the time of year, and several Landing Craft tank (LCTs) from a group en route from Gibraltar to the UK were being lost without trace in the ensuing storm. Wet weather gear was ordered for the bridge-keeping watch, the first time in 16 months that such an instruction had been given, so Ursula suits and towel scarves were brought out of storage.

2200 hours 12th November:
Unruffled surfaced into gale-force winds and heavy seas. Due to the thick atmosphere inside the submarine, the bananas began to ripen rapidly and, in order to deal with the problem, the menu was changed to include banana fritters, banana custard – or just raw banana. In the end, however, the bulk of the stock had to be ditched over the side.

No games were played and little food consumed as a large number of the crew who were not otherwise on watch simply lay in their hammocks or on the floor suffering the effects of the storm. The clocks had been put back and the necessary changes were made to the home station codes and wireless frequencies.

In such poor weather conditions, it would normally have been expected for the captain to maintain a depth of at least 60 feet during daylight hours so that the crew could get some sleep. Sometimes this depth would still not be sufficient to prevent the 'sea sickness effect', though it did provide a short respite from the unpleasant conditions above.

0745 hours 15ᵗʰ November:
A strong northerly gale was still blowing ten miles from Bishop Rock as *Unruffled* continued on towards Falmouth. Excitement levels rose to fever pitch amongst the ratings at 1730 hours when the boat reached its Falmouth anchorage and awaited inspection and examination of the boat before entering the harbour. With the custom duty paid on certain luxury goods being imported into the UK by officers and crew, the mood on board turned from the usual moans and groans to a happier, light-hearted tone.

The 'gash' buckets (rubbish) were lined up in the control room in readiness for ditching over the side of the conning tower bridge and those who were off watch were kept busy scrubbing and cleaning the boat in readiness for the inspection by the first lieutenants prior to entry into Dartmouth.

16ᵗʰ November:
Unruffled was escorted by Chasseur 13 (clipper) to Portsmouth, berthing at Dartmouth and Yarmouth Roads. There was no reception awaiting them at the jetty at Dartmouth but, following the order to 'finish main motors and steering', many of the crew, including the captain, enjoyed a welcome British pint at the nearest pub. Though the duty watch stayed on board, most matelots attempted to telephone home, have a few drinks and then, in some cases, stagger back to the boat in various stages of inebriation, perhaps bringing with them a few bottles of beer for those whose task it was to remain behind.

In the wardroom below deck, the celebrations continued throughout the night and into the early hours of the morning, as the officers held a party with some French and RN officers. Hardly anyone slept that night and many were still 'woolly headed' when the boat departed for the five-hour trip to Gosport.

18th November:

Arrived at HMS Dolphin, Fort Blockhouse, Gosport, home to the 5th Submarine Flotilla. *Unruffled's* white ensign and Jolly Roger were flying proudly above the bridge. All 21 symbols of achievement were sewn onto the black Jolly Roger material to highlight reconnaissance, rescue, invasion marker, five schooners and other craft, a cruiser badly damaged and clandestine missions accomplished. In all, nearly 40,000 tons of important Axis shipping had been either sunk or severely damaged.

True to tradition, the ship's company of HMS Dolphin mustered on the ramparts and jetties of the old fort and Commander (S) took the salute as *Unruffled* passed. Wives, sweethearts and parents packed the jetty shouting, cheering and waving, and some crying with joyful relief. *Unruffled* looked tired, a little rusty, but proud as she docked.

All too soon it was back to normality, with the stores, spares and personal items being unloaded. Then it was all crew members on board to be allocated a mess, after which they were to return to the boat for a final cleanse throughout. Two days' leave was granted, which was convenient for those who were close to home, but for those living further afield it inevitably meant that family reunions would have to wait.

21st November:

They then set sail for the short journey to Tilbury where the major ship repairer, R.H. Green and Silley Weir Ltd, would soon begin a refit, *Unruffled* becoming the first submarine to enter the company's dry dock. After disembarking and giving their fond farewells to the submarine that had brought them home safely, all personnel returned to Fort Blockhouse to await confirmation of their 14 days' Foreign Service leave to be issued.

Author's note: Because Unruffled's arrival at Gosport was at such short notice, and her movements generally were kept secret, there were very few wives and relatives on the dockside to welcome the boat and its crew. Most who were there were local family and friends who had been notified by telephone or telegram, while those from further afield would not have had time to travel to Gosport.

CHAPTER EIGHT

CELEBRATIONS IN
UNRUFFLED'S ADOPTED TOWN

———⊃∞⊂———

IN the Second World War the government introduced a war bonds scheme to support the war effort and help provide funds towards the cost of building ships for the Royal Navy. Prior to the Second World War several countries ran national savings schemes to finance both budget deficits and wartime expenditure, and in 1916 the UK's National Savings Movement was set up. It ran until 1978 and in that time allowed people to save any amount of money they liked.

The War Savings Campaign, however, was primarily launched for wartime purposes, allowing cities to raise the finance to adopt, say, a battleship or aircraft carrier, while towns and villages focused on cruisers, destroyers and submarines. The Lords Commissioners of the Admiralty, comprising a mixture of politicians with naval experience and professional naval officers, was left to decide which vessel should be designated to any given area.

There was massive production under this scheme during the war, with one battleship, four aircraft carriers, three cruisers, 24 destroyers, one monitor and 16 submarines being produced, as well as a number of smaller craft, and the amount raised for the war effort reached a staggering £955,611,589. As part of this campaign, the Essex garrison town of Colchester was afforded the responsibility of raising £250,000 worth of war bonds to fund the building of *Unruffled (P46),* the amount calculated on population of the town. Such was the enthusiasm and passion locally that a much larger total was raised, resulting in an impressive £435,223 worth of war bonds being purchased. In addition, local charity organisations, schools and churches provided the crew of *Unruffled* with gloves, woollen socks and balaclavas, and local children took on the task of writing letters and cards to the crew.

Finally, in December 1942, a grateful Admiralty presented Colchester with a plaque, which included the words 'Burdened but *Unruffled*', and it was hung on display in the town hall. For reasons that are not clear, the plaque at some time was removed and, subsequently, mislaid. Many years later it was rediscovered and on March 14, 2012, the date of the 20th anniversary of 1942 Warship Week, was reinstalled in its pride of place in the foyer of the town hall.

1125 hours 28th December, 1943:
A total of 28 officers and crew of *Unruffled* attended a day

of celebrations in Colchester and a civic reception at the town hall to mark their safe return home. Maurice Pye, the Mayor of Colchester, along with Percy Sanders, Deputy Lieutenant of Essex, welcomed the submarine's personnel and presented John Stevens with the Borough Arms Shield, which had earlier been lost in transit. In what was to prove an unusually arduous 24 hours for the submarine commander, Stevens made the first of six emotional speeches and at 1215 hours the mayor and crew assembled on the balcony of the town hall and introduced him to the gathered crowd, followed by lunch at the George Hotel in Colchester high street, the menu consisting of Crème St Germain, followed by roast goose, apple sauce, Brussels sprouts and roast potatoes, and then mince pie and coffee.

At 1400 hours the crew were invited by Odeon Theatres Ltd to make a personal appearance at the Regal cinema where, after being introduced by the manager, Alex Thomson, they received another heart-warming reception from the audience, and at 1700 hours tea was provided by the Moot Hall Forces canteen in the mayor's suite before supper at another high street hotel, the Red Lion, followed by a dance, with music provided by the Royal Berkshire Regiment band under conductor Joe Needham.

0100 hours 29th December:
The dance and the long day's exertions over, the crew retired for a few hours' sleep and then completed the celebrations in Colchester with a visit to local engineering firm Davey Paxman, the company which had provided the diesel engines for both *Unruffled* and its U-class sister ships. Finally, a poem written especially for the occasion by the

High Steward of Colchester, Sir William Gurney Benham, was presented to the crew in honour of her successful war patrols:

In days remote, whose date remains unknown,
NATURE, by some mysterious ways and means,
Produced at Colchester, beneath, the COLNE,
Unnumbered and unrivalled SUBMARINES.
Now the Right Worshipful, whose name is Pye,
Rules o'er the PYE-FLEET, as befits his name,
Where deep beneath the tide the Natives lie
And prove by price their undiminished fame.
Secret and silent in the depths below,
Emblems of peace amid a world at strife,
Guiltless of any sin of which we know,
They lead their blameless, uneventful life.
But how say you, our proudly honoured guests,
Adventurous STEVENS, Officers and Crew?
Perchance these virtues to warm your breasts,
But leave you cold, and maybe scornful too.
Therefore go on, UNRUFFLED everywhere,
Making your glory and Renown increase,
Until God speed the day, you grandly share,
The Great Adventure, VICTORY, HOME, and PEACE.

As time passed, more and more of the original crew members were either transferred to other submarines or attended courses leading to promotion, each one leaving with his own memories and deep affection for the submarine, which would stay with them for the rest of their lives.

Author's note: Tragically, less than five months after that historic civic reception for Unruffled, William Gurney Benham, who had penned the evocative poem, died at the age of 85. He came from the Benham family, owners of the famous Colchester-based printing and publishing group, and had been the town's mayor on three occasions. He was knighted in 1935 in recognition of his public service and for over 40 years was a director of the Colchester Gas Company, being chairman right up until his resignation on grounds of ill health the day before his death on 13 May 1944.

Percy Sanders, later to receive a knighthood, had a particular affinity with Unruffled, and not only because he was on the board of Paxmans, the submarine's engine builders, where he was a joint managing director up until the time of his death in 1962, aged 80. He also had a strong link with Unruffled's builders, Vickers-Armstrong, having served part of his apprenticeship with Metropolitan Vickers Ltd, the British heavy industrial company, based in Manchester. He was also elected mayor of Colchester on no fewer than five occasions. However, perhaps his greatest personal triumph was in saving Paxmans from the Official Receiver and then restoring the company to prosperity.

CHAPTER NINE

TRAINING IN BERMUDA

1ST MARCH 1944 - 27TH JUNE 1945

———∞———

HAVING completed a refit and passed an acceptance trial, *Unruffled* set sail for a new destination – Bermuda. At the helm was the boat's former second lieutenant, Oliver Lascelles. A new commander, maybe, but as an old hand, and someone who was no stranger to the unique habits, handling and capabilities of the submarine, he knew every inch of the boat. Under his leadership, *Unruffled* was to embark on a course far removed from the constants of rationing and battle conditions, as the boat adopted a new role as a training boat.

The submarine sailed from the UK in early February and, after a stop-off at Newfoundland, is thought to have arrived at Penno's Wharf, St George's Town, Bermuda, later that month, though no records are available. The next log begins on 1st March, 1944, where we find the boat docked at St George's, the crew employed cleaning the boat in the morning, with make-and-mend sessions in the afternoon. Leave was granted from 1330 to 0600 hours the next morning.

Due to the presence of numerous American and Canadian service personnel, the night life in Bermuda exceeded all expectations. Items not seen before the war could be purchased in the shops and the food was of the gods, with menus that included steak and peach melba – pure luxury compared to Europe. *Unruffled* was tasked with the role of ASDIC and role-playing training with a combined UK, Canadian and USA anti-submarine flotilla.

0830 2nd March, 1944:

Harbour stations was called and at 0842 hours *Unruffled* slipped her mooring and headed out to sea. At 0946 the boat dived for attack exercises with HMS *Upright* used as the target and at 1102 the roles were reversed. At 1300 hours, with practice completed, *Unruffled* secured to Penno's Wharf, St George's and leave was granted, from 1400-0700 hours for ratings and 1400-0730 hours for petty officers.

0820 hours 3rd March:

All hands fell in and were employed cleaning the ship. At 1000 hours the Davis Submerged Escape Apparatus (DSEA), which was oxygen rebreather emergency equipment designed primarily for submarine crew in 1927, was inspected, practised and found to be correct. At 1200 dinner was taken, after which the duty watch remained on board while two-thirds of the crew took leave from 1330 hours until 0700 hours the following morning.

0830 hours 4th March:

The men were employed cleaning the ship, stopping for dinner at 1200 hours, with leave beginning at 1330 hours.

0754 hours 5th March:

Crew members were brought to harbour stations and *Unruffled* slipped her mooring at 0800 for another training patrol. Lieutenant Lascelles called for diving stations and at 0924 hours the klaxon burst into life, sending *Unruffled* into the depths, though the boat was back on the surface at 1126. Twenty-one minutes later *Unruffled* dived again. The boat resurfaced at 1318 hours and made its way back to Penno's Wharf. Leave was granted at 1700 hours until 0600 the next morning.

0615 hours 6th March:

Harbour stations again and at 0630 hours *Unruffled* left for exercises. By 0910 hours the boat had dived and a mock attack on a convoy was carried out, after which it returned to the surface at 1026. The boat dived once more at 1155 for a further attack exercise and at 1334 hours it surfaced and gun action stations was called, with the 3-inch gun and Vickers machine-gun put through their paces. At 1658 hours the boat again secured to Penno's Wharf.

0645 hours 7th March:

Harbour stations was called and *Unruffled* left at 0656 hours. It dived at 0809 and resurfacing at 1015 dived once more at 1100 and returned to the surface two hours four minutes later. By 1537 *Unruffled* was back on its mooring. Leave was granted from 1700-0600.

0645 hours 8th March:
Unruffled left the wharf and headed out to sea for exercises. The boat dived at 0824, resurfaced at 1031, dived at 1100, resurfaced at 1305, dived again 13 minutes later to carry out an attack exercise and finally, 12 minutes later, resurfaced and returned to base at 1529 hours.

0645 hours 9th March:
Unruffled proceeded to the exercise area. It dived at 0802, resurfacing at 1006, dived again at 1037 then resurfaced at 1239 and proceeded to Penno's Wharf, arriving at 1430.

0650 hours 10th March:
Proceeded to sea. *Unruffled* dived at 0823, resurfaced at 1024, dived at 1046, resurfaced at 1225, dived at 1340 and resurfaced at 1548 before heading back to the wharf where it docked at 1742 hours. At 2100 the seals on the DSEA were inspected and found to be correct.

0200 hours 11th March:
The clocks on board were advanced one hour and at 0730 hours the boat headed for the training area. It dived at 0855 and resurfaced at 1101. Twenty-three minutes later it dived once more and returned to the surface at 1228. Five minutes later it dived again, returning to the surface at 1540, and at 1700 hours secured alongside Penno's Wharf.

0740 hours 12ᵗʰ March:
Proceeded to sea for more exercises. Again, the boat went through the routine of diving three times during the day on various exercises. Secured alongside Penno's Wharf at 1710.

0740 hours 13ᵗʰ March:
Proceeded to sea. The boat dived at 0854, resurfaced at 1057, dived at 1130, resurfaced at 1334, dived at 1343 and surfaced for the final time at 1517. Returned to the wharf at 1657.

0740 hours 14ᵗʰ March:
Left the wharf and headed for sea, diving at 0908, returning to the surface at 1111 hours. After diving again at 1127, the submarine became entangled and was forced to resurface at 1136. Having disentangled itself, *Unruffled* dived again one minute later. At 1320 hours the boat surfaced, then dived at 1419. It returned to daylight at 1622 and headed back to the berth on the surface, securing at 1733.

0830 hours 15ᵗʰ March:
All hands fell in for cleaning and maintenance work. This continued throughout the day until 1700 hours. The daily routine of either training or taking a day in port to clean the ship and attending to daily routines continued throughout the month, with only one notable addition being that, on the 25ᵗʰ March, *Unruffled* renewed acquaintances with the newly-arrived HMS *United (P46),* which was also involved in the attack on the damaged Attilio Regolo on 8ᵗʰ November, 1942 without scoring a hit. *Unruffled* had secured one torpedo hit on the Italian light cruiser the day

before. By the middle of April, *Unruffled* had returned to the UK with a newly-trained and sun-tanned crew. The boat was loaded with gifts and food for friends and relatives.

0830 7ᵗʰ May:
Unruffled sailed from Tilbury to Sheerness, in the Thames Estuary, for degaussing. On the way a surface speed test was carried out and it was noted that, at 460 revs, a distance of one mile could be covered in ten minutes. Secured alongside buoy at 1240 hours.

1200 hours 8ᵗʰ May:
Proceeded from Sheerness to the Medway town of Chatham, where the boat arrived at 1700 and commenced to embark torpedoes.

0700 hours 9ᵗʰ May:
All hands fell in to continue embarking torpedoes. At 1100 hours the boat left for Sheerness, where she arrived at 1315. At 1830 the boat left for the naval base of Portland, Weymouth.

1547 hours 10ᵗʰ May:
Arrived at Portland and secured to the outer coaling area. Crew granted leave from 1630-2330.

1641 hours 11ᵗʰ May:
Proceeded to sea heading for the Royal Navy base at Devonport, Plymouth, arriving at 1559 hours.

0808 hours 13ᵗʰ May:
Unruffled began a day of exercises, returning at 1715 hours. This training regime continued throughout the rest of May.

0825 hours 1st June:
The boat left its mooring at Devonport and headed for the submarine base of Rothesay, Isle of Bute.

1002 hours 3ʳᵈ June:
After an uneventful journey *Unruffled* secured alongside 'HMS Cyclops', depot ship for the 7ᵗʰ Submarine Flotilla.

0849 hours 5ᵗʰ June:
Proceeded to sea for exercises, returning to Rothesay at 1410 hours the following day.

1200 hours 7ᵗʰ June:
Half the crew was given seven days' leave.

0800 hour 17ᵗʰ June:
The crew said farewell to Lieutenant Lascelles, as his time with *Unruffled* was at an end. First Lieutenant Peter Stanley Worth assumed command until the arrival of the boat's new commander, Lieutenant Francis Park, RN.

0830 hours 24ᵗʰ June:
Unruffled left 'Cyclops' for Greenock, the torpedo manufacturing site on the Clyde, returning to Rothesay at 1456 hours.

0830 hours 25th June:

For the next two days torpedo, gunnery and diving exercises took place.

0130 hours 27th June:

Carried out dummy patrol, resulting on a practice attack on the sloop HMS Milford. Secured alongside Cyclops at 0618 hours and at 0830 the crew began the loading of stores, a procedure that continued throughout the afternoon.

1700 hours 29th June:

Left harbour in company with *Unseen* and Milford for St John's, Newfoundland.

0140 hours 1st July:

Unruffled parted company with *Unseen* and Milford.

1901 hours 8th July:

After travelling the majority of the journey on the surface, *Unruffled* met up with HMCS Eyebright (K150), a Royal Canadian corvette under the command of Lieutenant Howard Lee Quinn, RCNVR.

0836 hours 9th July:

The boat tied up alongside *Unseen* in St John's, Newfoundland.

1145 hours 11th July:

The boat slipped its mooring and proceeded, on the surface, to Halifax, Nova Scotia.

1107 hours 14th July:

Unruffled secured alongside *Unseen* at No1 jetty, Halifax.

1130 hours 22nd July:

The submarine left Halifax and plotted a course back to St George's Bermuda.

1409 hours 26th July:

Secured in St George's Harbour, Bermuda.

0800 27th July:

All hands spent time cleaning the submarine and removing personal items for storage at their permanent mess.

0652 hours 28th July:

Slipped mooring and proceeded for exercises. This involved an identical routine as previously experienced by *Unruffled*'s crew. For any new ratings on board who had never visited previously Bermuda the ordeal must have seemed like heaven-sent.

29th July-2nd October:

The usual daily routine of going to sea and returning to base five or six times a week to dive, surface and carry out dummy attacks continued throughout the following months.

0815 hours 3rd October:

All hands fell in to clean the boat.

0850 hours 4th October:

The ratings were brought to Harbour stations and *Unruffled* slipped her moorings at 0900 hours and proceeded to the Royal Naval Dockyard, St George's, securing at 1043 hours beneath a two-ton crane in the South Basin. At 1315 hours the commencement of disembarking torpedoes and ammunition began, and this work continued until 1800 hours.

0700 hours 5th October:

The disembarking of ammunition was finally completed and at 0900 hours *Unruffled* entered the floating dock inside the basin. At 1300 hours the boat was hauled out of the water and secured in a cradle.

0830 hours 6th October:

The crew was kept busy overhauling the gear. Dinner was taken at the usual time, 1200 hours, and everyone was back on duty at 1300. Work finished at 1600 hours.

0830 7th-17th October:

A similar routine continued throughout these 11 days, with the added task that the crew also had to paint the boat.

0830 hours 18th October:

Half the crew continued painting the boat, with the other half attending the rifle range for target practice. At 1330 hours the roles were reversed and at 1530 *Unruffled* moved from the floating dock to the South Basin.

1800 hours 20th October:

The starboard generator armature was removed for repairs.

0815 hours 21st October:

Ammunition was embarked on board as *Unruffled* was prepared for sea and at 1330 the mooring lines were slipped and the boat made its way slowly back to Penno's Wharf, arriving at 1500 hours.

0730 hours 23rd-27th November:

The routine of daily exercises began again in earnest. However, in November various exercises were cancelled because of the extreme weather conditions. On 8th November the repaired generator armature was returned and successfully replaced.

0700 hours 5th December:

Unruffled left its mooring to proceed for exercises. On board was Lieutenant Allan Harold MacCoy DSC. At 0822 the boat dived, but at 0830 a defect was found on the starboard generator and at 0900 there was a watch diving emergency exercise. At 1025 the submarine surfaced and, because of the poor weather, the decision was taken to cancel the day's exercises. The official hand-over of command to Lieutenant MacCoy from Lieutenant Park took place at 1200 hours and at 1247 *Unruffled* secured alongside Penno's Wharf.

1100 hours 20th December:

Sub Lieutenant R.A. Cobb was discharged to HMS Seawolf.

0655 hours 31st December:

Unruffled proceeded to sea for exercises. The boat dived at 0825 but, due to a serious leak in the stern gland, all further exercises were abandoned and the submarine returned to harbour, securing at 1221 hours.

January–June, 1945:

Exercises became increasingly few and far between, with an average of just six sailings a month. Periodically *Unruffled* was accompanied by *Upright*, with training consisting of mock convoy, anti-submarine and submarine attacks, using HMCS corvettes, frigates and tugs as target practice and evasive manoeuvres. These vessels included HMCS New Westminster (K228), HMCS Dunvegan (K177), HMCS Strathroy (K455), HMCS Forrest Hill (K486), HMCS Cape Breton (K350), HMCS Wetaskiwin (K175), HMCS Frontenac (K335), HMCS Three Rivers (10-20), HMCS Westmount (J318), HMCS Agassiz (K129), HMCS Long Branch (K487) and HMCS Dawson.

27th June:

Unruffled began its journey home to the UK, proceeding on passage to the USA where the boat docked at the vast Naval Submarine Base New London, on the Thames River at Groton, Connecticut, arriving on the 30th June, 1945.

After a short stay, *Unruffled* returned to the UK, though this time there was no fanfare or rousing reception awaiting her. Flying the white ensign, the Jolly Roger and a pennant, which fluttered astern of the submarine, signifying that the boat was returning from a foreign commission to be paid off, *P46* simply moored quietly alongside the quay at Fort Blockhouse, Gosport, and the crew disembarked in anticipation of leave. In time *Unruffled* was to follow in the wake of 44 other heroic veteran submarines; the boat which began life as just a number, and whose sole purpose was to seek and destroy, was destined for the scrap yard.

Sold in January 1946 for scrap, *Unruffled* would be

beached in Troon, Ayrshire, and torn apart, to be reborn as valuable metal and tin for the domestic market: a sad ending for such a valiant, sturdy, brave, inexpensive boat, which throughout the war had served her country with honour and, in the finest tradition of the Royal Navy, returned her shipmates safely home.

Jolly Roger Symbols

Lieutenant Commander Max Kennedy Horton (later Admiral Sir Max Horton G.C.B., D.S.O. Commander-in-Chief Western Approaches) began the practice of flying the Jolly Roger when in command of the First World war submarine HMS E9. On the 13th September, 1914, Horton sank the German Light Cruiser Hela off Heligoland Harbour with two torpedoes aimed amidships. Upon returning safely to his home port of Harwich, he flew the skull and crossbones from his periscope. As the number of sinkings mounted up, and there was no longer any more room for more flags Horton adopted the system of flying one large pirate flag with bars denoting the number of enemy vessels he had sunk. The sailors loved it, and so did the press. Indeed, most submariners took a delight in flaunting the idea, for they knew very well that senior officers of the old navy had spoken of them as pirates.

- ■ Red bar – Axis naval vessel sunk.
- ■ Red bar with U overlaid – Enemy submarine sunk.
- ■ White bar – Axis merchant vessel sunk.
- ■ Half a bar – Enemy vessel damaged but not sunk.

- Crossed guns with a star – Axis vessel sunk by gunfire.

- Chevron – Small Axis vessel sunk by gunfire.

- Lighthouse and torch – Beacon or beachmarking operations for amphibious landings.

- Lifebelt – Air-sea rescue operation.

- A dagger/sword – Cloak and dagger operations, including the landing of agents or commandos.

- 'Eugene the jeep' (character in Popeye cartoons) – Chariot recovery.

- Railway engine – Train or railway track destroyed by gunfire.

- Demolition charge – Enemy vessel sunk by placing demolition charges on board.

- Diver's helmet – Submarine went below safe diving depth.

- Aircraft – Shot down an enemy aircraft.

REFERENCES

National Archives

ADM 173/17411 ADM 173/19232
ADM 173/17412 ADM 173/19234
ADM 173/17413 ADM 173/19233
ADM 173/17901 ADM 173/20137
ADM 173/17416 ADM 173/20139
ADM 173/17902 ADM 173/20140
ADM 173/17415 ADM 173/19237
ADM 173/17414 ADM 173/19238
ADM 173/17417 ADM 173/20138
ADM 1/14321 ADM 173/19236
ADM 173/19735 ADM 173/19231
ADM 199/1822

Imperial War Museum

AX 139A A 20446
AX 137A A 20434
AX 138A A 20435
A 20441 A 20440
A 20436 A 20444
A 20438 A 20445
A 20443 A 20442
A 20439

Interview with Lieutenant John Stevens
Private papers of Lieutenant Oliver Lascelles
The Times of Malta

REFERENCES

Captain J.S. Stevens D.S.O., D.S.C., RN, *Never Volunteer* (J.S. Stevens, 1971)

John Wingate DSC, *The Fighting Tenth* (Periscope Publishing Ltd, 2003)

Peter Elliott, *The Cross And The Ensign* (HarperCollins Publishing, 1994)

Edward Young, *One Of Our Submarines* (Pen & Sword Books Ltd, 2004)

John Winton, *The Submarines* (Constable and Company Ltd, 1999)

Sydney Hart, *Discharged Dead* (Wyman & Sons Ltd, 1956)

John Frayn Turner, *Periscope Patrol* (Airlife Publishing Ltd, 1997)

Commander William King D.S.O., D.S.C., R.N., *The Stick And The Stars* (Hutchinson & Co, 1958)

Admiral Of The Fleet Viscount Cunningham of Hyndhope K.T., G.C.B., O.M., D.S.O., A *Sailor's Odyssey* (Hutchinson & Co 1951)

Rear Admiral G.W.G. Simpson C.B., C.B.E., *Periscope View* (Macmillan London Ltd, 1972)

Brian Izzard, *Gamp VC* (Haynes Publishing, 2009)

David J.B. Smith, *Being Silent They Speak*, (Stand Easy, 2012)

Michael Galea, *Malta Diary Of A War* (Publishers Enterprise Group, 1992)

Rear-Admiral Ben Bryant C.B., D.S.O., and Two Bars, D.S.C., *One Man Band* (William Kimber, 1958)

Arthur P. Dickison, *Crash Dive* (Sutton Publishing, 1999)

Alastair Mars, *Unbroken* (Frederick Muller Ltd, 1953)

Vice Admiral Sir Arthur Hezlet K.B.E., C.B., D.S.O., D.S.C., *The Submarine And Sea Power* (Peter Davies London, 1967)

Commander F.W. Lipscomb O.B.E., *The British Submarine* (Adam and Charles Black London, 1954)

Peter Dornan, *Diving Stations* (Pen & Sword Maritime, 2010)

Derek Walters, *The History of the British 'U' Class Submarine* (Pen & Sword Maritime, 2004)

R.A. Cunningham, *A Submarine At War*, (R.A. Cunningham, 1992)

Ralph Stanbury, *Survey By Starlight* (Hodder & Stoughton, 1949)

Jack Greene and Alessandro Massignani, *Rommel's North Africa Campaign* (Combined Books, Inc, 1994)